WITHDRAWN

THE
CORROSION
OF
CONSERVATISM

ALSO BY MAX BOOT

*The Road Not Taken: Edward Lansdale and
the American Tragedy in Vietnam*

*Invisible Armies: An Epic History of Guerrilla Warfare
from Ancient Times to the Present*

*War Made New: Technology, Warfare, and
the Course of History, 1500 to Today*

*The Savage Wars of Peace: Small Wars and
the Rise of American Power*

THE CORROSION OF CONSERVATISM

Why I Left the Right

MAX BOOT

LIVERIGHT PUBLISHING CORPORATION
A DIVISION OF W. W. NORTON & COMPANY
Independent Publishers Since 1923
NEW YORK   LONDON

Copyright © 2018 by Max Boot

All rights reserved
Printed in the United States of America
First Edition

For information about permission to reproduce selections from this book,
write to Permissions, Liveright Publishing Corporation, a division of
W. W. Norton & Company, Inc., 500 Fifth Avenue, New York, NY 10110

For information about special discounts for bulk purchases, please contact
W. W. Norton Special Sales at specialsales@wwnorton.com or 800-233-4830

Manufacturing by LSC Communications, Harrisonburg
Book design by Lovedog Studio
Production manager: Anna Oler

ISBN 978-1-63149-567-0

Liveright Publishing Corporation, 500 Fifth Avenue, New York, N.Y. 10110
www.wwnorton.com

W. W. Norton & Company Ltd., 15 Carlisle Street, London W1D 3BS

1 2 3 4 5 6 7 8 9 0

To Robert Weil,
Editor Extraordinaire

All I have is a voice
To undo the folded lie,
The romantic lie in the brain
Of the sensual man-in-the-street
And the lie of Authority
Whose buildings grope the sky

—W. H. Auden,
"September 1, 1939" (1939)

CONTENTS

Prologue

NOVEMBER 8, 2016

N OVEMBER 8, 2016, WAS ONE OF THE MOST DEMOR-
alizing days of my life. It was also, in ways that have become
impossible to ignore, devastating not just for America in general but
for American conservatism in particular.

I had never imagined that Donald Trump could be elected president. If you had suggested to me before 2016 that such a thing
was possible I would have replied that it was too far-fetched to
contemplate—it sounded like the plot of a dystopian science-fiction
movie. Arnold Schwarzenegger would have been a more plausible
president—and he wasn't even born in America. I didn't think
Trump would win a single Republican primary. Sure, he had been
polling strongly in 2015, but I figured that when the actual balloting began my fellow Republicans would sober up and realize that
the reality TV star and real-estate mogul was not remotely qualified
for the nation's highest office.

Trump had offended my sensibilities from the very first day of
the campaign, June 16, 2015, when he had come down the gar-
ish escalator at Trump Tower to castigate Mexican immigrants
in crudely xenophobic terms. "They're bringing drugs," he said.
"They're bringing crime. They're rapists. And some, I assume,
are good people."[1] A month later, he launched an odious attack
on Senator John McCain, a man whose presidential campaign I
had been proud to advise in 2008. This is what Trump, who had

gotten five draft deferments, had to say about a war hero who had endured nearly six years of hellish captivity in North Vietnam: "He's not a war hero. He was a war hero because he was captured. I like people who weren't captured."[2] A few months after that, in November 2015, Trump hit another low, mocking a disabled reporter who had the temerity to question his bogus claims to have seen thousands of Muslims in Jersey City, New Jersey, cheering as the World Trade Center came down. Trump then lied about what he had done—even though his cruel japery was recorded on videotape.[3]

There was no possibility, I figured, that the party of Lincoln, Roosevelt, and Reagan would endorse Trump for president. Was there?

When the primaries began and Trump began winning state after state, I thought I had entered *The Twilight Zone*. The torment worsened when he locked up the nomination and Republican after Republican dutifully lined up to endorse his candidacy after having lambasted him in the harshest terms possible. Former governor Rick Perry had called Trump a "cancer on conservatism" before endorsing said cancer—and being rewarded with a cabinet post. Former governor Bobby Jindal had called Trump a "madman who must be stopped" before endorsing said madman. Senator Rand Paul had called him a "delusional narcissist" before endorsing said narcissist. Most painful of all for me, Senator Marco Rubio, whose presidential campaign I had served as a foreign policy adviser, went from denouncing Trump as a "con artist" to endorsing said con artist. House Speaker Paul Ryan got my hopes up by hesitating to endorse Trump, but in the end, he too bent the knee. This was not the Republican Party I knew. Or thought I knew. How could so many Republicans for whom I had such respect have betrayed everything that they—and I—believed in? What was going on? How could all of these conservatives turn into Trump toadies? I was angry and bewildered. My faith in the Republican Party was shaken and has never recovered.

But at least I comforted myself that in the general election there was no way the American people could possibly elect someone like Trump. I had come to America as a six-year-old from the Soviet Union in 1976 and had grown to revere the country that had offered asylum to my family. I was convinced that America was the greatest and most selfless country in the world. Now I had faith that the voters would in their wisdom choose Hillary Clinton, who was a deeply flawed and seriously uncharismatic candidate, to be sure, but also extremely knowledgeable, resolutely centrist, and amply qualified. I had never voted for a Democrat in my life, but for me it was an easy call. Here I was, a conservative Republican, voting for Clinton; I figured that there would be plenty of others who would do the same. If Trump couldn't even count on the undivided support of the GOP, there was no way he could win.

Like countless other commentators, I was sure Trump was finished on October 7, 2016, when a videotape emerged in which he could be heard bragging that because he was a "star" he could do anything he wanted to women—even "grab them by the pussy." Numerous Republicans withdrew their endorsements and urged Trump to drop out. Yet when he refused to withdraw, many of the same Republicans came crawling back to re-endorse him. The race tightened as Election Day approached. Yet I was still certain— foolishly, naïvely, pathetically certain—that Trump could not win. My Pollyannaish faith in America had blinded me to what was to come, and that faith has not survived the debacle to come.

I agreed to spend election night at the Comedy Cellar nightclub in downtown New York, offering commentary on the results along with other pundits and comedians at a forum organized by *Foreign Policy* magazine. I was nervous in the afternoon but was reassured by rumors that the exit polls showed a Clinton victory. I was on stage, chatting with the other panelists, when around 8 p.m. I saw my partner, Sue, growing increasingly agitated across the room. She kept looking at her phone and getting more upset. I sneaked out my own phone and saw what was disturbing her—the *New York Times* had just moved Florida into Trump's column. It now looked as if he had a path to victory. As the night wore on, swing state after swing state went for Trump. Clinton went from the odds-on favorite to an increasing long shot.

By the time Sue and I got home to our apartment on the Upper West Side at 10 p.m. or so, it was obvious that the unthinkable was about to become the inevitable: Donald Trump was going to be elected the 45th president of the United States. A friend came over from the Clinton election-night party at the Javits Center; she was crying and in shock. I swilled a Scotch and took some sleeping pills—something I don't normally do—and tried to sleep. And, yes, I know you're not supposed to combine sedatives with alcohol, but you're also not supposed to elect a bigoted bully as president of the United States. This was a day for disregarding the rules. Even with chemical inducements, however, my sleep was fretful and disturbed because I knew that I would awaken to a nightmare. My America had become Trump's America. My Republican Party had become Trump's party. My conservative movement had become Trump's movement.

The first thing I did the next morning—the dawn of what I felt was a new annus horribilis—was to go online and change my voter registration. I had been a Republican since turning eighteen just before the 1988 presidential election. Now, at the age of forty-seven, I became an independent. Politics is a team sport. Suddenly I was without a team. I was politically homeless. In an instant I felt alienated from some of my oldest friends and fellow travelers—conservatives with whom I had been in one fight after another over the past quarter-century. How was it possible that 90 percent of

Republicans had supported a charlatan who had only recently been a Democrat and who had few fixed convictions outside of narcissism and nativism, racism and sexism? My sense of alienation has only deepened as I have watched the Trump presidency in action. No other president has been more hostile to the values of conservatism as I conceived it.

Conservatism, American-style, means different things to different people. There is, after all, an inherent tension in advocating a conservative vision in a liberal society in which social, economic, and technological change is constant. American conservatism is very different from the kind of "blood and soil" conservatism that has long been characteristic of Europe. Continental conservatism is chauvinistic and pessimistic; American conservatism is optimistic and inclusive. For me, conservatism means prudent and incremental policymaking based on empirical study; support for American global leadership and American allies; a strong defense and a willingness to oppose the enemies of freedom; respect for character, community, personal virtue, and family; limited government and fiscal prudence; freedom of opportunity rather than equality of outcome; a social safety net big enough to help the neediest but small enough to avoid stifling individual initiative, enterprise, and social mobility; individual liberty to the greatest extent possible consistent with public safety; freedom of speech and of the press; immigration and assimilation; and colorblindness and racial integration. Looming above them all are two documents that I revere, as should every American. The Declaration of Independence defines the United States as a nation bound together not by shared heritage or blood but rather by a shared belief in the "self-evident" truths "that all men are created equal, that they are endowed by their Creator with certain unalienable Rights, that among these are Life, Liberty and the pursuit of Happiness." The "pursuit of Happiness" is a critical concept, putting personal freedom at the center of our political enterprise. While the Declaration lays out the goals of self-government, the Constitution defines how we can achieve them. It protects our liberties, limits the government's power, and ensures that the rule of law prevails. We honor, defend, and respect the Constitution, and the offices, laws, and norms that derive from it. All Americans, of all political persuasions, are expected to defer to the Constitution, but it should be of particular concern to conservatives who proclaim their desire to conserve what makes America great.

That, to me, is American conservatism. That is what I believe. Those are the ideas I have tried to advance as a writer and commentator. To judge by his words and actions, Trump does not understand or believe in a single one of these principles. Yet he remains wildly popular among Republicans and conservatives. When 2016 began I could hardly find a Republican who had anything positive to say about Trump. By the beginning of 2018 it was hard to find a Republican who had anything negative to say about him—at least in public.

How can this be? Did I not understand all along what American conservatism was all about? Did I miss essential features that Trump had discerned and used to his benefit? Or had conservatism morphed under the magnetic pull of Trump's outsized personality to become something very different from the movement I had grown up in?

The modern conservative movement was inspired by Barry Goldwater's canonical text from 1960, *The Conscience of a Conservative*.[4] I believed in that movement, and served it my whole life, but under the pressure of Trumpism, conservatism as I understood it has been corroding—and so has my faith in the movement. Hence this book's title. I am perceiving ugly truths about America and about conservatism that other people had long seen but I had turned a blind eye to. I no longer like to call myself a conservative, a label that has become virtually synonymous with Trump toady. I now prefer to think of myself as a classical liberal.

I would like to be able to quote Ronald Reagan's quip when he became a Republican—"I didn't leave the Democratic Party, the Democratic Party left me"—but in truth my beliefs are shifting because of the rise of Trumpism and other contemporary developments such as the failure of the Iraq invasion, the Great Recession of 2008–2009, the #MeToo movement, and the spread of police videotapes revealing violent racism. My ideology has come into conflict with reality—and reality is winning. I have undertaken a painful and difficult intellectual journey, leaving behind many of the simple verities that I clung to for decades as a "movement" conservative. I am now forced to think for myself, and that is not an easy thing to do. But given the epochal events that have shaken America, this self-reflection is necessary, indeed overdue. I only wish more conservatives were willing to engage in similar self-examination instead of resorting to glib insults of "libtards" and "snowflakes" or reflexive defenses of the man who has usurped their party.

I am no longer a Republican, but I am not a Democrat either. I am a man without a party. This is a record of my ideological journey so far—and of my attempts to come to grips, honestly and unflinchingly, with the phenomenon known as Trumpism. The question that haunts me is: Did I somehow contribute to the rise of this dark force in American life with my advocacy for conservatism?

Whatever the case, I am now convinced that the Republican Party must suffer repeated and devastating defeats. It must pay a heavy price for its embrace of white nationalism and know-nothingism. Only if the GOP as currently constituted is burned to the ground will there be any chance to build a reasonable center-right political party out of the ashes.

How did we get to the point where I—a lifelong Republican—

now wish ill fortune upon my erstwhile party? To find the answer, I invite you to turn the page with me, literally as well as figuratively.

What follows is not a full-blown memoir or autobiography. But to make you understand why I—and other #NeverTrump conservatives, all too few in number—feel such a strong sense of betrayal at the hands of Trump and his Republican Party, it is important for you to understand how I became a conservative in the first place and what it felt like to be a conservative in the heyday of the movement. My history, I feel, can help the reader to make sense of late-twentieth-century conservatism—now, in the early twenty-first century, practically unrecognizable. I take the story up to the present day, explaining why I left the Republican Party because of my profound opposition to Trump, how Trump continues to traduce conservative principles, and what the future holds for me and other conservatives who cannot imagine being members of a Trumpista party. Put another way, this is a tale of first love, marriage, growing disenchantment, and, eventually, a heartbreaking divorce. Today we are locked in a bitter custody battle over the future of the Republican Party: Will it return to its previous principles or will it remain forever a populist, white-nationalist movement in the image of Donald Trump?

This book, I strongly suspect, will infuriate many of my old comrades on the right who will conclude that I have gone soft in the head or sold out my beliefs to gain popular acceptance in liberal circles. I, in turn, am convinced that they are the ones who have gone off the rails by embracing a demagogue who seems to equate bigotry with conservatism. There is a gulf between us that cannot be bridged, at least not while Trump is still in office. Likewise, what follows is unlikely to satisfy the hard left. No matter how strongly I come out against Trump and his hateful works, I find it is never enough for the most doctrinaire leftists who seem to think that no step short, perhaps, of ritual suicide will atone for my "war crimes," which upon closer examination seem to consist of supporting an invasion of Iraq that was backed by bipartisan majorities in both houses.

This book is not addressed to the far left or the far right. It is written with the center-left and the center-right in mind. My hope is that my ideological odyssey will inspire others—that I can be part of a larger, bipartisan movement in America toward greater moderation and civility in our politics. Or, if that doesn't happen, and if the present trend toward extremism continues, I will at least register my dissent in the strongest terms I know.

I love America. I am devoted to conservative principles. I want to defend what I hold dear when I see it under unprecedented attack from within—with the greatest threat posed by a man at the very pinnacle of power. This is how I became a conservative and why I no longer feel part of a movement whose betrayal of its principles is abhorrent to me.

THE
CORROSION
OF
CONSERVATISM

1.

THE
EDUCATION
OF A
CONSERVATIVE

I WAS BORN IN WHAT DONALD TRUMP WOULD CALL A "shithole" country. My experience of becoming a conservative is unique—but so is everyone else's. I cannot tell all of their stories, so I will tell mine in the hope that others will recognize at least a glimmer of their own experiences. My tale may not be typical, but my journey from embrace of the conservative movement to exit is nevertheless representative of a certain number of #NeverTrumpers. The major difference is that I had to come a much longer way than most of them to join the right. Before I could become a conservative, I first had to become an American.

The Soviet Union in 1969, the year of my birth, was a grim place ruled by a geriatric oligarchy that repressed its own people and ruined its own economy. Store shelves were bare and lines long. Moscow, where my family lived, was better off than the provinces, but it was still an impoverished and illiberal place. I am especially sensitive to growing signs of anti-Semitism in Donald Trump's America because that prejudice was so pervasive in Leonid Brezhnev's Soviet Union. Jews—their "nationality" stamped in their internal passports, just like in Nazi Germany—had to work harder to get into a university or find a job because they were routinely discriminated against. Most synagogues had been shuttered. There were no Hebrew schools. Despite the official passports, most Jews, including my parents, were thoroughly assimilated and thought of themselves as Russians, but that's not the way ethnic Russians viewed them. My father got his share of beatings as a boy from anti-Semitic bullies who called him a *zhid* (kike).

Little wonder that my parents—young, educated, urban Jews—were anxious to emigrate. But they couldn't find a way out of this countrywide prison. My father became a refusenik, one of the dissidents who was refused permission to leave. He agitated for freedom by passing around samizdat publications and talking to Western reporters. That my parents and hundreds of thousands of other Soviet Jews were finally able to leave was due largely to neo-conservative foreign policy.

American Jews began agitating in the early 1970s for their Soviet brethren to be allowed to emigrate—a fundamental right enshrined in Article 13 of the 1948 Universal Declaration of Human Rights. As Gal Beckerman recounts in his 2010 book, *When They Come for Us We'll Be Gone: The Epic Struggle to Save Soviet Jewry*, this became one of the first major human-rights campaigns in US foreign policy, presaging later agitation over apartheid, Bosnia, and Darfur. Senator Henry "Scoop" Jackson, a New Deal Democrat from Washington, became the most prominent advocate for the Soviet Jews. Jackson wasn't Jewish; his family, having come from Norway, were the kind of immigrants Trump would have liked. But, unlike Trump, he believed that the United States needed to stand up for human rights, and he worried that the Nixon administration was caving into Communism with its policy of détente. Jackson's nemesis was Secretary of State Henry Kissinger, who was a Jewish immigrant himself but also a Realpolitiker who did not believe that human rights should intrude into cold-blooded calculations of national interest.

Jackson, working with his aides Dorothy Fosdick and Richard Perle, won the battle by mobilizing the support of liberal Democrats and conservative Republicans—an alliance unthinkable today—to link US diplomatic and trade ties to the Soviet Union with its willingness to allow Jewish emigration. His triumph was symbolized by the passage in 1974 of the Jackson-Vanik Amendment, which forbade the United States from granting most-favored-nation trade status to any nonmarket (i.e., Communist) economy that did not respect the freedom to emigrate. Under pressure from the United States, Soviet leader Leonid Brezhnev opened the door a crack and allowed some Jews out.[1]

In later life I would support giving moral concerns a prominent place in US foreign policy, a stance that has been associated with neoconservatism. It's not hard to see why I came to this position: I wouldn't have become an American, at least not when I did, if the Realpolitik approach had prevailed.

MY FATHER DID, IN FACT, get out of the Soviet Union in 1973 a few steps ahead of the KGB; the KGB had just issued a warrant for his arrest, but the bureaucracy was so ineffective that the word did not reach the passport control office at the airport in time to prevent him from flying away. My father settled in Houston, where he went to work for NASA as a Russian-English translator on the Apollo-Soyuz space program, a centerpiece of the Nixon-Kissinger policy of détente. My parents had divorced when I was only two and when we—my mother, grandmother, and I—followed him to America in 1976, we did not wind up in the same city. We went first to Italy, where Soviet immigrants were expected to wait for an entry visa to the United States. I have a memory of New Year's Day 1976 in Rome—the holiday that Russians typically celebrated rather than Christmas or Hanukah. The only present I received was a little toy boot filled with candy. It was all my mother could afford. After a few months in Italy, we were allowed to move to Los Angeles. Why L.A.? Because my aunt and uncle—a sculptor and a physician—had just moved there with their two children. This is what nativists would call "chain migration": the practice of immigrants bringing relatives from the old country to join them in America.

My widowed and retired grandmother, a babushka who had once worked as an engineer in Russia, settled into an apartment in Hollywood, supported by my mother and by the Social Security Administration's Supplemental Security Income payments. (Thank you, America.) Before long, my mom—a thin woman with a regal bearing, a Bohemian taste in clothes, and an indescribable but vaguely European accent—and I moved some sixty miles to the east. She had gotten a job teaching at the University of California, Riverside, so we relocated to a small town in the desert as far removed as imaginable from the snowy metropolis where I had been born. At first, we lived in an apartment complex, and later, in a small home at the edge of a dun-colored mountain range full of rattlesnakes and mesquite. In Russia, mom had taught English to Russians. In America, she would teach Russian to Americans.

I am immensely, indescribably grateful to my mother for bringing me to America, a country that I would come to love as my own—because it indeed became my own. If I had remained in Russia, I can't imagine how I would have survived under the Putin regime, which is re-creating many of the worst elements of Soviet despotism that my father agitated against in the late 1960s and early 1970s. Putin may be even more ruthless than Brezhnev in killing inconvenient dissidents, although usually in ways that are difficult to trace back to the Kremlin. Little could I imagine then that an admirer of the Russian despot would eventually lead the Land of the Free.

In hindsight I marvel at the way my parents, in their twenties, were able to pack up, abandon everything and everyone they had known, and start new lives in a country they had never visited.

I do not know if I could be so brave. There was no going back in those days: on our way out of Russia we were stripped of our Soviet nationality. From the Soviet standpoint, we were becoming nonpersons. We would be lucky to reach our Russian relatives, including my father's parents, on the telephone; visiting them was out of the question until the Soviet Union collapsed in 1991, and of course no one knew in the 1970s that the USSR wouldn't last forever. We had no money and no prospects. If some generous country did not take us in, we would become stateless persons. The only two countries that were willing to succor us were Israel and America. Because my mother spoke English but not Hebrew, we decided to come to America. I am as thankful to America for taking us in as I am to my mother for getting us there, and I am greatly saddened that the United States has extended refugee status to so few others in the Trump era. I think of how bleak our lives would have been if we had not been allowed to come to this distant shore, and I feel the pain of those suffering and in want who are today denied entry.

Ours was a modern version of the immigrant saga shared by most Americans, only instead of arriving by ship at Ellis Island, we reached Kennedy Airport by jetliner. But the agonies of assimilation had not changed much since the turn of the twentieth century, even if my parents, unlike earlier generations of Jewish immigrants from Eastern Europe, did not have to toil as garment workers or junk peddlers.

Everything about this new country was strange and wondrous. We were mystified when we visited a temple of haute cuisine called McDonald's that served an exotic dish known as french fries. There were no McDonald's in Russia back then. No fast food of any kind. My mom's first car was a used Buick Electra with giant tail fins. I remember sitting in the back while she learned to drive; there were few private cars in Russia back then and no driver's ed. She couldn't simply leave me with a babysitter because she couldn't afford one. I was a "latchkey kid" who came home from school by myself while still in elementary school—an experience that induced a combination of befuddlement and dread in my young heart. Where, I wondered, was my mother? I cried tears of consternation and frustration, but she was doing the best she could. My parents had little money in the Soviet Union and were allowed to take next to nothing out. We were only able to finance the transition to a new life with loans from the Hebrew Immigrant Aid Society—loans that my scrupulously honest mother later repaid. And working as a junior lecturer at a state university wasn't exactly a lucrative job. My mother was lucky to have found employment at all. She would later say that it was either teaching Russian or washing dishes.

I was only seven years old when we arrived in the bicentennial year—and desperate to fit in. Everything and everybody was new, strange, and intimidating. It was such a traumatic experience that I have blotted a lot of it out of my memory. I do remember being bewildered by meeting African American, Asian, and Latino kids: while the Soviet Union was a polyglot empire, the only black people to be found in Moscow were a few African students who encountered terrible prejudice while being indoctrinated at Patrice Lumumba University. The idea of a racially and ethnically diverse society was, at first, strange to me, but I would quickly come to see it as one of the glories of America—a hard-won achievement that is now under siege.

My mother enrolled me in swim classes, piano lessons, and Hebrew school to give me the athletic, musical, and religious education that she had lacked. I became a slow if confident swimmer, but I can't speak a word of Hebrew or play a note on the piano. Still, I have to give her credit for trying. And even if most of my extracurricular education did not stick, all of those years of Hebrew school did ensure that I grew up identifying with the Jewish people and the state of Israel in a way that my parents had not been free to do back in the USSR.

There were no English as a second language classes in those days, at least none that I was aware of. I was thrown straight into regular elementary school classes—first in Hollywood, then in Riverside. It was like learning to swim by being thrown into the deep end of a pool. Eventually, after a period of floundering around, I dog-paddled to safety. Before long I became so proficient in English that, to my mother's initial dismay, I refused to speak Russian anymore. I even lost any trace of a Russian accent—an achievement that, I like to joke, may have hindered my future career as a foreign policy pundit because I lack the gravitas that comes from having a thick foreign accent like Henry Kissinger or Zbigniew Brzezinski. I later learned that my parents—my mother in Riverside, my father in Houston—discussed how to handle my refusal to speak Russian and decided to leave me alone. They didn't want me to become a linguistic half-breed who did not speak either language perfectly, and they were sufficiently alienated from their homeland that they didn't want me to have much to do with it either. So we developed an odd routine at home where my mother would speak to me in Russian and I would answer in English. Ironically, in later years, my mother would become a pioneer of heritage language studies, teaching the children of immigrants how to speak their parents' tongue. I like to think that I inspired her professional success with the C that I received in the only Russian-language class I ever took in college.

By now—more than forty years after coming to America—I have all but forgotten Russian and have few if any memories of Russia beyond what I can see in grainy black-and-white photos showing me as a Soviet toddler bundled up like a polar explorer to brave the harsh Moscow winter. I have never visited Russia since leaving. I feel entirely American. Or rather I felt that way before the rise of Trump and his demonization of immigrants.

THE FIRST BIG DISLOCATION of my childhood that remains in my adult consciousness was moving to America. The second and third were acquiring a stepfather and moving from Riverside to Los Angeles. The former event occurred in 1978, the latter in 1981. My mother proved such a proficient Russian professor that she was hired away by UCLA, a larger and more prestigious University of California campus. Three years before moving, she married a dark-haired and handsome, if socially awkward, geophysicist who was a fellow Russian émigré. In his heavy accent, he would recount tales of his adventures researching earthquakes during his travels in Soviet Central Asia—akin to the American West. He made a positive impression on me initially by whirling me around and playing with me. I remember nine-year-old me sitting on the floor of a room in our Riverside house, watching Saturday morning cartoons, when Mom came in to tell me that she was getting married. I was so excited I couldn't sit still. I had a stepfather! I even wanted to adopt his last name—an impulse that passed. He would not prove to be a hands-on parent. A typically unworldly scientist, he was always intensely focused on his work—predicting earthquakes using complicated and, to me, incomprehensible mathematical models. Everything else, including his new family, receded into the background.

I would see my biological father for only a few months each year when I was shipped off to Houston to spend the stifling southern summer with him and his younger second wife, a hairdresser also newly arrived from Russia. From a child's perspective, my father seemed to be living the quintessential American life of the swingin' seventies, complete with driving a big car made in Detroit, hosting pool parties at his new townhouse, playing tennis in short shorts, partying in shiny silk shirts, and, of course, consuming lots of cigarettes and booze. A character out of Philip Roth or Saul Bellow—a young Jewish striver on the make—he was full of strike-it-rich schemes that never quite materialized. Never lacking in self-confidence, he thought of himself as a major intellectual and resented the world for not sharing his self-assessment. But it was hard to hold his overactive imagination against him. He was a skilled raconteur who would hold listeners in thrall for hours talking about his favorite subject—himself. An irresponsible ne'er-do-well who did not contribute financially to my upbringing or attend my high school or college graduations, bar mitzvah, or wedding, my sybaritic father could nevertheless charm anyone he met—except possibly his own son. My ascetic mother, who died of cancer while I was writing this book, was considerably more responsible, sober, and hard-working but also more of a scold and not nearly as entertaining. My father was an exhibitionist; my mother, intensely private. He was portly; she, thin. It was no surprise they got divorced; the wonder was that they were ever married to begin with.

In the late 1970s and early 1980s, my father always seemed to be busy during the day, hustling for work as a freelance translator, soon to become an advertising copywriter, or . . . doing something else. I learned when I became a little older that he was a prodigious womanizer despite his beer belly, baldness, and generally unprepossessing appearance. While he was busy elsewhere—I never quite knew where—he would park me at an arcade with a bag of quarters to entertain myself playing Pac-Man, Space Invaders, and Frogger. But it wasn't as if he neglected my intellectual development.

WHEN I WAS THIRTEEN my father got me a subscription to *National Review*. As an émigré from a Communist country and a self-styled intellectual, he naturally embraced the most anti-Communist strand of American political life, and he wanted to introduce me to the ideas associated with the "conservative movement." Its Bible was *National Review*, a magazine launched in 1955 by William F. Buckley Jr., a wealthy young Yale graduate, to stand "athwart history, yelling Stop." I grew up reading *NR*, as it was known to its devotees, and thereby became immersed in the worldview of its regular writers—not only Buckley but also Richard Brookhiser, Joseph Sobran, Erik von Kuehnelt-Leddihn, Jeffrey Hart, Brian Crozier, John Simon, Ernest van den Haag, Ralph de Toledano, D. Keith Mano, and other stalwarts. They were hardly household names even in those days, but I can list their names more easily today than I can the star players on the Los Angeles Rams during their thrilling and unlikely run to the Super Bowl in 1979. The *NR* writers were a learned, worldly, elitist, and eccentric lot far removed from the simpleminded, cracker-barrel populists who have taken control of the conservative movement today. The Austrian-born Kuehnelt-Leddihn, for example, was a self-described monarchist who could speak eight languages and read seventeen others. Their brand of conservatism was known as fusionism, a term coined by the philosopher Frank Meyer for an inclusive approach combining free-market economics with traditional social views and a hawkish, anti-Communist foreign policy. This became my brand of conservatism too, at least when I was young—minus the Catholicism of Buckley and many of the magazine's other mavens.

In addition to faithfully reading *NR*, I read many of the books that had influenced its contributors or been written by them, including Whittaker Chambers's *Witness*, a searing chronicle of the author's break with Communism; F. A. Hayek's *The Road to Serfdom*, the influential free-market manifesto; Russell Kirk's *The Conservative Mind*, a compendium of the conservative canon; and

Edmund Burke's *Reflections on the Revolution in France*, the ur-text of modern conservatism, describing the English political philosopher's rejection of the radicalism of the French Revolution in favor of gradual, organic change. I doubt that Donald Trump has heard of any of these books, much less read them. I doubt, in fact, that his recreational reading has ever extended beyond *Golf* magazine or possibly *Playboy* when it still flourished. But these tomes were part of the common curriculum for conservatives of my generation.

My growing interest in politics was evident at my bar mitzvah in 1982 at the Wilshire Boulevard Temple in Los Angeles, a magnificent old pile of a synagogue that looked like a grand cathedral from Europe and that was located in a part of the city where few Jews lived anymore. It was presided over by another impressive relic, Rabbi Edgar Magnin. By then in his nineties, he was part of a department store dynasty and had been the "rabbi to the stars" since the birth of Hollywood in the 1910s. In my speech at the end of the ceremony I did not speak on the usual Torah theme. Even then I was more interested in worldly rather than religious affairs—of which I have remained lamentably and invincibly ignorant. I even had to read my Torah portions from an English transliteration. My speech, delivered in a newly purchased beige suit that I loved, was a defense of Israel's recent invasion of Lebanon. It displayed my precocity, my attachment to Israel, a country I had not yet visited— and my questionable judgment, since the invasion would turn out to be a fiasco that would embroil Israel in a Vietnam-like quagmire.

In case you haven't figured it out yet, I was a nerd. Massively so. I wasn't a math or science geek—I was never good at those subjects, which is perhaps one reason why I did not grow up to become a Silicon Valley billionaire. I was a humanities nerd, history division. That's why I used my bar mitzvah to share my views of geopolitics. Many people are drawn to conservatism by the study of economics or political philosophy. My route was via history. In my bedroom

I did not have pictures of typical teen idols. I had a giant portrait of Winston Churchill—the famous picture snapped by the peerless photographer Yousuf Karsh in 1941 showing the great man glowering. (Karsh induced that facial expression by plucking Churchill's cigar out of his mouth while he was posing.)

Like many American conservatives, I idolized Churchill and read everything by and about him that I could get my hands on. He impressed me not only because of his resolution and foresight in rejecting appeasement in the 1930s—he was a hawk who was amply vindicated by subsequent events—but also because of his graceful literary style and his appetite for adventure and the good life. In eighth grade at my public junior high school in the San Fernando Valley, I even made a deal with my English teacher to let me read Churchill's *History of the English-Speaking Peoples* instead of *The Adventures of Huckleberry Finn*. (I did eventually read Mark Twain's classic.) But the Churchill book I liked best was *My Early Life*, his rollicking account of growing up in an aristocratic British family and then serving as a young officer and war correspondent on the frontiers of the British Empire. From Churchill my interest expanded to World War II and then to military history generally.

My mother and stepfather, as typical members of the Russian intelligentsia, had highbrow tastes—they loved classical music, ballet, opera, and museums. Even living in Riverside, they would regularly shop at the one German deli in town where they could get sausages, beer, mustard, pickles, and other delicacies that reminded them of what they ate back in Russia. I lived in a halfway house between Russian and American culture but became increasingly Americanized as I grew older. While I never developed a taste for Wonder Bread, Coke, or cereal—those quintessential products of the American industrial-food complex—I did become an avid consumer of peanut butter and that American delicacy, french fries; a devotee of classic rock—the Beatles and the Clash, Tom Petty and Billy Joel—rather than of Bach, Beethoven, and Mozart; and an avid watcher of television in an era where there were only a handful of channels. *Mission Impossible*, *Rockford Files*, *Starsky & Hutch*, *Dukes of Hazzard*, *CHiPs*, *Greatest American Hero*—I loved all the action shows.

I read a lot but can't claim that all my reading was highbrow. Well, I could, but I wouldn't be telling the truth. I devoured a lot of comic books, which I carefully collected in plastic packets in the confident expectation that someday I would make a mint by reselling them. (I recently threw away all my comics in the process of cleaning out my parents' old home, thereby parting with another youthful illusion.) I didn't like the alienated superheroes, Spider-Man and the X-Men, that are so popular with angst-ridden teenagers. I liked the more mainstream, all-American heroes Batman and Superman; I particularly empathized with the Man of Steel because he was a visitor from another planet. As my TV-viewing and comic-book-reading habits make clear, I was becoming a typical suburban kid of the 1980s—achieving my great ambition of fitting into this new society to which I had been transplanted.

My mother and stepfather pretty well left me alone. They neither encouraged nor discouraged my headlong rush toward assimilation. They were busy at work, and this was a more easygoing era when no one thought anything of smoking around a kid or driving around without seatbelts. There were of course no cell phones or internet in the 1980s, so even though I watched too much TV and read too many comic books, there was plenty of time left over for thinking and dreaming. An only child, and not a particularly outgoing one, I spent a lot of my childhood by myself, lost in my own head. I recall that one of my persistent daydreams was to travel the world on a great big yacht with my father—a subconscious indication of how much I missed the old man even though I grew increasingly exasperated in my interactions with him as the years went by.

My dad's self-absorption and bumptiousness grated on me as I grew older; his stories became less amusing when I heard them for the fifth or sixth time. I saw less of him as I entered high school because I refused to spend my summers with him anymore. Perhaps for this reason our brands of conservatism diverged—a reminder of how many different views can lodge under that catchall title. He became a European-style reactionary who pined for the days of monarchy and admired the eighteenth-century anti-Enlightenment thinker Joseph de Maistre. After divorcing the Russian hairdresser, marrying an English woman, and moving to London in 1988, he often expressed his disdain for the United States as a proletarian place devoid of true culture. He liked the European Union even less: he compared it, absurdly enough, to Nazi Germany or the Soviet Union because of its supposedly undemocratic character. I, on the other hand, liked the European Union because it subsumed nationalist competition in Europe, and I loved the United States, my adopted homeland. His brand of conservatism seemed to me, a kid who had grown up in America, alien and strange. My brand of conservatism, which drew on the nineteenth-century English classical-liberal tradition, was firmly in the mainstream of American thought. At least in those days.

I WAS ALWAYS INTERESTED IN current events—hardly surprising given how closely the fate of my family had been tied to the twists and turns of the Cold War. My parents were faithful subscribers to the *Los Angeles Times* and *Newsweek*, and I recall unruly mounds of old issues of *Newsweek* piled up in our attic like fish on a deep-sea trawler. I read *Newsweek* along with *National Review* to get the facts from the former and opinions from the latter—a quaint distinction that still existed in those pre-internet days.

I was also a faithful devotee of the Sunday morning show on ABC, *This Week with David Brinkley*. Like millions of other Americans, I couldn't wait for the avuncular Brinkley to fill me in on "the news since the Sunday papers." My favorite part of the show was the roundtable at the end, when Brinkley would chew over the news of the day with Cokie Roberts, a genial Every Mom, and George F. Will, a bow-tied Tory delivering High Church judgments in crisp, complete sentences. It was a very civilized conversation, although I sensed that Will sometimes became exasperated with Roberts's liberal pieties.

Other kids dreamed of becoming athletes or astronauts. I dreamed of becoming a syndicated columnist like George F. Will or William F. Buckley Jr. I regularly watched Buckley's PBS show, *Firing Line*, in which he would engage in erudite conversation with a single guest, often a fellow intellectual, for thirty to sixty minutes. It was as far removed from the sound-bites and snark that dominate cable news today as quill pens and foolscap are from laptop computers and iPads. I can still picture in my mind's eye Buckley clutching his clipboard, his tie askew, slumping, in that peculiarly aristocratic way, ever lower in his chair until he was almost horizontal, arching his eyebrow, and delivering a devastating critique or cutting witticism with a slight smile flickering at the edge of his mouth. *Firing Line* elevated conservatism; the shows that conservatives watch today, primarily on the Fox News Channel, debase and dumb down the movement.

In 1984 Buckley came to speak at UCLA. I was in high school and drove with my mom across the hills from the San Fernando Valley to hear him deliver a typically dazzling oratorical performance punctuated by his Brobdingnagian vocabulary and coruscating wit. He radiated sophistication and joie de vivre. His books served up not only his conservative opinions but also his jet-set lifestyle—yachting across the Atlantic, skiing at St. Moritz, dining with John Kenneth Galbraith and David Niven. *This* was who I wanted to be. It goes without saying that Buckley, with his mid-Atlantic accent and aristocratic languor, would be derided by today's populists as a "globalist," "cuck," and "RINO" (Republican in name only) who doesn't sound or act like a "real" American.

One of the most important contributions that Buckley made from his perch at *National Review* was to drive assorted cranks and extremists out of the ranks of the right. He had initially sympathized with some of their views, particularly in his uncompromising anti-Communism and opposition to desegregation, but in the 1960s he exiled the John Birchers—conspiracy theorists so unhinged that they claimed Dwight D. Eisenhower was a Communist agent. Later he would excommunicate the writers Joseph Sobran, Samuel Francis, and Pat Buchanan for their blatant anti-Semitism. All the more painful, then, to see the intellectual heirs of these disreputable elements crawl out of the gutter to seize control of Buckley's movement.

Buckley clearly saw through Donald Trump, whom he identified as a narcissist and demagogue all the way back in 2000, when the real-estate developer was first flirting with a presidential campaign. "When he looks at a glass, he is mesmerized by its reflection," Buckley wrote. "If Donald Trump were shaped a little differently, he would compete for Miss America. But whatever the depths of self-enchantment, the demagogue has to say *something*. So what does Trump say? That he is a successful businessman and that that is what America needs in the Oval Office. There is some plausibility in this, though not much. The greatest deeds of American Presidents—midwifing the new republic; freeing the slaves; harnessing the energies and vision needed to win the Cold War—had little to do with a bottom line."[2]

But by the time Trump began running for president in 2015, Buckley had been in his grave for seven years. And even if he were still alive, he would not have exercised the same influence he once had. Buckley was a gatekeeper of the conservative movement. But there are no gatekeepers anymore. The democratization of politics via the internet has empowered the cranks and conspiracy-mongers, while making it impossible for more erudite eminences, to the extent that they still exist, to shape the conversation as Buckley once did.

IF BUCKLEY AND WILL were my intellectual heroes, my political hero was Ronald Reagan. How I loved that man. As a Soviet refugee, I thrilled to his anti-Communist rhetoric and his unapologetic defense of freedom. Discarding détente, Reagan said on May 17, 1981, "The West won't contain communism, it will transcend communism. . . . It will dismiss it as some bizarre chapter in human history whose last pages are even now being written." But it wasn't just his hard line against the Soviet Union and his championing of human rights and democracy that drew me to him. It was also his perceived goodness, his sincerity, his gentleness, his sheer niceness. Living in Riverside, a college town, when he was elected in 1980, I remembered predictions from liberals that if you voted for Reagan today, World War III would break out tomorrow. I never believed it. I believed in the Gipper. He was a movement conservative, just as I was becoming. He had read the books of the conservative canon—and subscribed to *National Review*—long before I was born.

I vividly recall the shock when I heard on March 30, 1981, that the president had been shot. The news arrived when I was sitting in the library of my elementary school in Riverside. A teacher wheeled out a large, clunky TV on a metal cart, antenna protruding from the back, and turned it on so we could watch one of the network newscasts. I was desperately worried until I heard that he would live.

I wished the best for Reagan, but always fretted when he sparred with the press. I was concerned that he would make one of his famous gaffes revealing that he wasn't in command of the facts, thereby providing ammunition for his numerous critics. Usually it was a needless worry, but he stumbled often enough to leave supporters like me on tenterhooks every time he spoke extemporaneously. When he was speaking from a teleprompter, however, there was no one better—as he proved on January 28, 1986. That was the day when the space shuttle *Challenger* exploded on takeoff, killing the entire crew and one passenger—Christa McAuliffe, who was to be the first teacher in space. Like countless other school kids across the nation, I was watching the launch. In an instant wonder turned to horror and we were left with nothing to see but the smoky contrail in the sky. Reagan was due to deliver the State of the Union that day. He turned it into a beautiful tribute to the dead astronauts. Peggy Noonan wrote the words, but no one other than Reagan could have said them so movingly: "We will never forget them, nor the last time we saw them, this morning, as they prepared for their journey and waved goodbye and 'slipped the surly bonds of earth' to 'touch the face of God.'" Along with the entire nation, I was touched and uplifted. That moment cemented my deep bond with the president. He became for me what JFK had been for an earlier generation: an icon and an inspiration. He made conservatism optimistic and inclusive—a sharp contrast to how dark and divisive the movement would become in more recent years.

The one time I saw Reagan in person was a thrilling occasion for me—and possibly even for him, although not because I was present. The last rally of his last political campaign was held on November 5, 1984. He was cruising toward a big reelection victory and decided to end his political career where it had begun—in Los Angeles. He spoke that day at Pierce Community College in Canoga Park, California, an unremarkable suburb full of strip malls and tract homes not far from the equally dreary suburb where I lived. I recall getting there hours ahead of time with a friend and roasting in the hot sun waiting for the president to make his appearance. The erstwhile matinee idol was natty as usual in his dark suit, his tie in a Windsor knot, a white handkerchief displayed in his breast pocket. He only spoke for about thirty minutes but did not disappoint. "I've come to the people of the San Fernando Valley to ask for support many times before," Reagan said in that soft-spoken, appealing, aw-shucks way of his, "and I'd like to ask you this last time to be with us tomorrow." The crowd of twenty thousand roared back, "Four more years! Four more years!" Normally I hate crowds and groupthink, but I happily joined in.

Nobody would ever confuse this lovefest with the kind of hate-mongering that would become characteristic of Trump rallies. Reagan did not attack his opponent or the news media or minority groups or anyone else. He simply offered an optimistic vision epitomized by his slogan "Morning in America." Today, by contrast, the conservative movement seems to think that it's two minutes to midnight and that an extremist agenda is justified in order to save the country from impending doom at the hands of liberals. I am incredulous that anyone could possibly compare Reagan to Trump. The former had dignity, grace, humor, and class that the latter can only dream of. Reagan may not have known as much about public policy as intellectuals expected, but compared to Trump, he might as well have been a political science PhD, having spent decades reading, writing, and speaking about the issues. Reagan offered hope; Trump, fear.

Reagan inspired me to work on my first political campaign as a high school student, volunteering for the Ed Zschau for US Senate campaign in 1986, the year that the Chernobyl nuclear reactor blew up in the Soviet Union and the Iran-Contra scandal blew up in Washington. I spent countless hours laboring without remuneration for Zschau, a young, moderate Republican running against the aged liberal lion, Senator Alan Cranston. Zschau fell just short, but the Republican governor, George Deukmejian, was easily reelected to a second term. That was back in the days when there was a viable Republican Party in California—before Senator Pete Wilson was elected governor in 1990 and embarked on an anti-immigrant agenda that alienated the state's growing Latino population. Wilson, a far more moderate and reasonable figure, did to the California GOP what Donald Trump may well be doing to the national GOP.

The Zschau campaign didn't win, but I loved the experience— even the drudge work, which is most of what I did. I stuffed envelopes, made copies, answered mail—whatever was necessary. The spirit of camaraderie among the campaign staff in the Sunset Boulevard office left a deep impression on me. I relished the sense that we are all conservatives working together to defeat a liberal Democrat notorious for his dovish approach to the Soviet Union and his hawkish approach toward Ronald Reagan.

THERE WERE OTHER INFLUENCES on my embryonic conservatism, not just politics and history but writing and criticism. The curmudgeonly and conservative Baltimore newspaperman H. L. Mencken, who died in 1956, was a particular favorite. I savored his hilarious, stylish, and lacerating essays even if I did not share his contempt for democracy or the ordinary Americans that he lampooned as the "booboisie." I was even less in sympathy with the racist and anti-Semitic sentiments he revealed in letters published long after his death. In more recent years, however, I have concluded that Mencken's skepticism about "the swinish multitude" was well justified. The ignorance and extremism he denounced in early-twentieth-century America—exemplified, in his view, by the populist rabble-rouser William Jennings Bryan, who argued against teaching the theory of evolution—is more evident than ever in the early twenty-first century. I often think of Mencken's description of democracy—"Democracy is the theory that the common people know what they want, and deserve to get it good and hard"—when I think of the triumph of Trump.

A master of the bon mot, Mencken had a description that could not be bettered of how he became a writer. He spoke for me when he wrote:

> It happens that I was born with an intense and insatiable interest in ideas, and thus like to play with them. It happens also that I was born with rather more than the average facility for putting them into words. In consequence, I am a writer and editor, which is to say, a dealer in them and concoctor of them.
>
> There is very little conscious volition in all this. What I do was ordained by the inscrutable fates, not chosen by me. In my boyhood, yielding to a powerful but still subordinate interest in exact facts, I wanted to be a chemist, and at the same time my poor father tried to make me a business man. At other times, like any other relatively poor man, I have longed to make a lot of money by some easy swindle. But I became a writer all the same, and shall remain one until the end of the chapter, just as a cow goes on giving milk all her life, even though what appears to be her self-interest urges her to give gin.[3]

I only differed from Mencken in never entertaining any hopes of becoming a chemist or businessman. I did think of becoming a lawyer—an ambition encouraged by my father—but only because I doubted my ability to make a living as a writer.

I felt the urge to write as early as junior high school, when a friend and I came up with a prototype for an unofficial school newspaper. My ambition would be realized in high school when some friends and I would start an "underground" newspaper called *The Forum*. We loved making trouble for the administrators at Grover Cleveland High School in Reseda, California, a public school that, with its low-slung buildings surrounded by fences and its windows covered in bars, looked from a distance like a minimum-security prison. *The Forum*'s publication was suspended by the principal after we published an article accusing the mathematics department of "rampant ineptitude" because of students' low scores on standardized state tests. We promptly called up the *Los Angeles Times* and were featured in an article as First Amendment heroes. It was, of course, a lot easier to champion free speech in an American public school than in the Soviet Union, but that experience impressed on me as a teenager the importance of freedom of the press—a realization that has not dawned on Trump even in his seventies. By my senior year, I was editor not only of the underground newspaper but also of the official student newspaper, *Le Sabre*. I was also the Los Angeles County champion in mock trial. You might say that my careers as a lawyer and a newspaper mogul both peaked before the age of eighteen.

I was respected by my peers but hardly beloved; I was voted "most likely to succeed," not "most popular." I was a good student but not a quiet or obedient one. I loved to mouth off in class, challenging the leftist views of my teachers at the Cleveland Humanities Magnet—a school within a school for kids especially interested in the liberal arts—with the conservative orthodoxy I was imbibing from *National Review*. I'm sure I was insufferable, but I reveled in dissenting. Did I mention that I was also captain of the debate team? I loved arguing with anyone about everything. My best friend in high school, who later became a lawyer, was an equally opinionated liberal, and we would spend hours happily debating with each other. When we got to college—we both went to the University of California at Berkeley, which cost next to nothing for in-state residents in those days—our girlfriends quickly tired of this forensic ritual. But we loved it.

In retrospect I think that arguing, in print and person, gave me a way to interact with the world that I found comfortable, whereas less antagonistic interactions were harder for me, because I was naturally shy. I loved getting a rise out of people, which helps to explain why I wrote contrarian if not particularly wise articles for *The Forum*, such as one arguing that money can buy happiness.

MY EXPERIENCE AT a liberal high school was perfect preparation for my undergraduate career as a conservative troublemaker in Berkeley, a town that never seemed to have left the sixties behind. The counterculture was the dominant culture in Berkeley even in the conservative 1980s. The Spartacist League bookstore still sold Marxist tracts; hippies still congregated in People's Park; and peace signs and tie-dyes could still be seen all along the main drag, Telegraph Avenue. My favorite all-night hot-dog stand, Top Dog, even served its wieners with a side of libertarian politics. There would be a riot during my senior year in 1991 to protest the university's attempts to place volleyball courts in People's Park, thus re-creating the riot that broke out in 1969 when the university tried to build a sports field atop this same weed-infested block that had become a magnet for drug dealers and addicts.

I lived initially in Slavic House, an elegant, university-owned house on fraternity row reserved for students of Slavic languages; my mother pulled a few strings to get me in, even though I had no intention of studying any Slavic language, because I had lost out in the housing lottery for space in the normal high-rise dormitories that looked like Soviet workers' housing. It was at Slavic House, as a sophomore, that I met my future wife during a party fueled by vodka-spiked punch. She first heard that I existed when another resident told her that there was a "fascist" living down the hall with a "Bush-Quayle '88" sticker on his door. It didn't take much to be branded a fascist in the ultraliberal atmosphere of Berkeley! But while I did not hide my views, I was eager to make my mark in campus journalism, not politics.

One of the first things I did upon arriving in the fall of 1987 was to head to *The Daily Californian*, the official student newspaper, which was headquartered in a pink stucco building a few blocks from campus. I spent much of my first two years covering the Berkeley City Council. It was a fascinating experience because Berkeley was one of the few towns in America with its own foreign policy. The city council was regularly passing resolutions condemning Reagan's hawkish foreign policy and Israel's occupation of Palestine. I rolled my eyes every time the council members launched into their predictable diatribes cribbed from the pages of *The Nation*. I also covered numerous rallies and sit-ins on campus. Once, demonstrators occupied Sproul Hall, the campus administration building, and, while I watched, they had a lively debate to figure out why—were they asking for a nuclear freeze, divestment from South Africa, greater diversity on campus, an end to animal testing, or some other demand? In other words, protest first, cause second. This juvenile posturing increased my scorn for the left—not that I was above juvenile posturing myself. I was just posturing from the right rather than the left.

Before long I transitioned from reporting to editorializing. In the fall of 1989 I did a semester abroad at the London School of Economics. When I came back, I ran in the *Daily Cal*'s election to become a columnist. In true communal fashion, all the editors and columnists were elected by the staff. A lot of people were inclined to vote against me because of my conservative views, but, as I recall, Jim Herron Zamora, a future editor in chief and a true newsman, urged a yes vote because he thought it would be fun to "wind up Max and point him at City Hall." I won and immediately penned a column in January 1990 about the cognitive dissonance I felt returning from Europe after the fall of the Berlin Wall, which I saw as vindication of Ronald Reagan's Cold War policies and proof of the enduring appeal of American-style liberal democracy. The US triumph in the Cold War made me proud to be an American— and a conservative. "While Eastern Europe is being transformed by a new longing for economic prosperity and political freedom," I wrote, "Berkeley remains mired in a rigid, New Left mindset created 30 years ago. Nostalgia for the politics and protests of the 1960s dominates this town's collective consciousness. The signs of it are everywhere. Note the prevalence of tie-dyes, lovebeads, and Birkenstocks—all symbols of a world that has not existed for 20 years."

That set the tone for the weekly columns that I would write for the next year and a half until my graduation. I loved making a bonfire of Berkeley's liberal pieties, including its rent-control regulations that made housing hard to find, its tolerance of homeless people that made the streets dangerous to walk, and its affection for the Communist dictator of Nicaragua that made a mockery of human rights. I expressed standard conservative views—for example, attacking affirmative action quotas and supporting the Gulf War. Like many conservatives of the day, I often protested political correctness that stifled free speech, writing that anyone who disagrees with the left "is labeled (pick one) 'fascist,' 'homophobe,' 'racist,' or 'elitist.'" "The biggest threat to the First Amendment," I wrote, "comes from the left, not the right." (That is a view I no longer hold in the age of Trump.)

My articles caused considerable consternation on campus, where conservative opinions were rarely heard. One reader tossed a brick through the window of the *Daily Cal* building in protest. Another sent me a bullet in the mail with my name taped on it. I wasn't the slightest bit intimidated. I loved the attention and notoriety. And the violent reaction only confirmed in my mind the rightness of my views, in both senses of the word.

In early 2018, I went back to Berkeley as part of a book tour, and, with an hour to kill before my lecture, visited the university library to read my old columns on microfilm. Some of them I still endorse, including my criticisms of rent control, an anticapitalist conceit that reduced the stock of rental housing not only in Berkeley but also in New York, where I would move a few years later. But some things I wrote now make me cringe—for example, my reaction to a 1990 hostage siege at an off-campus hangout called Henry's. A deranged, heavily armed gunman held thirty-three people hostage, killing one and wounding seven, before he was gunned down by the Berkeley police SWAT team. In my column, I for some reason endorsed the death penalty, even though the assailant was already dead. Presumably this was because support for capital punishment, which had been suspended by the Supreme Court in 1972 before being reinstated four years later, was such a big conservative cause in those days. Just as predictably for someone indoctrinated in conservatism, I resisted calls for stricter gun control. "We don't need even tougher restrictions, because the status of gun law has little relation with the ability of determined maniacs to acquire weapons," I wrote. "Gun control only deters law-abiding citizens from defending themselves. (Imagine how the outcome of the Henry's incident may have been different if one of the patrons had been armed.)"

Was I really suggesting it would have been a good idea for some

boozy customer to whip out a Glock and open up? Apparently
so. Then, as now, this was the conventional wisdom on the right,
which exaggerates the defensive use of firearms by law-abiding citizens and minimizes their use in homicides and suicides. I joined
in fetishizing the Second Amendment as a license to sell just about
any gun to just about anyone—even though the historical record
and plain text clearly indicate that this language was intended to
prevent the federal government from shutting down state militias.
It has taken me decades to break free of the pro-gun orthodoxy. I
now favor stricter gun controls, which are permissible even under
the Second Amendment, because the only explanation for the prevalence of gun violence in America—we have six times as many
firearms homicides as Canada and nearly sixteen times as many as
Germany—is the ready availability of guns.[4] But in those days I
faithfully echoed the conservative party line.

While mine was an often lonely voice in "Berzerkeley," there
were plenty of other conservatives on other college campuses in the
1980s and 1990s. Reagan had made conservatism cool, and right-
wing donors were funding conservative newspapers to battle what
they regarded as a stifling leftist orthodoxy on campus. The most
notorious publication was the *Dartmouth Review*, which produced
the future far-right superstars Dinesh D'Souza and Laura Ingraham.
As *Mother Jones* magazine later noted: "While [D'Souza] helmed the
Review, it published a 'lighthearted interview with a former Klan
leader'—accompanied by a staged photo of a black person hanging
from a tree—and an assault on affirmative action titled, 'Dis Sho
Ain't No Jive, Bro,' which was written in Ebonics. ('Now we be
comin' to Dartmut and be up over our 'fros in studies, but we still
be not graduatin' Phi Beta Kappa.') The 'Jive' article caused Jack
Kemp, a conservative icon mindful of the right's problems with
minority outreach, to resign from the *Review*'s advisory board."[5]
The *Review* also outed members of the Gay Students Association at

a time when "coming out" was still a risky thing to do; one of the outed students reportedly "became severely depressed and talked repeatedly of suicide."

While there was undoubtedly some overlap between my writings and those in publications like the *Review*, my college journalism was less sensationalistic and less offensive. I was not a racist; as a Jewish immigrant, I identified with other minorities. To my shame, I must admit that I shared some of the homophobic attitudes of that less-enlightened time—prejudices that I have long since outgrown—but I would never have dreamed of singling out anyone for public humiliation. There were, from the start, sharp limits on how far I would go in pushing my political views. Provoking people, for me, was not an end in itself. I liked Ronald Reagan's approach—or what I took to be his approach—of offering an outstretched hand rather than a clenched fist. That was not the case with many of my conservative contemporaries, who made a career of becoming ever more transgressive to get attention. Little did I suspect that this all-out assault on liberalism would set the stage for the political triumph of a boorish real-estate developer who in the 1980s was regularly mocked as a "short-fingered vulgarian" in the now-defunct *Spy* magazine, one of my favorite periodicals besides *National Review*.

In the 1990s, I felt solidarity with other young conservatives who were determined to complete the conservative revolution that Reagan had begun. My faith in the movement was strong; it would be decades before my certitudes would begin to corrode as I watched conservatism morph into something I could not recognize. When I graduated from college in the spring of 1991, shortly after the American victory in the Gulf War and shortly before the collapse of the Soviet Union, I knew I wanted to contribute to the great cause.

I just had to figure out how.

2.

THE
CAREER
OF A
CONSERVATIVE

M Y PERSPECTIVE ON CONSERVATISM WOULD SHIFT as I went from being an outsider—a fanboy on the left coast—to an insider: a professional journalist, historian, and foreign policy pundit in the Acela Corridor. I would become personally acquainted with many of the conservative sages whose writings I had grown up reading. In some cases, familiarity would breed contempt. But in many other instances, my respect would only grow as I got to know my boyhood heroes personally. At one point, I would declare that the smartest people I knew were conservatives: a statement I now regard as the height of folly. That I would say such a thing is indicative of the mindset that I developed as a "movement" conservative. I was not just drinking the Kool-Aid; I was bathing in it. I understand what Fox News viewers experience because I experienced a version of the same brainwashing myself. This was a process of indoctrination—largely self-indoctrination, I should add—that took decades and that I am only now escaping.

That's not to say that I am leaving behind all, or even most of, what I believed then. Rather, as I approach my fifties, I am sorting out for myself what makes sense and what doesn't in the conservative Weltanschauung. That is not something I was capable of doing in my twenties, when I was just being initiated into the world of the right. Back then, my enthusiasm for conservatism was excessive and indiscriminate, as is so often the case with a proselyte.

I COULD HAVE GONE to work as an entry-level reporter for some newspaper after graduation, most likely the *Los Angeles Times*; I had had college internships at the *Times* bureau in Sacramento and the *Baltimore Sun* bureau in Washington, and I had worked as the *Times*'s stringer in Berkeley. But I didn't relish covering the "night cops" beat or working in some dull suburban bureau—the normal initiation rituals for cub reporters. So instead I went to graduate school, studying history at Yale University. Between my college graduation and the start of grad school I got married to my college girlfriend. While I was taking classes at Yale, she applied to law school—and got into Harvard but not Yale. In 1992, having received an MA from Yale after just a year amid the urban decay of New Haven, I moved with her to Cambridge so she could go to Harvard Law School.

Living in a small duplex in north Cambridge—this was Tip O'Neill's old district—was an education for me. In California, where I had grown up, people of pallor were an unvariegated mass known collectively as Anglos. In the Boston area, by contrast, they were not simply white people—they were Italians, Irish, Poles, Portuguese, etc. This was my introduction to the white ethnic, working-class politics that Donald Trump would exploit so skillfully across the Rust Belt. Our landlord was an Italian American barber who had lived in this area his whole life and regarded a trip to Harvard Square—a mile away—as a journey to a strange and bewildering land. Above his mantel he had a picture of his hero, John F. Kennedy. He was socially conservative but strongly identified with the Democratic Party. If he is still alive, I wonder if today he might not be displaying a Trump photo.

I left grad school—temporarily, I thought—to work as a junior editor at the *Christian Science Monitor* in Boston. The newspaper had a distinguished pedigree; at one time it had been one of only two national newspapers in America, the other being the *Wall Street Journal*, and it was known for its outstanding international coverage and a sober, serious approach to the news. But the national rollout of the *New York Times* usurped the *Monitor*'s position, and its costly and ill-conceived foray into television sapped it of precious operating capital. By the time I arrived, many of its most distinguished editors and correspondents had left. That was perfect from my perspective because it gave me—a twenty-two-year-old kid—the chance to assume responsibilities far beyond my modest level of experience. I not only worked as an assistant editor on the national desk but also wrote numerous articles, reveling in the thrill of having my byline appear in print.

I had actually applied to, and gotten into, the Harvard history department, but by the time it was time to go back to grad school in the fall of 2003, I decided to stay in journalism. Editing and writing was more fun than going to class and then heading to a dive bar to commiserate with fellow grad students about the awful job market for history PhDs. I knew that it would be especially hard for me to find a job in the academy because of my conservative views and interest in military history—both intellectual deviations frowned upon by the liberal professoriate. Journalism seemed like a more promising and interesting alternative.

Because the *Monitor* was distributed by the US Postal Service, it had absurdly early deadlines—around 1 p.m. in those days. I recall trudging through fields of snow up to my knees at the crack of dawn to reach the Alewife T stop in north Cambridge to take the train to Back Bay. It was a culture shock for a Californian, but a return to my heritage as a Muscovite. The early deadlines made it hard to stay on top of the news, so we focused more on analysis, but in a rigorously even-handed way. For the time being I put aside my conservative views and concentrated on learning the newspaper trade as a "straight" journalist—not an editorialist. The *Monitor* was strict about maintaining its neutrality and integrity, so I was trained quite differently from young writers today who are hired by click-hungry websites with the expectation that they will inject "attitude" and opinion into their writing from the start. Indeed, online publications such as *Infowars* and *Breitbart* and broadcasters such as Fox News Channel and RT have entirely destroyed the demarcation line between opinion and news—they peddle their self-serving fantasies as if they were reality. My time at the *Monitor* taught me to be more devoted to getting the facts right. Hence I am especially offended that America now has a president who repeats the same lies over and over, long after they have been called out by the fact-checkers.

One of the oddities of the *Monitor* was that almost everyone who worked in the home office—a massive modernist building located next to the Romanesque Mother Church in Boston's fashionable Back Bay neighborhood—was a Christian Scientist. I was practically the only non-Scientist in headquarters, although many of the correspondents in far-flung bureaus were also nonbelievers. Luckily, as a Russian Jewish immigrant in America and a conservative Republican at Berkeley, I had had plenty of experience being a minority. I discovered that Scientists were nice people, but it took a while to adjust to the peculiarities of their religion. Because they believe that the entire physical world is only a figment of "the immortal Mind" of God, they don't celebrate birthdays, acknowledge deaths (people are said to "pass"), or use medical metaphors (no "budget headaches" for them). They are best known for relying on faith healers known as "practitioners" rather than medical doctors. When someone was absent from the office for a few days, you never knew whether she had a cold or terminal cancer—either way, she wasn't going to admit that anything was physically wrong. I got tired of having people ask, when I told them I worked for the *Monitor*, whether I had health insurance. The answer was yes—heretics like me could use our health benefits to see a real doctor. In truth, some of the Scientists would sneak aspirin themselves.

My exposure to the Christian Science faith deepened my appreciation for the diversity of America and made me realize I could like people very different from myself even if there were far more of "them" than there were of people like me. I wish more Trump supporters, anxious about the changing demographics of America, would have a similar epiphany.

WHILE I ENJOYED WORKING AT the *Monitor*, my dream was to enter the world of conservative punditry. I set my sights on the editorial page of the *Wall Street Journal*, which I had taken to reading in college. The *Journal* was known for its advocacy of supply-side economics, the notion that cuts in taxes and regulations can spur economic growth. It was a philosophy that Ronald Reagan adopted as his own. *Journal* editorials were reported and influential and did not hesitate to disagree with the more liberal views of the *Journal*'s news pages. I wasn't particularly interested in the financial markets, but the *Journal* had expanded to become a more general interest newspaper that set the tone for much of the Republican Party. It reached a far bigger audience than a niche publication like *National Review*—it was, in fact, the largest circulation daily newspaper in America, with 1.7 million subscribers.

I would regularly mail clippings of my *Daily Californian* and *Christian Science Monitor* articles to the *Journal* editorial page (this was in the days before the internet and email), receiving in reply nothing more than form letters. I did not have much hope that my aspirations would be realized until one day in early 1994, when

I was notified that Robert L. Bartley, the editorial page editor, would be in Boston and wanted to meet me. He was a legendary journalist who had taken over the editorial page in 1972 at age thirty-four and had won a Pulitzer Prize in 1980. He did not just run an editorial page; he ran his own news-gathering operation in competition not only with other newspapers but also with the *Journal*'s news side. Bartley was one of the most influential opinion shapers among conservatives. I was intimidated and excited to meet him.

I trudged through the snow to the stately old Parker House hotel (this was where Parker rolls had been invented) for one of the more unexpected and important meetings of my life. I had imagined that Bartley would quiz me about my political views. In preparation I had prepared elaborate disquisitions on my Burkean conservative philosophy. Instead he preferred to talk about my work in journalism. He wanted skilled journalists, not untrained ideologues, working for him. He would later say, "Journalistically, my proudest boast is that I've run the only editorial page in the country that actually sells newspapers." Our conversation was halting and stilted; Bartley, slight and bespectacled, was shy and retiring in person, not an easy person to talk to in spite of his perpetual Mona Lisa smile. I thought I had blown the interview until he casually mentioned that he had a couple of job openings—one for an editorial writer on economics, the other for an assistant op-ed editor. Which one would I prefer? Somehow I had been hired.

I was horrified at the prospect of becoming the economics editorialist for the nation's premier business newspaper. I had never taken a class in the subject and had no interest in it. Bartley was serenely unperturbed. I later learned that he liked to take writers who did not know much about the subject and train them in his way of thinking. He did not want to hire an economist because most professional economists disdained supply-side economics—

the philosophy that he had embraced at the urging of economists Arthur Laffer and Robert Mundell and former editorial-page writer Jude Wanniski. In spite of Bartley's confidence in my abilities to write economics editorials, I opted for the op-ed editing job and prepared to move to New York.

I was thrilled to have gotten this opportunity. When I joined the *Wall Street Journal* in 1994 at the age of just twenty-four, I felt as if I had already fulfilled my life's ambitions. My mother was predictably proud; my father was just as predictably unimpressed. I considered myself supremely lucky to be at the epicenter of conservative politics and journalism. I had joined what Michael Kinsley had called "a central cog in the vast right-wing conspiracy." It was a description meant to be disparaging but one that we embraced. I was dazzled by new colleagues such as John Fund, a walking encyclopedia of American politics; Paul Gigot, the Pulitzer Prize–winning "Potomac Watch" columnist (and Bartley's eventual successor), who seemed supremely plugged into Washington; and Dorothy Rabinowitz, an unconventional woman of indeterminate age who dressed in all black and was always making amusing and acerbic observations on the passing scene.

Now that I was working in the heart of the conservative moment, I got to meet its other luminaries. I was invited on a cruise around Manhattan to celebrate *National Review*'s fortieth anniversary, and I went to Bill Buckley's townhouse for dinner with him and his editors. I found the experience every bit as enchanting as I had imagined, if also a bit intimidating. Buckley was the height of geniality, but his social X-ray wife, Pat, was more ferocious and standoffish. The evening ended, as I recall, with Buckley playing the harpsichord.

This was part of my introduction to conservative society in New York—a small but intense circle of right-wingers who tended to stick together in this liberal city. There was a conservative social circuit that included annual fundraising dinners hosted by the Manhattan Institute and *Commentary* magazine, where big-bucks donors mingled with down-at-the-heels writers like me; modest Christmas parties for the highbrow crowd at the offices of the *New Criterion*; monthly gatherings of the Monday Meeting, a networking opportunity for a motley collection of conservative activists promoting every cause from the gold standard to the horse-drawn carriages of Central Park; regular fundraisers hosted by wealthy GOP donors such as Paul Singer and Mallory Factor to fete and cross-examine candidates for high office; book talks hosted by the influential philanthropist and deeply learned patron of history Roger Hertog; and more informal occasions such as an annual holiday gala in the airy SoHo loft of James and Heather Higgins, prominent conservative activists and philanthropists who were close to Newt Gingrich and other leading Republicans in Washington. A special mark of favor was to be invited to spend the weekend at the Hamptons estate of one of these wealthy luminaries. Needless to say, such invitations would be extended only to those who faithfully toed the party line. (I haven't been receiving a lot of them lately from Trump supporters.)

I'm sure that similar pressures exist on the left that can be just as straitening. This is how all social, ideological, or religious movements police their members—by making clear that agreement will be rewarded with greater social standing and support, and disagreement punished with ostracism. This pressure is so amorphous and pervasive that, like oxygen, you are only aware of it when it is gone.

My arrival as a "made guy" of the conservative moment was ratified a few years later, in 2007, when I won the Eric Breindel Award for Excellence in Opinion Journalism, given annually to a writer who exhibits "love of country and its democratic institutions" and "bears witness to the evils of totalitarianism." The award had been established by Rupert Murdoch in honor of the late editorial page editor of the *New York Post*, one of many newspapers that he owned. I received the honor, along with a munificent $20,000 check, at a dinner cohosted by Murdoch and Roger Ailes, the impresario behind Fox News. I strained to understand Murdoch's Australian-accented mumbling and roared at Ailes's coarse humor. I could not possibly imagine then that a few years later I would be bemoaning their creation, Fox News Channel, as a pernicious influence on American life—as, in fact, a threat to this country's democratic institutions.

In joining this conservative counterculture, I got to meet Norman Podhoretz and Irving Kristol, two of the most prominent "neocons," meaning literally "new conservatives." They had been Democrats who had drifted to the right in the 1960s and 1970s and eventually became enthusiastic supporters of Ronald Reagan. Kristol was the editor of the *Public Interest*, Podhoretz of *Commentary*—two little magazines whose intellectual impact was out of all proportion to their meager circulations. I became friendly, too, with their sons, John Podhoretz and William Kristol, who were neocon royalty of a sort. Together with the well-known pundit Fred Barnes, they launched a new magazine called the *Weekly Standard* in 1995 to serve as a standard-bearer for a new generation of conservatives. I became a contributing editor to the *Weekly Standard* and spent a decade (2007–2017) as a blogger for *Commentary*. Bill Kristol became a mentor and good friend, whose genial, wisecracking company I regularly sought out when I was in Washington or he was in New York.

Perhaps because the Kristols and Podhoretzes were Jewish and could trace their ancestry back to Eastern Europe, just like me, I found myself drawing closer to these neoconservatives than to the heavily Catholic and more socially conservative *National Review* crowd. Before long I would find myself described as a "neocon," a term that was often used as a slur to mean "Jewish conservative" or simply "ultrahawk." I bristled at the description because I wasn't a "new" conservative, never having been a Trotskyite or even a Democrat. Neither had Bill Kristol or John Podhoretz. We were all "right from the beginning" as much as the arch-nativist Pat Buchanan, who used that phrase as the title of his autobiography. Buchanan's attacks, however, were good preparation for the routine charges of disloyalty and demands that we move "back" to Israel or Russia or some other country that Jewish conservatives have faced in the age of Trump.

I FOUND IT HARD AT FIRST to figure out how things worked at the *Wall Street Journal* editorial page. The newspaper not only preached laissez-faire doctrine but also practiced it. There was a daily meeting in the doorless office of Dan Henninger, the deputy editorial page editor, but the most striking characteristic of these gatherings was the long periods of silence. This took some getting used to for a hypervocal Jewish kid from Los Angeles. A product of Minnesota and Iowa, Bob Bartley was so shy and introspective that he was comfortable sitting for long minutes without saying anything, just staring at the ceiling. The meetings became almost a staring contest to see who could go the longest without speaking. I had to resist the urge to fill the dead air. People would wander in and out and nothing ever seemed to get decided, yet somehow at the end of the day, every day, a complete editorial page emerged as if by magic. Bartley managed by indirection, making vague, cryptic comments and leaving his subordinates to intuit what he would want them to do. Remarkably enough, this hands-off approach worked.

Bartley did not write editorials himself every day, but when he did they were inevitably razor sharp. Somehow this diffident bookworm would turn into a ninja warrior on the printed page, severing his adversaries' rhetorical aortas with a few flicks of his metaphorical sword. I am similarly paradoxical: mild in person, fierce in print. My partner Sue would later tell me that she was surprised when she met me, having known me only through my writing, to discover that I wasn't an "asshole."

I advanced rapidly at the editorial page, in part because I was deemed good at my job, but also because of the high turnover. My first boss at the op-ed page was Amity Shlaes. Then she left for another division of Dow Jones, the publisher of the *Journal*, and was replaced by David Brooks. Then he left for the *Weekly Standard* and was replaced by David Asman. Then he left for a new TV network called Fox News. I was the last man standing. In 1998, at the age of twenty-eight, I became the op-ed editor of the *Wall Street Journal*. I was in charge of three signed articles, called editorial features, that appeared every day next to the editorials, known in-house as "randos" because they appeared under the banner of "Review & Outlook."

I fully subscribed to the views of the editorial page. Its motto was "Free Men and Free Markets" (later changed to the gender neutral "Free People"), and it advocated tax cuts, free trade, immigration, a strong defense, and an internationalist foreign policy. We didn't talk much about social issues. Bob was hardly a fundamentalist, but he also didn't want to offend the religious right, whose support Republican candidates needed to win, so he generally steered clear of saying anything at all on the subject. I was becoming more liberal on social issues, but I didn't disagree with his pragmatic judgment, in part because my own views had been molded over the years by reading the *Journal*'s editorial page.

Bartley's obsession in the 1990s was "Whitewater," a catchall phrase for alleged financial wrongdoing by the Clintons. We ran rando after rando on this subject; one of them ("Who Was Vince

Foster?") was even blamed for contributing to the suicide of a White House lawyer who had been a Hillary Clinton law partner in Little Rock. Phrases such as "Rose law firm" and "Mena airport" constantly cropped up; I had a flash of recognition years later when I saw the Tom Cruise movie *American Made*, which featured a real-life drug smuggler and sometime CIA operative operating out of the Mena, Arkansas, airport. The evidence of Clinton misconduct was hardly conclusive, and the editorials were so carefully lawyered that it was hard for me to figure out just what they were supposed to have done wrong. I still can't say, for example, what the connection was supposed to be between Governor Clinton and Mena Airport. But Bartley was so proud of his work that he published six volumes of Whitewater editorials as stand-alone books.

These editorials could be seen as contributing to the growing tendency in American public life not just to disagree with one's political opponents but also to try to annihilate them—a trend that ultimately culminated in the election of Donald Trump, a Republican who vituperates Democrats as traitors and charges that "they certainly don't seem to love our country very much."[1] The left was far from innocent in this regard—"to Bork" had become a political term for character assassination after the mauling that Judge Robert Bork had received in his Supreme Court confirmation hearing in 1987—but the right certainly bore its share of guilt. Both sides used the past outrages perpetrated against their partisans to justify their own outrages against the other side. It was an eye for an eye, a tooth for a tooth, until the body politic would be in danger of becoming sightless and toothless.

In the end President Clinton would be brought low, at least temporarily, not by his greed but his libido. His ill-conceived dalliance with his White House intern Monica Lewinsky opened the way for the Republican-controlled House to impeach him for perjury because he lied under oath about their assignations. I shared the outrage of other conservatives over Clinton's tawdry behavior and the way he had demeaned the presidency, and I was dismayed that liberals excused his conduct. Unlike many other conservatives, however, I did not think that Clinton was the devil incarnate. He was a center-of-the-road president who cooperated with a Republican Congress to eliminate the budget deficit and reform the welfare system. I thought he was a deeply flawed man, but I appreciated the achievements of his presidency.

Ever a contrarian, I decided, as one of my first initiatives as the *Journal*'s op-ed editor, to commission an article critical of supply-side economics from a Princeton professor named Paul Krugman—not yet a celebrated *New York Times* columnist. That didn't work out so well. Bartley saw the article on the lineup and came into my office to let me know in his soft-spoken way that he didn't want to run it. I had to call Krugman to apologize and pay a kill fee; he graciously passed up an opportunity to publicly embarrass the newspaper. There was an official liberal slot opposite the editorial page—a rotating column written by authors such as Christopher Hitchens and Alexander Cockburn—and Bartley wasn't interested in seeing a lot of contrary viewpoints beyond that. His reasoning was that other newspapers such as the *New York Times* provided plenty of space for the liberal orthodoxy; he wanted the *Journal*'s editorial pages to be a forum for the right. I barely managed to avoid losing my job over the Krugman debacle; Bartley apparently thought about removing me but decided to give the tyro another chance. This was an early indication to me that groupthink could be just as tenacious on the right as on the left.

While I could not run too many head-on attacks against the *Journal*'s editorial line, I did manage to sneak all sorts of nonpolitical articles onto the page by authors who weren't conservative ideologues. For instance, I convinced a former hedge fund manager named Andy Kessler to write on business news, and a former boxer turned philosophy professor named Gordon Marino to write on boxing news. I have always had an intolerance of orthodoxy, even when I agreed with it, and I was interested in producing a lively page full of unexpected insights rather than simply rote repetitions of the party line. I was greatly aided in this task by an outstanding cast of assistant editors, including a young Bret Stephens and a young Kimberly Strassel. The civil war that would eventually rip apart the conservative movement would lead Bret to become a prominent #NeverTrumper and Kim a prominent pro-Trumper.

ALTHOUGH WORKING PRIMARILY AS an editor, I also got a chance to write unsigned editorials. It was a heady experience for a twenty-something to write in the royal "we" with all the eminence and majesty of America's largest newspaper behind his every word. I'm sure that the people reading my words imagined that their author was some sixty-year-old graybeard rather than a twenty-seven-year-old know-it-all punk. Because our legal columnist had just left the editorial page, there was nobody to write about legal issues so, without anyone assigning me to do it, I started to cover the legal beat. That meant writing editorials castigating ambulance-chasing "tort lawyers," who were blamed by the editorial page for winning unfair judgments from corporations.

I even broke a story in 1996 when I went down to Houston to interview several employees of John O'Quinn, a well-known Texas trial lawyer, who accused him of paying "accident runners" to sign up clients after airplane crashes—an ethical no-no that might have gotten him disbarred. O'Quinn had gotten rich with a good-ole-boy swagger that he used to charm juries in backwoods jurisdictions to award his clients vast sums from large, out-of-state corporations. He had won billions from makers of breast implants, cigarettes, and

pharmaceuticals. This was populism for profit—O'Quinn had figured out how to monetize the resentment of small-town Americans
against the coastal elites.

O'Quinn's rage after my article appeared was something to
behold. He sent letters to the *Journal* calling me "goofier than a
road lizard" and threatening to sue the newspaper for every penny
it possessed. Given O'Quinn's track record as one of the most successful litigators in America—he was said to have earned 40 million
dollars the previous year—this was no idle boast. I was genuinely
worried, even if I did have the *Journal*'s legal team behind me.
But O'Quinn turned out to be, as they say in Texas, all hat and
no cattle. No lawsuit was ever forthcoming. He was just trying to
intimidate us into backing down. Donald Trump employs exactly
the same kind of bluster, right down to threats of lawsuits that are
never filed. He might as well be O'Quinn's long-lost New York
cousin. Actually, Trump has gone him one better, because he's
figured out how to take advantage of ordinary people not only to
grow richer but also vastly more powerful than O'Quinn could
have ever imagined. My run-in with O'Quinn, who died in 2009,
was an early education in the kind of scoundrels who hide behind
the banner of populism.

My focus on the legal profession led me to write my first book,
Out of Order: Arrogance, Corruption and Incompetence on the Bench,
which came out in 1998. It was a jeremiad against judges who
offended conservative sensibilities by either allowing plaintiffs'
lawyers to win unreasonably large judgments or who engaged in
"judicial activism," legislating their own views from the bench.
These were standard conservative critiques that I was parroting
without truly understanding the underlying issues. I did not deal
convincingly with the inherent tensions in the case against judicial
activism: I condemned the 1954 decision in *Brown v. Board of Education*, for example, by claiming that school desegregation was not

mandated by the Constitution, yet I applauded the blow that it had struck against racism. Despite (or perhaps because of) my shallow reasoning, I convinced Robert Bork, a hero on the right, to write the foreword. If he had written the whole thing, it would have been a much better book. I am not proud of *Out of Order*; I feel about it much as a well-established actress might feel about a porno film that she did when she was just starting out. The best thing about the book is that it provided an advance that enabled my wife and me, with our first baby on the way, to make a down payment on a house in the New York suburbs.

I WAS DETERMINED THAT my next book would be better. Over the next four years, I spent nights, early mornings, and weekends, while working full time at the *Journal*, writing a history of America's small wars. I got interested in the subject because the 1990s was the decade of US interventions in Somalia, Haiti, Bosnia, and Kosovo. I wanted to find the historical antecedents of these operations and wound up writing a history that stretched from the Barbary Wars of the early nineteenth century up to the Vietnam War and beyond. I felt much better about this book than about *Out of Order* because history, and specifically military history, was my first love. This time I was not simply parroting the conclusions of other scholars; I was striking out into virgin intellectual terrain.

I had a manuscript of the book finished by September 11, 2001. The day started off normally enough—I took a Metro-North train from Westchester County to Grand Central Station. En route, I heard rumors that an airplane had crashed into the World Trade Center. I imagined a Cessna flying into one of the buildings by accident and proceeded downtown as usual by subway. It turned out to be the last train running. When I got off at City Hall, a scene straight out of hell confronted me. Sirens were wailing, people were running, and everything and everybody was covered in a ghostly film of white dust. I stumbled forward and watched the second tower fall. And then a giant ball of soot and smoke came roaring down the street like the massive boulder at the beginning of *Raiders of the Lost Ark*. I ran away along with everyone else. After having walked all the way to midtown, I caught a commuter train back to sylvan Larchmont. Arriving in my comfortable suburb from what was now a war zone was surreal: I had gone in the space of a few hours from watching people plummet to their deaths to taking the recycling container out to the curb. I worked remotely that afternoon, helping the paper come out as usual even though our headquarters was a shambles—the *Journal* was located in the World Financial Center across the street from the World Trade Center, and the collapse of the Twin Towers punctured its windows, covering everything inside in soot and ash. None of my colleagues were killed in the attack but some had close calls. The editorial page staffers would spend the next few weeks working out of a temporary office in Princeton, New Jersey. It was an intense period full of work and purpose—we felt as if we were helping America to make sense of the worst terrorist attack in history.

I made my own small contribution to the national conversation with a cover story in the *Weekly Standard* that appeared a month after 9/11: "The Case for American Empire."[2] For a number of years this was the most influential article I had written; it helped to spark a broader debate about "American empire" that was taken up by Niall Ferguson, Andrew Bacevich, and others. I would lose track of how often that article's signature line was quoted—"Afghanistan and other troubled lands today cry out for the sort of enlightened foreign administration once provided by self-confident Englishmen in jodhpurs and pith helmets." I now recognize that in my youthful zeal to shock, my use of the word "empire" may have backfired by generating more heat than light. I wasn't calling for the United States to acquire colonies but rather to engage in Kosovo-style nation-building in countries such as Afghanistan to prevent them from becoming once again a breeding ground for extremism. I still believe this is a good idea, and one that doesn't require a massive American military presence. Without a political solution, no amount of military action can achieve decisive results. But it doesn't help to generate political support for this idea in the postcolonial age by invoking the example of nineteenth-century empires. It's been years since I've made the case for the United States to become more unapologetically imperialist. I still argue, however, for paying more attention to nation-building, albeit of the "small footprint" variety that doesn't involve sending lots of American soldiers.

In the spring of 2002 my second book—*The Savage Wars of Peace: Small Wars and the Rise of American Power*—came out. Its thesis was that "small wars" had played an important, if unrecognized, role in shaping American power and would remain as commonplace in the future as they had been in the past. The US military, I argued, did not have the luxury of concentrating only on the kind of big, conventional wars that it preferred to fight. *The Savage Wars of Peace* was much better received and much more successful than my first book. I would be gratified in subsequent years to hear from many soldiers and marines who read it either before deploying to Iraq or Afghanistan or while on deployment; they would tell they had benefited from the historical perspective that it provided. I had, of course, written the book before 9/11, but it was more timely than ever when it came out after the attacks and while the United States was engaged in a new "small war" in Afghanistan.

Not long after the book's release, I got a call from Leslie Gelb, president of the Council on Foreign Relations, a think tank and membership organization in New York that was viewed with suspicion by conservatives who thought it was a bastion of liberal globalists. An idiosyncratic and accomplished figure who had been both a high-ranking government official (he had overseen the preparation of the *Pentagon Papers* for the Johnson administration) and a *New York Times* columnist, Les told me that he was impressed by my book and wanted to hire me as a senior fellow because he wanted greater ideological diversity on his staff. You might say I was an affirmative action hire—for my views, not my skin color. I was not immediately won over; I liked my job at the *Journal*. But Les was hard to say no to when he was enthusiastic about something—and he was enthusiastic about bringing me to the Council. In hindsight I am very glad he won me over. I have found working at the Council to be the best job that I have ever had, and quite possibly the best job that anyone has ever had—anyone, that is, who isn't concerned about making a fortune. Neither Les nor his successor as Council president, the distinguished policymaker and scholar Richard Haass, has ever told me what to write or say. They fully supported me as I plunged deeper into military affairs in the years ahead, writing a series of books that focused on military history and too many articles to count on the controversies of the day. It was like being at a university without student papers to grade—and without the stifling political correctness of the classroom.

One of the great benefits of being at the Council was getting to know our visiting military fellows—colonels and captains from the military services who are in residence with us for a year. Spending time with them introduced me to American military culture. I was able to expand my understanding by making regular trips "down range" to observe military operations in Afghanistan and Iraq. Sometimes I would travel by myself or with other think tankers; at other times I would lead tour groups of prominent Council members interested in educating themselves about the post-9/11 wars. This is the kind of education that Donald Trump never bothered to get before becoming president. Although he lived and worked for decades only a few blocks from the Council's headquarters in an elegant Upper East Side townhouse, he never showed any interest in its work or in US foreign policy more broadly. Even as president he has never once visited a war zone. He loves military symbols—hence his desire for a military parade in Washington—but shows no understanding of how the armed forces actually operate.

JUST LIKE DONALD TRUMP and most other people, I was a supporter of the war in Iraq. The difference is I'm willing to admit it, not pretending that I was opposed to the war all along. I backed the overthrow of Saddam Hussein, one of the worst tyrants on the planet, and I had faith—obviously unwarranted—that the United States could build a democratic Iraq after his downfall. But I would not have advocated military intervention if I were not convinced that containment wasn't working and that Saddam posed a threat to the United States and its allies with his weapons of mass destruction program. None of this set me apart from most Americans in 2003. The war had the support of 72 percent of the public initially, and it was authorized by both houses of Congress. Among those who voted for the use of force were Senators Hillary Clinton, Joe Biden, Chuck Schumer, and John Kerry. What made me different from many of these fair-weather hawks was that, as the situation spun out of control from the summer of 2003 on, I did not change my ornithological coloration to become a dove. I criticized the mistakes made by the Bush administration—for instance, after the 2004 Abu Ghraib prisoner-abuse scandal, I scandalized fellow conservatives by calling for the ouster of Secretary of Defense Donald Rumsfeld, who, I felt, was mismanaging the war.[3] (This made for an awkward meeting with Midge Decter, wife of Norman Podhoretz and an influential neoconservative thinker in her own right, who had just published a hagiography of Rumsfeld.) I was anguished by the deteriorating course of the conflict and felt some measure of responsibility for this quagmire. But I was convinced that an American pullout would make the situation even worse—a judgment amply vindicated by subsequent experience. President Obama's troop withdrawal in 2011 made possible the rise of the Islamic State of Syria and Iraq.

Instead of leaving Iraq, I became convinced that US troops needed to implement a classic counterinsurgency strategy of the kind I had described in *The Savage Wars of Peace*. This required sending more troops and pushing them out to provide security to the populace, rather than hunkering down in sprawling Forward Operating Bases isolated by Hesco barriers and blast walls from the Iraqi people. General David Petraeus implemented precisely this strategy when he took command in early 2007, and the result was a fall in violence by 90 percent over the next two years. I was not sure that the surge would work, but I became an advocate of giving this strategy a chance. I had previously met Petraeus, a rare general with an Ivy League PhD, while he was a division commander in Iraq in 2003, and we became friends. He invited me to visit Iraq—and later Afghanistan—to offer him my recommendations. These trips were occasionally dangerous (on one occasion in Mosul, a Humvee directly in front of mine hit a roadside bomb and we took machine gun fire from a nearby building), but always fascinating and inspirational. I came away deeply impressed by the morale, skills, and dedication of our troops. There has been no finer fighting force in history, and, though ill-prepared to fight a counterinsurgency, they rapidly improvised and figured out what to do.

My advocacy of the Iraq War and my refusal to support a pullout led the far left and far right to call me a "neocon warmonger" and "chickenhawk" who was part of a "cabal" that had "lied" America into the war. The aspersion that this was a "neocon war" seemed designed to play into ancient prejudices, on both the far left and far right, about conniving and disloyal Jews, since the "neocons" blamed for the conflict—Paul Wolfowitz, Douglas Feith, Richard Perle—were Jewish officials of limited influence. This is exactly the kind of calumny that Trump now spreads in inveighing against "globalist" elites who are supposedly betraying America. In truth the decision to go to war had been made by President George W. Bush, in consultation with colleagues such as Dick Cheney, Condoleezza Rice, Colin Powell, and Don Rumsfeld, none of whom was remotely a "neocon." Those of us who supported the invasion were, as one of my friends said, like hapless passengers who got into a vehicle with a drunk driver and could not escape as the car careened across the center divider.

For years I felt defensive about my support for the war and refused to repent. Stubborn and self-righteous, I did not want to cede any ground to my critics. Now, looking back with greater introspection and humility after the passage of more than fifteen years, I can finally acknowledge the obvious: it was all a big mistake. Saddam Hussein was heinous, but Iraq was better off under his tyrannical rule than the chaos that followed. I regret advocating the invasion and feel guilty about all the lives lost. It was a chastening lesson in the limits of American power. It is not nearly as easy to remake a foreign land by force as I had naïvely imagined in 2003, and even the conservative "best and brightest"—Cheney, Powell, Rumsfeld, Rice, and all the rest—can make mistakes that are every bit as dumb as those that their more liberal counterparts made in Vietnam.

One of the perverse consequences of this catastrophe was that—along with Hurricane Katrina in 2005 and the Great Recession in 2008–2009—it disillusioned many Republicans with the traditional leadership of their party and made them receptive to an outsider like Donald Trump who was unabashed in his hatred of the war and its architects. So, much to my chagrin, I now realize that the failed policies I advocated in 2003 helped, thirteen years later, to elect a president who stands in opposition to nearly everything that I believe in.

It was a lesson in the unintended effects of a militaristic foreign policy that I should have learned earlier. But some conservatives still have not learned it, as witness the agitation in some quarters in 2017 for a preventative war against North Korea before President Trump launched talks with Kim Jong Un. For my part, Iraq cured me of any enthusiasm for what my boss Richard Haass has labeled "wars of choice." Listening in early 2018 to hard-liners like future National Security Adviser John Bolton advocate a first strike against North Korea—an act that could easily trigger a nuclear war—I recognized an echo of my callow, earlier self. Bolton, a conservative firebrand since his days as a student at Yale University in the early 1970s, is whom I used to be.

MY POLICY ADVOCACY WAS not limited to the printed page. I was also becoming involved in politics at a higher level than the drudge work I had done as a teenager on the Zschau campaign. In 2007 I became a foreign policy adviser to the presidential campaign of Senator John McCain, whom I had gotten to know after he had read and liked *The Savage Wars of Peace*, which, unbeknownst to me, featured the exploits of one of his ancestors—an army officer who had fought Pancho Villa in 1916. McCain became one of those rare politicians, like Ronald Reagan, that I revered. He had exhibited superhuman courage in enduring more than five years of torture in North Vietnam. He could have won early release because his father was an admiral who commanded the US Pacific Fleet. But the POWs had a strict rule—first in, first out—and McCain was not going to betray his honor even if the cost of staying was nearly unendurable physical suffering. I still cannot believe that Trump, who sat out the Vietnam War with five draft deferments and claimed that avoiding sexually transmitted diseases was "my personal Vietnam," has the temerity to criticize one of America's greatest war heroes for being captured. I find it much easier to believe that Trump's graceless example encouraged one of his White House aides to "joke" that McCain's opposition to Gina Haspel's nomination to run the CIA didn't matter because the senator had brain cancer and "he's dying anyway."

McCain showed his character not just as a POW but also as a politician. In 2008, he corrected a woman at a rally who told him, "I can't trust Obama. I have read about him and . . . he's an Arab." "No ma'am," McCain replied. "He's a decent family man, a citizen that I just happen to have disagreements with on fundamental issues, and that's what this campaign is all about." How easy would it have been for McCain to traffic in conspiracy theories and demagoguery. But he refused to do it—and his refusal, along with his own missteps (such as choosing Sarah Palin as his running mate), helped cost him the presidency.

McCain spent his career in Congress as a leading champion of America's role as a global leader. Every year he led a delegation of lawmakers to the Munich Security Conference, a gathering of transatlantic movers and shakers. I was lucky enough to accompany the congressional delegation on their air force airplane on a few occasions. It was a heady experience, trading small talk and wisecracks with famous lawmakers and former policymakers. But what most impressed me was when I walked up to the front of the aircraft once and saw McCain reading a fat volume of history. I thought often of that scene in later years as I witnessed the ascendancy of a Republican president who was incapable of reading long briefing papers, much less books. Advising McCain on foreign policy was the easiest job I've ever had because he knew more about the subject than any of his advisers. His standing on economic and domestic policy was shakier, however, and it cost him badly when the financial markets began to melt down in the fall of 2008. Barack Obama took advantage of the turmoil and his opposition to the Iraq War to win a longshot bid for the presidency.

Four years later, in 2012, I advised another honorable man who won the Republican presidential nomination even though I had some doubts about his conservative bona fides. Many other conservatives were also lukewarm about Mitt Romney even though his personal character, thoughtfulness, and work ethic were unimpeachable. Romney needed more help in the foreign policy field because he had been a governor, not a senator, and I tried to provide it even though I was hardly a member of the inner circle. Obama was a formidable adversary, not only because of his natural charisma and oratorical skill but also because he could boast of having killed Osama bin Laden and kept General Motors alive. I remained highly critical of his presidency, however, because I feared that his "lead from behind" foreign policy was ceding American global leadership. Obama had won the presidency in no small measure because of his opposition to the Iraq War, which showed the high cost of American interventionism. But he swung too far in the other direction, toward noninterventionism, by pulling US troops out of Iraq in 2011 and refusing to intervene in the Syrian civil war. The result would be the rise of ISIS and the creation, in Syria, of what Petraeus would call a "geopolitical Chernobyl" spewing its toxins across the region and the world.

One of the turning points of the 2012 campaign was Romney's assertion that Russia was "without question our No. 1 geopolitical foe"—a claim that Obama ridiculed with the devastating line, "The 1980s are now calling to ask for their foreign policy back because the Cold War's been over for twenty years." Looking back, it's obvious that Obama was wrong and Romney right—even if not even Romney could anticipate how the Kremlin would subvert American democracy. All the more incredible, then, that Republicans have gone from backing a candidate who saw Russia as the enemy to one who refuses to say a negative word about its leader, even though Russia is a far greater menace today than it was in 2012.

By 2015, with another presidential campaign once again looming, I was convinced that we needed a president who, in the manner of Ronald Reagan, would unapologetically assert American power, stand with our allies, and defend freedom from the onslaught not only of terrorist groups but also of rogue states such as Iran and North Korea and rising near-peer competitors such as China and Russia. Jeb Bush came into the Republican race as the early frontrunner, but he wasn't conservative enough for me. That's how uncompromisingly conservative (and naïve) I was—Jeb Bush wasn't good enough for me! Today I would give anything in the world to make him president.

Rather than support Bush, I signed up as a foreign policy adviser with the presidential campaign of Senator Marco Rubio, an eloquent young senator from Florida who appealed to me because he was also a son of immigrants (in his case from Cuba) and spoke movingly of the need to defend and expand the sphere of freedom. I knew there was a good chance he would lose—but I figured that if he did, it would be to an eminently qualified if somewhat boring candidate like Bush.

I had fatally overestimated my fellow Republicans. My disillusionment was to be painful and prolonged; in fact, existential. In the process of being disabused of my illusions about the GOP I would also lose my faith in the conservative movement in whose bosom I had been nursed for decades.

I now wonder: What did I miss? How could all these eminences that I had worked with, and respected, sell out their professed principles to support a president who could not tell Edmund Burke from Arleigh Burke? Even as late as the winter of 2016 I would not have thought it possible.

3.

THE

SURRENDER

A T FIRST, LIKE MOST PEOPLE IN THE POLITICAL AND policy worlds, I did not take the Trump campaign all that seriously; I assumed that Donald Duck would have as much chance of becoming president as Donald Trump. He appeared to be a second-rate entertainer and first-rate self-promoter running for the presidency to expand his name recognition and boost the ratings of his TV show, *The Apprentice*. He had no government experience or policy knowledge. His past was full of affairs and divorces, of corporate bankruptcies and of stiffed vendors, of shady ventures like Trump University that led to lawsuits and recriminations. He was an opportunist who had regularly flip-flopped between the Democratic and Republican Parties, and he had given copious campaign donations to liberal Democrats. He hardly looked like the natural candidate of a Republican Party that, ever since the ascendancy of Newt Gingrich in the 1990s and then of the Tea Party in the 2000s, had been veering to the right. My assumption, like most others, was that Jeb Bush and Chris Christie would fight it out in the "Establishment lane," while Marco Rubio and Ted Cruz would compete for the hearts of conservatives. Rand Paul, an arch-isolationist, looked to be the most dangerous candidate in the race. Trump just seemed like a freak show—a less-qualified and less-knowledgeable version of Ben Carson, another candidate who was not remotely prepared to be president.

"I don't expect Trump's inability to articulate comprehensible policies to end his ascendancy in the polls anytime soon," I wrote in mid-August 2015, a couple of months after Trump had launched his campaign, "but I do have enough faith in the American political process to hope and even expect that his outright buffoonery will stop him from winning the Republican nomination, much less the presidency." I added a caveat, however, that I should have taken more seriously. Citing the examples of inept officeholders from James Buchanan, the president who had brought America to the brink of the Civil War, to Jesse "The Body" Ventura, a former wrestling star turned governor of Minnesota, I wrote: "But given the history that so many democracies have of making such foolish mistakes in choosing leaders, and given Trump's own history of surviving an advanced case of foot-in-the-mouth disease, there is a small part of me that wonders whether I am being Pollyannaish in expecting that the White House will not eventually have a neon 'Trump' sign on top of it."[1]

My warning would turn out to be prophetic. And yet in the months ahead I would forget my own insight, so convinced was I that no candidate could possibly win by violating so many of the supposed rules of the American presidential selection system. This is one of the traps that a historian can all too easily fall into: assuming that because something hasn't been done before, it can never be done in the future. Trump, supremely ignorant of the past, would prove to have a surer grasp on how to shape the future.

In the Rubio campaign, like most others, we were stockpiling policy advisers, pumping out position papers, and briefing the candidate to respond in a cogent and yet calculated manner to the news of the day. Trump didn't bother with any of that. He didn't have a normal campaign apparatus, and he didn't read briefing papers. He just flew around the country in his own airplane, speaking seemingly off the cuff, making promises to "build the wall," "take their oil," "drain the swamp," and "win so much" that resonated well with his audiences but that struck sophisticates like me as nonsensical. Pressed on the specifics of his plans, he would reply with vapid generalities, promising "we're going to have great plans," "I want to get you something great," and "we will make it stronger and smarter than ever, ever, ever before."[2]

In December 2015, at a Republican debate in answer to a question from radio host Hugh Hewitt, Trump revealed ignorance of the "nuclear triad"; Rubio had to patiently explain to him that the term referred to the US armed forces' ability to launch nuclear weapons from land, sea, and air. Sitting at home, watching the debate, I chortled. *Gotcha!* Advantage, Rubio. These were the kind of gaffes that would embarrass a normal candidate, but Trump and his acolytes couldn't care less. "The real problem with The Donald is not that he is ignorant but that he is aggressively ignorant," I wrote at the time. "He thinks that his lack of knowledge is a virtue, demonstrating his regular guy quality."[3] The *real* real problem would turn out to be that Trump was right and I was wrong—the kind of policy cramming that most candidates did prior to running or while running did indeed turn out to be superfluous. Trump was revealing that ignorance was no bar for a presidential candidate. It would prove to be a greater obstacle when he was elected; not having done the normal preparation work for a presidential run, he would prove to be spectacularly unqualified to assume the most difficult and powerful position in the world.

IT WASN'T JUST THAT Trump was ignorant. The larger problem was that much of what he said just wasn't so. He had a proclivity for conspiracy theories, having spent years pushing the "birtherism" hoax that Barack Obama had forged his birth certificate. He lied incessantly: PolitiFact found in mid-2016 that 78 percent of all of Trump's fact-checked statements were either mostly or entirely false, compared to only 16 percent for Hillary Clinton.[4]

Trump also had a long history of creepy, sexist comments that long predated the release of the *Access Hollywood* tape in the fall of 2016. In August 2015, after Megyn Kelly asked him tough questions during a presidential debate, he implied that it was because she was menstruating. The next month he suggested that no one would vote for his Republican rival Carly Fiorina because her face was so unattractive.

Trump's history of racism was just as long as his record of sexism, stretching all the way back to 1973, when Trump and his father settled charges brought by the Justice Department that their company had refused to rent to African Americans. When Ronald Reagan was endorsed by the Ku Klux Klan, he eloquently rejected the "politics of racial hatred and religious bigotry." When Trump was given three chances by CNN on February 28, 2016, to reject an endorsement from Klan leader David Duke, he refused to do so—and used as excuse the astonishing claim that he didn't know enough about the Klan. Trump subsequently blamed his failure on a malfunctioning earpiece, his version of "the dog ate my homework." This was part of a pattern with Trump. One study in early 2016 found that an incredible 62 percent of his retweets were of white supremacists.[5]

Trump's defenders pointed out that he palled around with black celebrities such as Jay Z, Don King, and Mike Tyson, and that his daughter converted to Judaism when she married Jared Kushner. But at most this demonstrated that Trump is not a doctrinaire neo-Nazi; he is too scattershot to be doctrinaire about *anything*. The evidence suggested he was a more casual bigot along the lines of Archie Bunker, the fictional *All in the Family* TV character from the New York borough of Queens, where Trump was born. That Trump may like particular individuals did not prevent him from stereotyping and stigmatizing entire minority groups—not just African Americans but also Mexicans and Muslims.[6]

Trump began his campaign by castigating all Mexican immigrants, not just those who had arrived illegally, as "rapists and murderers," promising to build a wall along the Mexican border that Mexico would pay for, and to deport all eleven million undocumented immigrants in the United States. Trump was unwittingly imitating the animus of earlier generations of nativists against earlier waves of newcomers, including the Irish, Italians, Jews, Chinese, and Japanese. Each one of those ethnic groups was once accused of being alien to Anglo-Saxon America—ethnically, culturally, or religiously—and yet each one assimilated, just as Latinos are now doing.

Trump seemed to forget—if he had ever known—that even German Americans like him had encountered pervasive hatred and discrimination during World War I. That did not stop him from slinging accusations of disloyalty against Muslims—the latest group caught on the wrong side of one of America's wars, just as I had been as a Russian American in the last decade of the Cold War. He falsely claimed that "thousands" of Arab Americans in Jersey City had cheered on 9/11, and when a reporter showed that this simply did not happen, Trump made fun of his disability. Trump upped the ante in early December 2015. After a terrorist attack in San Bernardino, he called for a "total and complete shutdown" of all Muslims entering the country—an abhorrent proposal that was contrary to the freedom of religion guaranteed by the First Amendment.

WHILE SCAPEGOATING MEXICANS, African Americans, and Muslims, Trump had nothing but praise for an actual enemy of America. In an interview on *Morning Joe* on December 18, 2015,

Trump praised Russia's dictator Vladimir Putin as a better "leader" than President Obama. When Joe Scarborough asked him about allegations about Putin killing journalists and political opponents, Trump replied, "I think our country does plenty of killing also, Joe, so you know."

Conservatives like me had spent decades inveighing against the tendency on the left to engage in moral relativism—to suggest that America, because of its sins, was no better than any other country. We had labeled this "anti-Americanism." Reagan's United Nations ambassador, Jeane Kirkpatrick, whose name graces the position I occupy at the Council on Foreign Relations, said: "There is no more misleading concept abroad today than this concept of . . . superpower equivalence." In 2011, Representative Paul Ryan said, "If you ask me what the biggest problem in America is, I'm not going to tell you debt, deficits, statistics, economics—I'll tell you it's moral relativism." Now here was Trump doing the very thing that conservatives had been criticizing, and in the process he was siding with Russia, a country whose aggressive designs Republicans had been opposing since the Bolshevik Revolution in 1917.[7]

Trump did not just admire Putin. He gave every indication of wanting to emulate his authoritarian example. "Be careful," Trump often told anyone speaking out against him, as if he were a dictator or at least a mob boss. He expressed a desire to change the libel laws so that when journalists wrote negative articles about him, "we can sue them and win lots of money." Trump would routinely instigate violence at his rallies against protesters. At a February 2016 rally in Las Vegas, Trump said, from behind a phalanx of Secret Service bodyguards, that he'd like "to punch a demonstrator in the face" and lamented that the man "wasn't being carried out a stretcher."[8] The parallels with fascist rallies in the 1930s were inescapable and alarming—even if "see no evil" Republicans purported not to notice them.

And those rallies did not *just* occur in Europe: In 1939, as recounted by historian Gordon F. Sander, the German American Bund filled Madison Square Garden with twenty thousand cheering Nazis—America's own version of the Nuremberg rallies. The führer of "Swastika Nation" was a German American auto worker named Fritz Julius Kuhn. After being introduced as "the man we love for the enemies he has made" (sound familiar?), he proceeded to denounce those enemies with anti-Semitic twists on their name. Like Trump, Kuhn had a gift for derogatory nicknames—at least derogatory to his anti-Semitic followers. He dubbed Franklin D. Roosevelt, who had called Nazism "a cancer," "Frank D. Rosenfeld." District Attorney—and future governor and Republican presidential candidate—Thomas Dewey was "Thomas Jewey." Mayor Fiorello LaGuardia, who was part Jewish, was "Fiorello Lumpen LaGuardia." His insults were greeted with cries of "Free America!"—a precursor of "Make America Great Again." A Jewish demonstrator became so agitated that he tried to rush the podium to make Kuhn stop spewing his filth, but he was tackled and beaten by the Bund's own brownshirts. Americans were horrified by newsreel footage of Nazis beating a Jew in New York City. Yes, it can happen here—and did. District Attorney Dewey got his revenge later that year by prosecuting Kuhn for tax evasion; the Nazi leader was sentenced to two-and-a-half years in prison.[9] There would be poetic justice if Trump were to face a similar fate: brought down not for his hate-mongering but for his shady business practices.

To the extent that Trump had coherent policy proposals, they were a throwback to the isolationism and protectionism of the 1930s—and a repudiation of the free trade and internationalism that the Republican Party, and the conservative movement, had championed since World War II. Trump threatened to pull US troops out of Germany, South Korea, and Japan, and to impose

massive tariffs on our trade partners. He even adopted as his slogan "America First," the very same phrase that had been used by
Charles Lindbergh and a cohort of other isolationists in the prewar
period—de facto allies of the German American Bund who were
sympathetic to Hitler and hostile to Jews. This should have been
a tocsin ringing loudly—but it was ignored by Republican voters,
ignorant of history, who seemed to have no conception of how
toxic this phrase was.

MY OPPOSITION TO TRUMP went far beyond disagreement
with his policy impulses; I would not dignify them by calling them
"ideas" or "proposals." I was morally offended by him, and apoplec-
tic that anyone could think that he was remotely qualified to fill the
office of Washington, Lincoln, and Roosevelt. In November 2015 I
tweeted: "Trump is a fascist. And that's not a term I use loosely or
often. But he's earned it."[10] This was not an epithet I casually tossed
around, having been branded a fascist myself at Berkeley for holding moderate conservative views. The word has no exact, commonly agreed upon definition, but many of the attributes of fascism
cited by Georgetown University historian John McNeill clearly
applied to Trump—including "hyper-nationalism," "militarism"
(Trump had just bragged at a GOP debate: "I'm the most militaristic person on that stage"), "glorification of violence," "fetishization
of masculinity," "leader cult," "lost-golden-age syndrome," "self-
definition by opposition," "mass mobilization," "tendency to purge
the disloyal," and "theatricality."[11]

Trump's lack of restraint caused me to loosen my own restraints.
I had grown up in a culture in which, even after the convulsions
of the 1960s and 1970s, the President—a title that was always
capitalized—was treated with deference and respect. I was influenced by watching old black-and-white movies from the fifties in

which the chief executive was such a mighty personage that he could only be glimpsed in silhouette or from the back—seeing his face would have seemed as sacrilegious as glimpsing the face of God. That attitude had carried over to my work as a political pundit. Even when I disagreed with presidents such as Barack Obama or George W. Bush, I was careful to treat them with the respect that their accomplishments and office demanded. A similar habit of deference carried over to presidential candidates, any one of whom (almost) could be the future commander in chief. But I could not treat Trump as a normal candidate when he was transgressing every norm not just of presidential politics but also of civilized society. I had some trepidation about calling out a presidential candidate— and a Republican to boot—in terms normally reserved for foreign tyrants, but my indignation propelled me forward. I could not stay silent.

In early 2016, I wrote that Trump was "a liar, an ignoramus, and a moral abomination." I added: "I have never previously described any presidential candidate in such harsh terms—not even close— but there is no other way to accurately describe him. There simply isn't."[12] In March I wrote that Trump was "emerging as the number one threat to American security. Yes, that's right—a bigger threat than ISIS, North Korea, Russia, China, Iran, or all the rest."[13] I have not revised my view in the intervening time: I still believe that Trump poses the greatest threat to US security. Writing in the *Weekly Standard*, my conservative Council on Foreign Relations colleague Benn Steil and I warned that Trump's "policies would not make America 'great.' Just the opposite. A Trump presidency would represent the death knell of America as a great power."[14] That, too, is a view that I believe has been vindicated by events.

I may have gone a bit further rhetorically than some other conservatives, but I was hardly alone in my alarm at the rise of Trump. One of the few conservatives who endorsed Trump early on felt compelled to do so anonymously. Michael Anton, a dandy in bespoke suits who had also graduated from Berkeley and who would subsequently become the spokesman for Trump's National Security Council, used a Roman pseudonym, Publius Decius Mus, to pen a pro-Trump essay in the *Claremont Review of Books*. I knew Anton and assumed that, having worked for President George W. Bush and Mayor Rudolph Giuliani, he was a normal, middle-of-the-road conservative who just happened to have an unusual degree of interest in the details of men's wear ("Prints are safe. Everyone wears prints") and French cooking. So I was unprepared for the role he now assumed as the leading Trumpian intellectual—admittedly an honor for which there was slim competition, given how anti-intellectual the candidate and most of his followers were. Anton argued: "2016 is the Flight 93 election: charge the cockpit or you die. You may die anyway. You—or the leader of your party—may make it into the cockpit and not know how to fly or land the plane. There are no guarantees. Except one: if you don't try, death is certain. To compound the metaphor: a Hillary Clinton presidency is Russian Roulette with a semi-auto. With Trump, at least you can spin the cylinder and take your chances."[15]

This was an argument, as even Anton had to concede, that sounded "histrionic" to "ordinary conservative ears." It didn't just sound histrionic; it *was* histrionic. It was, in fact, the kind of argument that apologists for dictators—dandies, aesthetes, and eccentrics among them—had made in the past, claiming that the alternative to their revered leader was so dire that it justified the imposition of despotism. Such beliefs typically had gained popularity at a time of existential crisis, usually following an economic meltdown or military defeat, when the threat came from Marxists or those who could credibly be depicted as such. That had been the pattern of fascism in countries such as Italy, Argentina, Chile, Hungary, Japan, Spain, and Germany. Anton's innovation was to sound this apocalyptic alarm at a time of peace and prosperity about *Hillary Clinton*—a boring, middle-of-the-road policy wonk who was considered far too conservative by Bernie Sanders–style progressives.

I remember serving on a Defense Department advisory board with Clinton when she was in the US Senate. The alphabetical order of our names led to us being seated next to each other. I found her to be congenial and smart. Not only was she utterly free of political cant, at least in this private setting, but she was interested in the details of defense planning to a degree that was unusual for a politician. It never occurred to me that this amiable lady whom I chatted with and liked would be depicted as the harbinger of doom by my fanatical compatriots on the right.

Anton's screed was widely mocked in the conservative circles in which I traveled. There was not a single mainstream conservative early on who was willing to embrace Trump, which helped to explain why he could not sign up any credible policy advisers and had to hire dubious characters such as Carter Page and George Papadopoulos, who were subsequently revealed to have links to the Kremlin. Along with more than a hundred other Republican national security experts, I signed an open letter that appeared on the War on the Rocks website pledging eternal opposition to Trump. The letter, organized by my friends Eliot Cohen and Bryan McGrath, concluded that "as committed and loyal Republicans, we are unable to support a Party ticket with Mr. Trump at its head. We commit ourselves to working energetically to prevent the election of someone so utterly unfitted to the office."[16] A few of those who signed the letter would subsequently try to disown it to win positions in the Trump administration, but they would not succeed in erasing this mark of Cain. Trump put stock in personal loyalty above all, and the national security experts who signed the War on the Rocks letter had disqualified themselves from service in his administration by showing that they were more loyal to the country than to its president.

Similar opposition to Trump was expressed by a bevy of prominent conservatives who wrote essays that *National Review* published shortly before the first primaries in January 2016 under the headline: "Against Trump." *NR*'s editors warned: "Donald Trump is a menace to American conservatism who would take the work of generations and trample it underfoot in behalf of a populism as heedless and crude as the Donald himself."[17] Contributing to this issue was a who's who of the conservative movement, including Ronald Reagan's attorney general Edwin Meese III, economist Thomas Sowell, syndicated columnist Cal Thomas, radio hosts Glenn Beck and Michael Medved, *Weekly Standard* editor Bill Kristol, *Commentary* editor John Podhoretz, evangelist Russell Moore, Club for Growth president David McIntosh, and former attorney general and judge Michael Mukasey.

With the stars of the right aligned against Trump, I figured, what chance did he have to win over ordinary conservative voters?

THE CONSERVATIVE MOVEMENT had always been an uneasy alliance, not only between different strains of ideology (cultural conservatives, libertarians, supply-siders, deficit hawks, internationalists, isolationists, etc.) but also between the leaders in Washington and New York and the masses in the rest of the country. Conservative elites like to accuse liberal elites of being "out of touch." It was an appeal to the supposed wisdom of the crowd that I had used on occasion myself—imagining that, even though I was part of a small, embattled minority among the liberal cognoscenti of Manhattan, I was in sync with the good people of Manhattan, Kansas (a place that, of course, I had never visited). "Middle America" was, along with "entrepreneurs," one of those imagined archetypes that conservative intellectuals employed much as Marxists appealed to the authority of "the workers" and "the proletariat." But it turned out that conservative eggheads were just as far removed from the heartland of America as the "limousine liberals" and "smoked-salmon socialists" that we hypocritically loved to ridicule. (Personally, I enjoy smoked salmon, a.k.a. lox, so much that I have it on a bagel nearly every weekend.)

Republican voters could not have cared less what elite conservatives like us were saying. Trump went over our heads by speaking directly to the country at his televised rallies. His lowbrow slogans resonated much better with ordinary Republican voters than our highfalutin arguments. The news networks covered Trump obsessively, providing him with what was later estimated to be $2 billion of free television advertising. He was getting more TV coverage than all of his rivals combined because there was a seductive frisson of excitement about his rallies that was lacking in the more scripted and sedate rallies of his rivals. Everyone wondered: What crazy thing would he say next?

Trump may not know much about policy, but he is a genius at self-promotion—a Jay Gatsby for our time. He has much in common with the land promoters who bamboozled English immigrants into coming to the New World in the seventeenth century with fanciful tales of riches—what Trump would describe as "truthful hyperbole." Or with the kind of charming con men who peddled patent medicines in the nineteenth century and then, in the twentieth century, penny stocks and time-shares.[18] But his bunkum would take on a more sinister aspect when he deployed it not to just to dupe people into handing him their money but also supreme power.

DESPITE HIS LEAD IN THE POLLS, Trump narrowly lost the Iowa caucuses, finishing just behind Ted Cruz and just ahead of

Marco Rubio. This stronger-than-expected showing for Rubio prompted a brief flurry of hope in our camp that he could win the New Hampshire primary and then run the table. But Rubio sabotaged himself in a February 6, 2016, debate when he robotically repeated the same canned lines four times in response to attacks from Chris Christie. Watching the debate on TV, I felt as if I were witnessing an automobile accident; all that was missing was the horrible screech of crumpling metal. But when I contacted the campaign, staffers feigned insouciance, claiming the situation wasn't as bad as it seemed. It was. Although we didn't realize it at the time, the Rubio campaign was basically finished that night. Trump won a commanding victory in New Hampshire, followed far behind by Cruz and Rubio.

Yet the other candidates still refused to engage in all-out attacks on Trump on the theory that his ramshackle campaign would inevitably fall apart, leaving one of the "serious" candidates to inherit his supporters. The professional politicians were being too clever by half, in the manner of aristocratic German conservatives such as President Paul von Hindenburg and Chancellor Franz von Papen, who welcomed Adolf Hitler's ascension as German chancellor in 1933 on the assumption that the jumped-up, loudmouthed little corporal would be easily manipulated by his social betters. The Republican candidates would have been better advised to be forthright from the beginning about Trump's unsuitability for high office and let the voters make up their minds. With the momentum Trump was gaining, he was becoming unstoppable.

Conservatives hoped that the South Carolina primary, on February 20, would slow Trump down. South Carolina voters had a reputation for being conservative and religious, and we told ourselves that they would punish Trump's blatant immorality and his trashing of the last Republican president, George W. Bush. No such luck. Again Trump won. Cruz was lucky to hold his home state of Texas on March 1. Rubio was not so lucky: on March 15 he lost Florida in spite, or because, of his desperate attempts to slow down Trump by imitating his personal insults. With his genius for needling his opponents, Trump had called Rubio "Little Marco"; Rubio retaliated by mocking Trump for having "small hands" and a "spray tan." It turned out, however, that while personal insults worked *for* Trump, they did not work *against* him. Voters seemed to expect nothing better from the reality TV star, while they wanted more from a senator like Rubio, who would subsequently apologize for his descent into the gutter.

With Rubio gone, John Kasich and Ted Cruz were the only Trump alternatives left. I voted for Kasich in the New York primary on April 19, but by then it was obvious that Trump was going to claim the GOP nomination.

As Trump began to emerge as the inevitable Republican nominee, something ominous occurred: Republicans genuflected before their new master. This could be explained by the Republicans' demonization of Democrats; by their knee-jerk loyalty to the GOP brand, regardless of whether its nominee shared any of their professed principles or not; by their fear of the Republican masses, whose passions Trump had shown a disturbing skill in whipping up; and by the sheer lust for power that is unfortunately characteristic of most officeholders and seekers. As countless toadies had done with demagogues of the past, so now most Republican leaders showed that that they were willing to discard their principles as mindlessly as a Styrofoam fast-food container if by doing so they could enhance their own positions and avoid the wrath of a powerful and vindictive leader.

Marco Rubio went from proclaiming "Never Trump" to endorsing Trump within a matter of months. How could he possibly support someone he had just described as a "con man" who was "too erratic" to be entrusted with the nuclear codes? Distraught, I called one of his aides, who lamely explained to me that "Never Trump" had only applied to the primaries. I was incredulous. Clearly I had misread Rubio. I had thought he was a man of principle, overlooking his track record of backtracking if those principles risked making him unpopular with the base. He had, for example, disowned attempts to reach a compromise on immigration in the Senate in 2013 after a backlash from nativists. Now he was showing a similar lack of courage and consistency, in fact a decided opportunism. This same phenomenon was evident across the conservative movement: all too many people who had only recently shared my abhorrence of Trump were boarding the Trump train as it picked up speed.

I remember having a conversation over a backyard cookout in Washington, D.C., with one of my closest friends, someone with whom I had worked on the Rubio campaign. He was more conservative than I was on social issues, but if anything that should have caused him to recoil even more strongly against the thrice-married libertine. So I was shocked when he told me that Trump would not only win the general election against Hillary Clinton but that, despite all his faults and flaws, he *deserved* to win. It did not take long for his seemingly reluctant endorsement to turn to full-blown enthusiasm. Today my old friend propagates conspiracy theories about how Democrats and the Deep State are supposedly plotting against Trump.

I had already said publicly and repeatedly, to the horror of many of my fellow conservatives, that I would vote for Clinton; even many fellow #NeverTrumpers could not bring themselves to support the Democratic nominee. I did not find it hard to cross this psychological Rubicon. In one of my less-considered quotes, I had told the *New York Times* that "I would sooner vote for Josef Stalin than I would vote for Donald Trump."[19] That was not, as Trump supporters disingenuously claimed, because I was sympathetic to Stalin, who had exiled my own grandfather to Siberia after World War II for having been taken prisoner by the Germans while serving in the Red Army. (Like Trump, Stalin did not like people who were captured.) It was just my clumsy if emphatic way of saying I was "Never Trump" all the way. As I told the *Times*: "There is no way in hell I would ever vote for him. I would far more readily support Hillary Clinton, or Bloomberg if he ran." My friend, who had served in a previous Republican administration, had a different view. He told me that politics is inherently tribal, and he had signed up with the Republican tribe, no matter who its chief was.

The difference between my friend and me is that I had always seen my primary allegiance as being to conservative principles rather than to the Republican Party. I had become a Republican because I viewed the GOP as the party most sympathetic to my ideals, but if it was now anointing a standard-bearer hostile to my views, I was not going to support the GOP. I had not realized how tribal politics was and how divorced it could be from principles or conviction. I was about to get an education that would dispel my naïve faith in the conservative movement and the American political system.

The rate of Republican surrender to Trump varied, as did the amount of anguish expressed along the way. But in the end almost everyone submitted in an astonishing domino effect. Senator Mitch McConnell, the Senate majority leader, went quietly, issuing a tepid press release in early May 2016 announcing that "I have committed to supporting the nominee chosen by Republican voters, and Donald Trump, the presumptive nominee, is now on the verge of clinching that nomination." Representative Paul Ryan, the House Speaker, said he was "not there yet" in terms of endorsing Trump, raising my hopes that he would prove to be a principled tribune of Reaganesque conservatism, but on June 2 he too caved.

With classic bad timing, Ryan delivered his endorsement just before Trump attacked a federal judge overseeing a civil case against him because of his Mexican ancestry. Ryan rightly described this as "the textbook definition of a racist comment," but he had little to say when the textbook expanded into multiple volumes. Ryan, a conservative of my own age who had worked for such movement icons as Bill Bennett and Jack Kemp, had been one of my heroes. I had viewed him as smart, principled, and brave because of his willingness to touch the third rail of American politics— he advocated reforming expensive entitlement programs such as Social Security and Medicare that were bankrupting the country. But now he showed that he was simply another politician like all the rest. Either he lacked real principles or he convinced himself that backing Trump could somehow advance those principles—a calculation that would predictably backfire.

Ted Cruz pleasantly surprised me by holding out longer against a nominee who had insulted both his wife and father. Like most people in Washington, I had seen Cruz as an insufferable opportunist who cynically exploited the populist whims of the Republican electorate when he knew better. During his Senate campaign in 2012, for example, he had denounced my employer, the Council on Foreign Relations, as a "pit of vipers" that was "working to undermine our sovereignty," even though his accomplished wife, Heidi, a Goldman Sachs banker, was herself a Council term member. I was in an unaccustomed position, therefore, in rooting for Cruz when he braved boos from the delegates by refusing to endorse Trump at the Republican convention. But eventually he reverted to form by running up the white flag, reportedly under pressure from his donors. He went from calling Trump a "pathological liar," "utterly amoral," "a narcissist at a level I don't think this country's ever seen," and "a serial philanderer" . . . to endorsing Trump. By 2018, he would be celebrating Trump as "a flashbang grenade thrown into Washington by the forgotten men and women of America."

Cruz proved he was every bit as opportunistic and unprincipled as Trump—but not nearly as successful at faking candor. His oleaginous manner oozed insincerity. Ironically such flip-flops only confirmed Trump's attacks on the Washington "swamp"—not that he had any intention of draining the swamp. He would actually make Washington swampier than ever.

THE PRESSURE ON MOST Republican officeholders to support "the nominee," as reluctant endorsers preferred to call him, was simply too strong to resist, coming as it did not only from their base, which thrilled to Trump's politically incorrect rhetoric, but also from their donors, who were mobilizing behind Trump in the expectation that he would push through a tax cut that would benefit them. Similar pressure was being felt by radio and television hosts, who felt the need to appease their pro-Trump audience. Even Hugh Hewitt, who had shown up Trump's staggering ignorance and had earned the candidate's wrath in return, became an enthusiastic supporter—apparently after having been instructed by his employer, Salem Media Group, to get aboard the Trump train.[20] I had often been a guest on Hewitt's radio show, and had found him to be a smart, well-informed interviewer. I had thought he was a cut above the Fox rabble-rousers; I was wrong.

Fox News Channel, of course, went all-in, with personalities such as the cast of *Fox & Friends*, Jeanine Pirro, Sean Hannity, and Bill O'Reilly—and later Laura Ingraham and Tucker Carlson—competing to outdo one another in their sycophancy to Trump. Was this out of principle or expedience? Were they telling their audience what it wanted to hear or did they actually believe what they were saying? Probably a bit of both, although I suspect Carlson of greater cynicism than Hannity, simply because I believe Carlson is smarter and knows better—or should. Indeed, Carlson often resorted to the shabby rhetorical device of bashing Trump critics rather than simply praising Trump—anti-anti-Trumpism being the last resort of the conservative scoundrel. Radio hosts such as Rush Limbaugh and Mark Levin likewise swallowed their doubts; they too were all-in.

The few conservative radio or TV personalities who resisted—for example, Charlie Sykes in Wisconsin and Erick Erickson in Georgia—soon found themselves losing their audience. Those who worked for think tanks and advocacy organizations were just as vulnerable to pressure from their funders. The president of one small, conservative think tank told me that he agreed with me about Trump but couldn't say so in public for fear of offending his board of directors.

Even most of those who had contributed to *National Review*'s "Against Trump" issue backtracked. A year later, David Frum noted that of the twenty-one signatories, "only six continue to speak publicly against his actions. Almost as many have become passionate defenders of the Trump presidency, most visibly the Media Research Center's Brent Bozell and the National Rifle Association's Dana Loesch."[21] The few who held out from Trump's blandishments tended to be either religious minorities—Jews or Mormons—who had ancestral memories of persecution or national security experts who knew the high stakes involved in the presidency. As it happens, I checked off both boxes.

In March 2016, I had written that Trump was a "character test" for the GOP: "Do you believe in the open and inclusive party of Ronald Reagan? Or do you want a bigoted and extremist party in the image of Donald Trump?"[22] To my growing horror, most Republicans were failing the test. Conservatives with whom I had been working on anti-Trump briefing papers for the Rubio campaign emerged, in the blink of an eye, as enthusiastic Trumpkins. I still have their anti-Trump emails to me, and while writing this book I reread them with amusement and disbelief. Like so many other conservatives, they evidently viewed the GOP as a cult from which there is no escape even if the cult leader changes.

ONLY A PRECIOUS FEW prominent conservatives refused to endorse Trump. The roll call of honor included former presidential candidates Mitt Romney and Jeb Bush; former RNC chairmen Michael Steele and Ken Mehlman; Senators Susan Collins, Lindsay Graham, Ben Sasse, Lisa Murkowski, and Jeff Flake (John McCain, Rob Portman, Mark Kirk, Cory Gardner, Dan Sullivan, and Kelly Ayotte initially endorsed and then repudiated Trump); a few House members, including Adam Kinzinger, Charlie Dent, Mia Love, and Barbara Comstock; Governors John Kasich, Charlie Baker, and Larry Hogan; and a smattering of #NeverTrump pundits, political consultants, intellectuals, and writers like me. A partial list of the latter includes Stuart Stevens, Michael Murphy, Steve Schmidt, Mark Salter, Matthew Dowd, Nicolle Wallace, Jennifer Rubin, William Kristol, Robert Kagan, David Brooks, Ross Douthat, Michael Gerson, John Podhoretz, Jonah Goldberg, Tom Nichols, David Frum, David French, Linda Chavez, Anne Applebaum, Bret Stephens, Stephen Hayes, Ana Navarro, Rick Wilson, Evan McMullin, Mindy Finn, Joe Scarborough, Charlie Sykes, and George F. Will.[23]

I was proud to stand with all of them, but we were too few in number. There were enough of us for a dinner party, not a political party. I expected many more to join our ranks and was shocked by how many others—men and women whom I had known and admired for years—sold out their professed principles. It was as if they had descended into the "sunken place" in *Get Out* to be brainwashed like the African American characters in that classic horror film. The historian Richard Brookhiser, a longtime stalwart at *National Review*, summed up the Trump effect: "Now the religious Right adores a thrice-married cad and casual liar. But it is not alone. Historians and psychologists of the martial virtues salute the bone-spurred draft-dodger whose Khe Sanh was not catching the clap. Cultural critics who deplored academic fads and slipshod aesthetics explicate a man who has never read a book, not even the ones he has signed. . . . Straussians, after leaving the cave, find themselves in Mar-a-Lago. Econocons put their money on a serial bankrupt."[24]

The Republican Party as I had known it was "dead," I wrote in May 2016, adding that, "as far as I'm concerned," the anti-Trump holdouts "are the real Republican Party, in exile. I only hope that they—and I—can return from the wilderness after November."[25] That was not an easy article to write; it represented my first public break with my tribe, and of course I hoped that the rupture would eventually be repaired. I was being overoptimistic. Little did I suspect that the Trump wing would become the dominant one, and that the rest of us would be consigned to an exile that gives every appearance of becoming permanent.

AS THE TRUMPKINS GAINED ascendancy within the GOP, attacks on conscientious objectors like me increased in vehemence. We were told that we were suffering from "Trump derangement syndrome" and were guilty of "virtue signaling" so that we could win social acceptance at "Georgetown cocktail parties." In reality I had been happy for years to be an outspoken conservative in liberal cities like Los Angeles, Berkeley, New Haven, Cambridge, and New York, and had never felt any desire or need to kowtow to liberal sensibilities. I reveled in being a minority and a dissenter;

remember, I love to debate. I had never attended a single "George-town cocktail party" before opposing Trump and still have not been to one. I had, however, developed a network of conservative friends and supporters, and now I felt increasingly alienated from them. I might have called this book *Ex-Friends* were that title not already taken by Norman Podhoretz, who lost friends when he moved from left to right.

Some of my ex-friends told me that I sounded "angry" when talking about Trump, implying that emotion clouded my judg-ment. They suggested I needed to be "helpful" to Trump, rather than critical. In my view, they were the deluded ones whose judg-ment has been clouded by power worship. I do, however, plead guilty to being angry. I was and remain furious at what Trump is doing to our democracy and how he is demonizing the most vul-nerable among us. And I'm angry with all those people who are *not* angry—who are, in fact, complacent in the face of his attack on our institutions or even serve as his willing accomplices.

Often these conservatives would preface their remarks with "I'm no fan of Trump *but*, . . ."—the "but" being key—and then proceed to make clear that they were indeed fans but were ashamed to admit it because they knew how vile Trump was considered to be by polite society. This was almost identical to the way certain people would say "I'm no racist but, . . ." before proceeding to prove that they were indeed racists by opining that people of color were "stupid," "criminal," or "lazy." But a large section of the Republican base was unashamed by Trump's transgressions and indeed celebrated him for breaking "politically correct" taboos.

I had lived in the United States for more than forty years with-out experiencing overt anti-Semitism; admittedly I had resided in liberal enclaves such as Los Angeles and New York, where a lot of Jews live. In 2015–2016, however, my Twitter account and some-times my email inbox filled up with anti-Semitic, pro-Trump vitriol. I was called "a traitor to America" and told that "Jews want Whites to think . . . ethnic identity's a vice." Some charming Twitter troll posted a picture of me being executed in a gas chamber by a smiling Trump dressed in a Nazi uniform. Others suggested that I should leave America and move to either Israel or Russia.

My experience was hardly unusual; other Jewish commentators critical of Trump received similar treatment—in some cases much worse than I did because they had more obviously Jewish-sounding names. The Anti-Defamation League found that from August 2015 to July 2016 there were 2.6 million anti-Semitic tweets, reaching 10 billion total impressions. Admittedly about 70 percent of them came from just 1,600 accounts, suggesting a small but fanatical movement.[26] The ADL also determined that the number of anti-Semitic acts in the United States increased from 942 in 2015 to 1,267 in 2016 and 1,986 in 2017.[27]

Most Jews, even conservative Jews, were alarmed by Trump despite his pro-Israel statements and his Jewish son-in-law because of his covert appeals to anti-Semitism. Witness all of his retweets of white nationalists and all of his attacks on "international banks" that were supposedly plotting "the destruction of U.S. sovereignty in order to enrich these global financial powers." To illustrate the danger posed by "global special interests," Trump's closing campaign commercial flashed photographs of such readily identifiable Jews as financier George Soros, Federal Reserve chair Janet Yellen, and Goldman Sachs CEO Lloyd Blankfein. It sounded all too similar to what Nazi propaganda minister Joseph Goebbels had said at the Nuremberg rally in 1935 when he warned of "the absolute destruction of all economic, social, state, cultural, and civilizing advances made by Western civilization for the benefit of a rootless and nomadic international clique of conspirators."[28]

The racist Alt Right—a new name for age-old bigotry—was energized by Trump's candidacy, and why not? They liked what they heard from the most unapologetically racist major-party nominee in many decades—and quite possibly ever. One of their own—Stephen Bannon—even went from publishing the openly racist Breitbart website to chairing Trump's campaign and later working in the White House.

THE RUSSIAN GOVERNMENT also turned out to be a big fan of Trump—hardly surprising given how effusively he praised Vladimir Putin. By the time of the Democratic National Convention in late July 2016, it was obvious, at least to me, that the Russians were meddling in America's democracy to help elect Trump. WikiLeaks, a left-wing, anti-American website run by the fugitive Julian Assange, released twenty thousand emails stolen from the DNC. These leaks forced the resignation of DNC chairwoman Debbie Wasserman Schultz because they seemed to show that the DNC had been biased in favor of Hillary Clinton over challenger Bernie Sanders. This served Trump's purposes by encouraging Sanders supporters to sit out the general election or to vote for a third-party candidate, Jill Stein, who was suspiciously friendly toward Putin.

CrowdStrike, a cybersecurity firm hired by the DNC, traced the source of the leaks to two groups of hackers—"Cozy Bear" and "Fancy Bear"—associated with two Russian intelligence agencies. As I noted at the time, "Moscow's virtual fingerprints are all over this operation, including hyperlinks in Cyrillic and Internet protocol addresses linked to previous Russian hacks. In short, this appears to be a Russian intelligence operation designed to damage Clinton."[29] Yet Trump denied that Russia was behind the hacks—"It could be Russia, but it could also be China. It could also be lots of other people," he said during the first presidential debate in the fall. "It also could be somebody sitting on their bed that weighs 400 pounds." That Trump would not admit reality—that the Russians were behind the hacking—revealed a guilty conscience on his part because he was making active use of the stolen emails. Former CIA director Michael Hayden described Trump as a "useful idiot" of Vladimir Putin; former acting CIA director Michael Morell called him an "unwitting agent."

In September 2016, President Obama dispatched national security officials to Capitol Hill to plead for bipartisan unity in confronting the Kremlin. Senate Majority Leader Mitch McConnell shamefully put party above patriotism by refusing to cooperate. This was another low point for the Republican Party—which in those days was still my party. The GOP was so determined to win the presidential election that it was willing to overlook Russian meddling in the electoral process. Obama should have done more to stop the Russians, but if he had done so without Republican support, he would have been vulnerable to Trump's cynical charges that the election was "rigged." By refusing to confront this foreign threat, the GOP had made itself complicit in something close to treason.

THROUGHOUT THE FALL, Trump traduced the most basic norms of American democracy: he called for his opponent to be locked up and refused to say that he would accept the election results if he lost. Republicans pretended not to notice. All considerations of morality or ethics had to be suspended in the name of defeating Hillary Clinton. This was the reductio ad absurdum of the "win at all costs" mindset that the Republican Party had cultivated for decades. The GOP wanted to prevail even if its nominee was a faux Republican who was likely to do lasting damage to American democracy.

The final blow to Republican self-respect occurred in October with the release of the *Access Hollywood* tape. Trump is clearly heard

bragging about groping women: "When you're a star, they let you
do it. You can do anything. . . . Grab them by the pussy. You can
do anything." Before long nineteen women would come forward
to testify that this was no mere "locker room talk"—that Trump
had in fact assaulted them. The future of Trump's candidacy was
briefly in doubt. Prominent Republicans withdrew their endorsements and called on him to pull out. His poll numbers plum-
meted. But he refused to budge, and as his support began climbing
again, some of the very same Republicans who had un-endorsed
him, re-endorsed him. In lieu of principles, these politicians had
poll numbers.

Evangelical Christian leaders didn't even bother going through
the charade of temporarily abandoning Trump; their devotion to
him was so total and unshakable that Trump might as well have
been the Messiah. Another notorious rascal, Governor Edwin
Edwards of Louisiana, had once said in what would become a
familiar trope: "The only way I can lose this election is if I'm
caught in bed with either a dead girl or a live boy." In Trump's
case, it's doubtful if even that would have been enough to alienate
his evangelical acolytes. He could literally have killed someone in
the middle of Fifth Avenue, as he bragged, and he still would not
have lost their backing.

"My view is that people of faith are voting on issues like who
will protect unborn life, defend religious freedom, create jobs, and
oppose the Iran nuclear deal," said Ralph Reed, the chairman of
the Faith and Freedom Coalition. "I think a 10-year-old tape of a
private conversation with a TV talk show host ranks pretty low on
their hierarchy of concerns."[30] If only Reed and other evangelicals
had extended similar sympathy and understanding to Bill Clinton
after his own sex scandal. In the past they had always maintained
that political leaders needed to be unimpeachable in their personal
conduct. But they were theological silly putty: they had no problem

twisting their supposed convictions to support whatever political outcome they favored.

Of all the GOP's toadies and hypocrites, the fundamentalists were the most egregious: these supposed champions of morality were willing to support a candidate who regarded the sins proscribed in the Ten Commandants as his personal to-do list. The more commandments he violated, the better they liked him. It called to mind H. L. Mencken's quip: "Religion is a conceited effort to deny the most obvious realities."

TRUMP WAS BUOYED not just by his fervent partisans but also, ironically, by a law enforcement professional whom he would subsequently fire and vilify. FBI director James Comey announced just eleven days before the election, in contravention of Department of Justice guidelines, that he was reopening an investigation of the Hillary Clinton email scandal based on new emails found on a laptop belonging to Anthony Weiner, the estranged husband of Clinton aide Huma Abedin. *Uh-oh*, I muttered when I heard the news in a Manhattan studio where I was preparing to tape a podcast. *Here we go again.* Just a few days later Comey announced that this new investigation had not found any criminal wrongdoing, any more than a previous investigation had. I rejoiced when I heard the news. But by then it was too late: Comey had thrust the Clinton emails, the source of Trump's endless calls to "Lock her up," back into the center of the campaign. I don't believe Comey did this to help Trump—he was trying to protect the FBI's reputation from right-wing critics who would have claimed a cover-up if Clinton had won—but the effect was the same.

Along with the stolen emails from the Russians, the FBI's unwise updates on the Clinton investigation—while keeping quiet about the ongoing investigation into Trump-Russia ties—would help seal the fate of Clinton's campaign. But that was obvious only in hindsight. In the days before the election, sealed off in my coastal enclave, I was serenely oblivious of the fate about to befall the country. I made the fatal mistake for an analyst of conflating my own preferences with those of other people.

I ended the campaign with an explanation in *Foreign Policy* magazine of why "This Lifetime GOP Voter Is with Her." I knew that my scribblings would not make any difference to the outcome, but I wanted to do everything I possibly could to stop Trump so that, no matter what happened, my conscience would be clear. "In the final analysis, the strongest case for Clinton is what she is not," I wrote. "She is not racist, sexist, or xenophobic. She is not cruel, erratic, or volatile. She is not a bully or an authoritarian personality. She is not ignorant or unhinged. Those may be insufficient recommendations against a more formidable opponent. But when she's running against Donald Trump it's more than enough."[31]

Few other Republicans agreed with me. Trump won 90 percent of GOP votes, roughly the same percentage as previous nominees. He lost the popular vote by nearly three million votes but eked out a narrow Electoral College victory by a margin of fewer than 80,000 votes in three Rust Belt states.[32]

THE NEW YORK REAL-ESTATE SCION had figured out a way to appeal to what used to be known as the Reagan Democrats—the white working-class voters in the Midwest who had been part of the New Deal coalition but by the 1960s had become disenchanted by the party's liberal positions on issues such as national security, crime, abortion, and civil rights. Many of them had supported George Wallace in 1968, Richard Nixon in 1972, and Ronald Reagan in 1980 and 1984. Bill Clinton and Barack Obama, two of the most gifted orators in modern American politics, had won at least some of them back; Hillary Clinton—a woman whose intimidating intelligence was not leavened by a common touch—had not.

Trump had beguiled these unsophisticated voters with the same kind of appeal to nostalgia made by so many demagogues in the past. He promised to return America to an imagined paradise of the 1950s, a time when blue-collar workers had high-paying jobs and people of color were powerless and invisible to mainstream white society. This message resonated among people struggling with a devastating opioid epidemic and years of economic stagnation. Between 1980 and 2014, the top 1 percent of the country experienced 205 percent growth in personal income; the bottom 50 percent saw only 1 percent growth.[33] And in those same years, nearly 40 percent of US factory jobs disappeared.[34] Those statistics, as much as anything else, helped to explain why so many people were so desperate for salvation that they were willing to turn to a reality TV host as their savior. They had lost confidence in Washington because of such epic blunders as the Iraq War—yes, the war I supported—and the financial meltdown in 2008—yes, the economic crisis that my laissez-faire ideology helped to bring about.[35] Trump gave them hope that he would blow up what they viewed as a dysfunctional political system—and that somehow something good would grow from the ruins.

I knew that shuttered steel mills and abandoned coal mines would not reopen even if Trump were elected, as subsequent events have confirmed, but I failed to grasp the extent of despair in the heartland or the ways in which my own free-market ideology and faith in globalization had contributed to this economic devastation. Those of us who support capitalism—even with welfare-state protections—tend to take for granted that it will result in the greatest prosperity for the greatest number of people. That is an easy ideology to hold when, like me, you are one of the well-educated beneficiaries of a rapidly changing economy living in a booming coastal enclave surrounded by other upwardly mobile strivers. And it may even be true in the long run but, in the meantime, the costs of "creative destruction" can be prohibitively high for those who lack the skills to benefit from the transformation wrought by the Information Revolution.

I was insensitive to those costs even though I was not nearly as insulated from ordinary life as Trump is. I do not, after all, shuttle between my many properties on a private airplane; I have only one property, an apartment in Manhattan, and I fly economy class like everyone else. Yet somehow, despite his "champagne wishes and caviar dreams" lifestyle, Trump managed to position himself as the tribune of the "forgotten men and women of our country."[36] It was a stroke of brilliant marketing rooted in his undoubted ability to read and exploit the mood of customers, viewers, and now voters.

Thanks to his expert demagoguery, Donald Trump was president-elect, and Republicans controlled all three branches of the federal government for only the second time in the last 84 years, along with a majority of governorships and state legislatures. It was an epochal achievement—and a cause for celebration—if you were a Republican. But I no longer was. The day after the election, I reregistered as an independent after a lifetime of supporting the GOP. As I explained in the *Los Angeles Times*: "I can no longer support a party that doesn't know what it stands for—and that in fact may stand for positions I find repugnant."[37]

4.

THE
CHAOS
PRESIDENT

A CONGENITAL OPTIMIST, I TRIED TO FIND CAUSE FOR good cheer immediately after the election—kind of like the Jewish troublemakers in Monty Python's *Life of Brian* who sing "Always look on the bright side of life" while being crucified. On the day after the most unexpected and dispiriting election result in American history, I cited Adam Smith's words upon being told that British troops had been defeated by the American rebels at Saratoga in 1777: "There is a great deal of ruin in a nation." "That proposition is about to be put to the test by President-elect Donald Trump," I wrote in *Foreign Policy*. "Yes, I can barely believe that I am actually writing those words: 'President Trump.' I never thought he was remotely qualified for the highest office, and I never thought he would win. I was obviously wrong about the latter. Now I have to pray that I was wrong about the former. . . . I'm hoping against hope that he will grow in the White House—that the office will make the man. Because if that doesn't occur, the consequences are too ghastly to contemplate."[1]

Okay, I wasn't *that* optimistic. But I was so desperate for the country to avoid catastrophe that I was even willing to hold out a small olive branch to the newly triumphant Trumpites. In *USA Today* four days later, I noted: "The temptation now for me and my fellow #NeverTrumpers is to want nothing to do with a candidate we considered unfit for office. The temptation for Trump is to want nothing to do with people who considered him unfit. For the good of the country, I hope the two sides can come together."[2] I had no personal ambitions—I would not have worked for Trump even in the unlikely eventuality that I had been asked to do so— but I encouraged friends to take administration positions. A few of my friends would indeed assume administration jobs—some quite senior. I supported their willingness to serve, even if they felt compelled to cut off all ties with a dissenter like me lest they be accused of disloyalty by the thought police. One official—a close friend of many years—pointedly crossed my name off a guest list at a party thrown in her honor by a Washington powerbroker. I was dismayed but not surprised. As the saying, attributed to Harry Truman, has it: If you want a friend in Washington, get a dog.

Like many other policy experts, I hoped that Trump would allow himself to be guided by wise advisers. Those hopes were briefly buoyed when he appointed what I wrongly judged to be a strong cabinet, with the exception of Rex Tillerson, who seemed completely unqualified to be secretary of state. The events of January 20, 2017, and the weeks that followed, would reveal how hollow those hopes that Trump would grow in office were—they were as naïve as my expectation that Trump would lose the election.

TRUMP SIGNALED THE DIRECTION of his administration with the most dystopian, dispiriting, and divisive inaugural address ever. Not for him the inspirational tone of a John F. Kennedy, Ronald Reagan, or Barack Obama. He spoke of an America full of "rusted-out factories scattered like tombstones across the landscape of our nation," a land rife with "crime and gangs and drugs that have stolen too many lives and robbed our country of so much unrealized potential." This was a very jarring vision of America—paranoid, angry, xenophobic—for someone like me who came here in 1976

from the Soviet Union as a six-year-old boy. To me, and to countless other immigrants (including, ahem, Trump's own grandpar-
ents), America appeared to be not the hellhole he describes but a
land of unimaginable wealth and opportunity.[3] Trump, by contrast,
was echoing the darkest depiction of America promulgated by a
long line of Russian dictators, culminating in Vladimir Putin.

In his first days in office, Trump claimed that the "fake news
media" had lied about the size of his inauguration crowds and that
he would have won the popular vote were it not for "millions" of
ballots cast by illegal immigrants. White House aides, called upon
by the president to defend his falsehoods, had to resort to the disturbing explanation that his "alternative facts" were just as good as
the actual facts. Trump then pulled out of the Trans-Pacific Partnership, a proposed free-trade zone incorporating twelve Pacific
Rim nations, and signed an ill-conceived executive order barring
visitors from seven Muslim countries. No one knew the details:
Were existing visas canceled? Did the ban apply to US green card
holders? The result: mass confusion at airports. Within hours, federal judges began intervening to block this Draconian decree, forcing the administration back to the drawing board.[4]

Other inexperienced presidents had gotten off to a bad start—
the Kennedy administration had been shaken by the failure of the
Bay of Pigs invasion on April 17–20, 1961—but none had begun his
term with so many self-inflicted debacles in the very first days. The
impression of chaos was reinforced when Trump's national security
adviser, retired lieutenant general Michael Flynn, was fired after
just twenty-four days on the job—the shortest tenure on record.
Flynn would subsequently plead guilty to a felony for lying to FBI
agents about his dealings with Russia's ambassador. That Flynn had
been appointed in the first place, after having taken money from
the governments of Turkey and Russia, was an indication of the
new administration's astonishing lack of ethics—and sheer incom-

petence. The ineptitude would be on display daily, with White House aide Kellyanne Conway referring to a nonexistent "Bowling Green massacre" and the president himself talking as if the abolitionist orator and ex-slave Frederick Douglass, who died in 1895, were still alive.

THIS TRAGEDY OF ERRORS was chalked up by Trump apologists to his inexperience as a businessman serving for the first time in government. Eventually, on July 31, 2017, White House chief of staff Reince Priebus was fired and replaced by John Kelly, who was supposed to bring greater discipline to a White House in crisis. And yet a year later Kelly was losing influence and the chaos was rising. By early 2018, Trump had gotten rid of anyone likely to stand as an impediment to his impetuosity. Secretary of State Rex Tillerson and National Security Adviser H. R. McMaster—who had counseled Trump to stay in the Iran nuclear deal—were fired. Economic adviser Gary Cohn, who had counseled against trade wars, quit when Trump imposed steel and aluminum tariffs. John Bolton, an advocate of regime change in Iran and North Korea, became Trump's third national security adviser in fifteen months, and the hardline CIA director Mike Pompeo took over as secretary of state. Trump was already on his sixth communications director, and hundreds of critical positions across the government remained empty. John Dowd stepped down as the president's lead outside lawyer, to be replaced by former New York mayor Rudolph Giuliani. Even Trump's emotional support dogsbodies, bodyguard Keith Schiller and Communications Director Hope Hicks, departed.

Trump's White House saw an astonishing 43 percent turnover among senior staff in its first year, compared to 9 percent for Barack Obama and 6 percent for George W. Bush.[5] Trump averaged one major firing or resignation every nine days.[6] Amid this turmoil,

Trump was forced to admit that he had paid off a porn star who had alleged that they had engaged in an affair. Before long FBI agents were raiding the offices of Trump's personal lawyer, Michael Cohen, who had facilitated the payoff. He was revealed to have taken millions of dollars from companies, including one linked to a prominent Russian oligarch, that were eager to influence the administration.

In explaining why he would not join Trump's legal team, the prominent conservative attorney Ted Olson, a former solicitor general in the George W. Bush administration, explained: "I think everybody would agree: This is turmoil, it's chaos, it's confusion, it's not good for anything. We always believe that there should be an orderly process, and, of course, government is not clean or orderly ever. But this seems to be beyond normal."[7]

Actually, this was the new normal. If Trump's administration has proven anything, it is that Jeb Bush was right when he said that Trump was "a chaos candidate," and that he would be "a chaos president." Trump's tenure, in fact, felt more like the reign of a Roman emperor than a normal American president. There were echoes of Rome's most capricious rulers: emperors like Tiberius, who moved his whole court to the isle of Capri, where he could frolic with young boys and girls ("Pans and nymphs") and pronounce death sentences by the score while he left the commander of his Praetorian Guard, Lucius Sejanus—a forerunner of generals such as John Kelly, H. R. McMaster, and James Mattis—to run the government in his absence. Or Tiberius's infamous successor, Caligula, who may have been clinically insane: he proclaimed himself a god, was famously said to have made his horse a consul, and, when he ran out of gladiators to be slaughtered at the Coliseum, had his guards throw an entire section of spectators into the arena to be eaten by wild beasts. (This was the ancient version of the kind of professional wrestling match in which Trump participated before his election.) Or Nero, who did not actually fiddle while Rome burned in AD 64 but did impale and burn to death scores of Christians to propitiate the people's anger over the deadly conflagration. This was a precursor of the kind of scapegoating of minorities that Trump specializes in.

Trump's recreational pursuits were tamer than the Romans'—he cavorted with strippers and playmates, not underage "Pans and nymphs," and instead of attending gladiator matches he played golf, *lots and lots* of golf. Indeed, if he keeps playing golf at the current pace, he will spend nearly one-fourth of a four-year term at the golf course.[8] And, much to his regret no doubt, he could not simply impale his enemies as the emperors had done. But his sloth and ineptitude were nearly as great. Trump was unable to function effectively because he was functionally illiterate: He could read in theory but chose not to, getting his information from television instead, Fox News to be exact. A former aide said that "everything that needs to be conveyed to the President must be boiled down to . . . 'two or three points, with the syntactical complexity of 'See Jane run.' "[9] Trump routinely made decisions based on his "gut" rather than the kind of study and staff work that had characterized previous presidents. As Susan Glasser noted in the *New Yorker*: "Many of this President's major decisions—from appointing Cabinet secretaries to pulling out of the Iran nuclear deal—are completely opaque and, in many cases, shockingly process-free."[10] The result was frequent fiascos such as the aborted nomination of the White House physician, Rear Admiral Ronny Jackson, to be secretary of veterans' affairs, his chief qualification having been his effusive praise of Trump's health. Or, far worse, the mishandling of Hurricane Maria in Puerto Rico, which resulted in at least 1,400 deaths—and possibly as many as 4,000.[11]

Most Americans recoiled from the "carnage," just as most Romans recoiled at the excesses of their emperors. (Hence the fact that many more emperors were killed or overthrown—voting an emperor out of office not being an option—than died on the throne of natural causes.) Despite robust economic growth, the public gave Trump record-low approval ratings that averaged around 40 percent—higher than warranted but lower than just about any previous president at a similar point in his tenure. By early 2018, after a slight uptick in his ratings, Trump would be in Jimmy Carter territory. And yet between 80 percent and 90 percent of Republicans stuck with him, applauding enthusiastically when the rest of the country was lustily booing or simply looking away in disgust.

WHAT WAS IT THAT these Republicans saw that the rest of us did not? The case for Trump was based on:

★ A strong economy—even though Trump inherited, and did not create, the robust economic conditions, including low unemployment, low interest rates, and a roaring bull market. In fact, Trump's policies jeopardized the economy. His tariffs and attacks on companies such as Amazon spooked the markets, making stocks as volatile as the president himself. The Dow average had risen 37 percent between Obama's inauguration and April 2010; between Trump's inauguration and April 2018, only 19 percent.[12] Likewise average monthly job creation since Trump's inauguration—186,200 new jobs a month—was lower than under Obama, who over the previous four years had averaged 215,875 new jobs a month.[13] Trump deserved some credit for presiding over the expansion but not nearly as much as Obama for presiding over the recovery from the Great Recession of 2007–2009. Indeed, a researcher at the Brookings Institution found that, measured against the five other presidents who inherited a growing economy since 1960, Trump's record, far from being exemplary, is tied for last place, lagging behind even Jimmy Carter's.[14]

★ Trump's "defeat" of ISIS—even though that organization is far from eradicated and even though the game plan for combating it was largely devised and implemented by Obama. By early 2018, moreover, Trump was threatening to pull the remaining 2,000 US troops out of Syria, thereby jeopardizing all of the gains against ISIS and opening eastern Syria to Iranian expansion.

★ Trump's pullout from treaties abominated by the right—the Paris Climate Accord and the Iran nuclear deal. His supporters refused to admit that global warming is real and that the Paris accord did not mandate job-killing regulations; compliance was entirely voluntary. As for the Iran nuclear deal, I had opposed it myself, but I did not think it made sense to pull out when Iran was complying with its terms, as even Trump's own secretary of state admitted.[15] Trump had no Plan B for containing Iranian power, beyond imposing unilateral sanctions and hoping for the best.

★ Trump's move of the US embassy in Israel from Tel Aviv to Jerusalem, fulfilling a pledge that other presidents had made but failed to implement. But while the location of the US embassy had obvious symbolic importance, it was of scant strategic significance. Far more important to Israel's security was the growing Iranian domination of Syria, which Trump showed little interest in combating, forcing Israel to launch an increasing number of air strikes on Iranian positions next door.

★ Trump's summit with Kim Jong Un. Trump did not succeed in winning any significant concessions beyond empty promises to "work towards the complete denuclearization of the Korean peninsula"—the same kind of assurances North Korean leaders had been making, and breaking, since 1992. In return, Trump legitimized North Korea on the world stage, effectively undermining the international sanctions regime. Trump showered sickening praise on one of the world's worst human-rights violators—in his telling, Kim has "got a great personality," "he's a funny guy, he's very smart, he's a great negotiator," and "he loves his people." Trump even agreed to cancel US–South Korea joint military exercises, which he called, in an echo of Pyongyang's propaganda, "provocative . . . war games." Conservatives had criticized President Obama for far less after he shook hands with Cuban dictator Raul Castro and signed a nuclear deal with Iran that Trump said was the "worst deal ever." Trump's deal with North Korea was far worse than the Iran nuclear deal. And yet conservatives showered Trump with praise after he returned from Singapore and proclaimed, "There is no longer a Nuclear Threat from North Korea"—his version of Neville Chamberlain's 1938 boast that the Munich Conference would result in "peace for our time."

★ The passage, near the end of Trump's first year in office, of a massive tax cut bill, even though, as we shall see, the cost of that legislation could prove to be prohibitive and its impact on the economy negligible. This was Trump's major and virtually sole legislative achievement—and it was the product of congressional negotiations into which Trump had little input. While Trump's tax-and-spend policies helped further stimulate the economy, his former economic adviser Gary

Cohn worried that their impact could be wiped out by the trade wars Trump started.

★ A host of regulations that Trump ordered repealed—even though the extent and impact of that deregulatory push was wildly exaggerated by the White House. Trump claims that "in the history of our country, no president, during their entire term, has cut more regulations than we've cut," but Ronald Reagan achieved far more deregulation. *Bloomberg BusinessWeek* found that Trump was using typical sleight of hand to obscure the fact that "hundreds of the pending regulations had been effectively shelved before Trump took office. Others listed as withdrawn are actually still being developed by federal agencies. Still more were moot because the actions sought in a pending rule were already in effect."[16] Goldman Sachs researchers determined that the actual scale of the Trump deregulation was so limited that it had no appreciable impact on the economy.[17]

★ Trump's selection of conservative judges Neil Gorsuch and Brett Kavanaugh to the Supreme Court and a host of lesser-known conservatives to the lower courts—even though in all other ways Trump would attack the rule of law that judges are supposed to uphold. For much of Trump's first year in office, any criticism of the president would be greeted by a predictable refrain: "But, Gorsuch . . ."

★ Trump wasn't Hillary Clinton. From Clinton's attempts as First Lady to reform health care to the murder of the US ambassador in Libya while she was secretary of state, conservatives had done an effective job of turning this centrist and capable, if uncharismatic, politician into a caricature of a far-left, anti-American "feminazi." The coup de grace was Trump's nickname—"Crooked Hillary"—bestowed because she had violated State Department regulations, although apparently not the law, by using a private server for some of her official emails. (As president, Trump would use a private cell phone for sensitive conversations that represented a much more significant potential security breach.)[18] If you are convinced that there is no greater evil that can be visited upon America than a Clinton presidency, then you are prepared to see a Trump presidency as your salvation. I cannot count how many emails and tweets I have gotten from Trump fans who respond to my criticisms of the president with: "But, Hillary . . ."

★ Last, and perhaps most important, Trump "triggered" liberals. The very fact that he sparked so much opprobrium was taken by conservatives as a compelling argument—probably, in fact, the *most* compelling argument—in his favor. Sure, conservatives would concede, sometimes Trump goes too far or says something he should not, but "at least he fights." For much of the right, there is no higher end in politics than to annoy liberal "elites"—or now also conservative #Never-Trump elites.

That's it: the conservative case for Trump.

For progressives, of course, few of these arguments, save Trump's outreach to Pyongyang, are remotely persuasive. They are not in favor of deregulation or tax cuts because they are acutely conscious of the costs to society, and of course they were not petrified (if also not enthusiastic) about the prospect of another Clinton presidency. Trump's achievements, such as they are, are harder to dismiss for conservatives. Even those who are critical of Trump have to acknowledge that his presidency hasn't been all bad—there have been a few good things achieved. For example, I favored the move of the US embassy to Jerusalem, the intensification of efforts to defeat ISIS, the imposition of harsh sanctions on North Korea, and the cut in the corporate tax rate to bring the US tax code into conformity with other major industrialized countries (although I thought it should have been done in a revenue-neutral way). If Trump can convince North Korea to carry out its pledges of denuclearization, that will obviously be a great thing—if also nearly impossible to verify.

But the presidency is not an á la carte buffet. It is a prix-fixe set menu. You cannot pick and choose what you want. You have to digest everything, good and bad. And in the course of achieving these minuscule policy victories, conservatives would have to swallow enough rancid garbage to give them a severe case of indigestion—even if most of them would never admit it.

5.

THE

COST

OF

CAPITULATION

As a historian, I am partial to parallels from the past, but it is nearly impossible to find equivalent events, at least in US history, to the rise of Donald Trump. He resembles demagogues such as Huey Long, Joseph McCarthy, and George Wallace, who made skillful use of the mass media, first radio and then television, to prey on the fears of their constituents and vilify minorities—whether "the rich," Communists, or African Americans—in order to accrue power. The major difference, of course, is that none of those men became president. Trump did. No historical comparison is ever exact, but for anyone wondering what the Kingfish, Tailgunner Joe, or the Fighting Judge would have done in office, Trump provides some hints.

The parallels between Wallace—the segregationist governor of Alabama who repeatedly sought the presidency, achieving his greatest success as a third-party candidate in 1968—and Trump are particularly striking. Wallace might as well have been speaking for Trump when he said, "Hell, we got too much dignity in government now, what we need is some *meanness*." So, too, other descriptions of Wallace from his biographer Marshall Frady have an uncanny resonance.

Frady wrote: "It has become Wallace's conviction—more than conviction, visceral sensation—that he exists as the very incarnation of the 'folks,' the embodiment of the will and sensibilities and discontents of the people in the roadside diners and all-night chili cafes, the cabdrivers and waitresses and plant workers, as well as a certain harried Prufrock population of dingy-collared department-store clerks and insurance salesmen and neighborhood grocers: the great silent American Folk which have never been politically numbered as the Wallace candidacy has now numbered them."

Also: "In fact, he seems to regard formal political organization with a vague contempt, as a sign of political effeteness, an absence of vitality—as if he is already naturally blessed with what political organization exists to create. His simple directness is, at once, part of his absurdity and part of his genius."

And: "He seems empty of any private philosophy or persuasions reached in solitude and stillness. He is made up, in mind and sensibilities, of the clatter and chatter and gusting impulses of the marketplace, the town square, the barbershop. His morality is the morality of the majority. 'The majority of the folks aren't gonna want to do anything that ain't right,' he insists. He is the ultimate product of the democratic system."

Finally: "Not only are abstract ethics alien to him, but he entertains a particular antipathy to people who live and act from them. It's something like the Dionysian principle applied to politics. 'Hell, intellectuals, when they've gotten into power, have made some of the bloodiest tyrants man has ever seen,' he maintains. 'These here liberals and intellectual morons, they don't believe in nothing but themselves and their theories. They don't have any faith in people. Lot of 'em don't really *like* people, when you get right down to it.'"[1]

The major difference is that Wallace reflected the style of white, rural Alabama, Trump of white, urban Forest Hills, Queens—but the similarities are striking, especially their anti-elite and anti-intellectual appeals, their contempt for the normal way of running campaigns, their unwillingness to abide by ethical norms, their championing of working-class whites, and their demonization of minorities. Both men were even alike in their disdain for alcohol.

Trump has not imposed fascism, as many, including me, had feared, but then neither did Wallace, even if he did uphold American apartheid as long as he could. It's hard to wreck a democracy in a short period, even in a political system much less robust than America's. Even for Vladimir Putin the task of turning Russia from a rickety democracy to a full-blown dictatorship took years after he was first appointed president in 1999. The courts, press, oligarchs, regional governors, opposition leaders, and other checks on his authority had to be painstakingly removed, and sometimes killed, one by one. A cult of personality had to be constructed, featuring the Russian dictator engaged in manly pursuits such as bare-chested horseback riding. Recep Tayyip Erdogan in Turkey and Abdel Fattah el-Sisi in Egypt have followed Putin's example in snuffing out the remnants of democracy in their countries. A similar process, not yet as advanced, has taken place in countries such as Hungary, the Philippines, and Poland, where far-right populists have won power in recent years.

If Trump were operating in a republic with a less-lengthy constitutional tradition or weaker institutional safeguards, he might well be another Vladimir Putin or a Benito Mussolini, Juan Peron, or Hugo Chavez. He would not be another Hitler: The Nazi leader was uniquely evil, and it does a disservice to the victims of Nazism to suggest that Trump is the second coming of the Führer, even if there are some disturbing parallels. (Likewise, it unfairly glorifies his critics to suggest that we are "the Resistance," as if we were the French Maquis risking torture and death to fight the Nazi-backed Vichy regime.) Trump is more of a garden-variety strongman, and if he were ruling in Italy in the 1920s, Argentina in the 1950s, or Russia or Venezuela in the 2000s, he would undoubtedly be a dictator by now.

America's robust checks and balances—a free press, an independent judiciary, and an apolitical civil service, in particular—keep

Trump from fully acting on his authoritarian impulses. He can't even go as far as his fellow populists Viktor Orban in Hungary or Rodrigo Duterte in the Philippines, or the Law and Justice Party in Poland. But Trump has cozied up to dictators and sought to redefine America's role in the world, picked fights with US allies, started trade wars, demonized the free press (and sought to financially punish the *Washington Post*'s owner), spewed nonstop lies, and whipped up hatred of minorities such as rich African American athletes and poor Mexican immigrants—all the while waging unrelenting war on the rule of law in order to save himself from criminal investigation. And, just like those earlier demagogues Huey Long, Joe McCarthy, and George Wallace, Trump has won plaudits from a substantial portion of the American electorate while assaulting the highest ideals of America because he has claimed to be protecting the country from insidious threats—disloyal elites, criminals of color, immigrants, terrorists, perfidious trade partners and allies—that threaten America's "greatness."

The Founding Fathers anticipated the rise of demagogues. *Federalist 10* warns: "Men of factious tempers, of local prejudices, or of sinister designs may, by intrigue, by corruption, or by other means, first obtain the suffrages, and then betray the interests, of the people."[2] But the Founders could not have foreseen the ability of this particular demagogue to directly reach millions of people via Twitter, Facebook, or Fox News Channel. Nor could they have anticipated the spread of "fake news" that allows Trump's followers to live in a world of "alternative facts" at odds with reality. We are in uncharted territory—the kind of unexplored land that, on at least one sixteenth-century globe, was marked "Here be dragons."

It's impossible to know where we are headed: How can you predict what a president who is capable of saying or doing just about anything will do next? Trump is so unpredictable that sometimes he even does sensible things, much as his critics may hate to admit it. His very volatility is the source of his power; if he were ever to become boring and predictable like other politicians, he would be finished. But even if we cannot know where he is going next, we can at least chart the surrealistic journey up to this point.

What follows is a brief and incomplete list of Trump's transgressions against common decency and good sense—and quite possibly the law itself. Some—perhaps much—of what follows may be familiar to you, but there has been so much craziness emanating from the administration that it's hard for even the most dedicated consumer of news to keep track of it all. It is, therefore, imperative to briefly summarize just what Trump has done that is so wrong. This is the grim reality that should offend any person with a shred of decency. This is what the president's acolytes either ignore or excuse. This is why I am so disgusted with Trump—and his toadies.

I. RACISM

Any recounting of the toll of the Trump presidency must begin with the damage that the president is doing to race relations in America. This is the most vexing, emotional, and important issue in American history, and it is one on which conservatives, as we shall see in the next chapter, have had a checkered record. But the Republican Party is, or perhaps more accurately *was*, the party of Lincoln—the party that freed the slaves. That commitment to civil rights lasted at least into the 1960s. A higher percentage of House and Senate Republicans supported the 1964 Civil Rights Act and the 1965 Voting Rights Act than did Democrats.[3] In more recent years Republicans had justified their opposition to racial "quotas" and "set-asides" by claiming that the right response to the racial discrimination of the past was not a new form of discrimination but, rather, strict adherence to the creed of color blindness. We liked to quote the immortal words of the Rev. Dr. Martin Luther King Jr.: "I have a dream that my four little children will one day live in a nation where they will not be judged by the color of their skin but by the content of their character."

There is no reason to assume that Donald Trump shares this dream—and much reason to suspect that he does not. His entire career has been full of racist slurs and acts. His presidency has been no different. After neo-Nazis clashed with counterdemonstrators in Charlottesville, Virginia, on the weekend of August 11–12, 2017, Trump claimed there were "very fine people on both sides." He went on to side with the neo-Nazis in opposing the removal of Confederate monuments. "Many of those people were there to protest the taking down of the statue of Robert E. Lee," the president said. "So this week, it is Robert E. Lee. I noticed that Stonewall Jackson is coming down. I wonder, is it George Washington next week? And is it Thomas Jefferson the week after? You know, you really do have to ask yourself, where does it stop?" This is moral sophistry of a high order. Washington and Jefferson were indeed slave owners. But they also created a system of government that, while stained by the original sin of slavery, nevertheless established certain "unalienable rights" that would eventually be vindicated after the struggles of the Civil War, Reconstruction, and the civil rights movement of the 1950s–1960s. By contrast, what is it that we are supposed to be grateful to the Confederates for? For triggering the bloodiest conflict in American history? For fighting to keep their fellow citizens in bondage? The fact that Trump cannot make these basic distinctions is indicative of his deeply prejudiced worldview.[4]

Yet more evidence of Trump's racism came just a few weeks after Charlottesville, when he pardoned Joe Arpaio, the sheriff of Maricopa County, Arizona, who had been found guilty of criminal contempt of court for ignoring a federal judge's order not to arrest Latinos solely because he suspected them of being in the country illegally.

The trend continued in the fall of 2017, when Trump launched a crusade against African American NFL players who kneeled during the playing of the national anthem to protest police brutality. At a rally on September 22, Trump said, "Wouldn't you love to see one of our NFL owners when someone disrespects our flag to say, 'Get that son of a bitch off the field right now . . . he's fired!'" Trump kept going in a similar vein as the NFL season unfolded, and even after—for example, saying that any player who didn't kneel during the anthem "shouldn't be in this country."[5] This was exactly the kind of impingement on free speech that conservatives routinely complained about when it was committed by college leftists—but they applauded Trump's attempts to stifle peaceful protests. Finally, in the spring of 2018, the NFL owners caved in and mandated fines for any players who kneel during the anthem. "The issue of kneeling has nothing to do with race," the president insisted. "It is about respect for our Country, Flag and National Anthem. NFL must respect this!" But there was no doubt that the racist undertones of his attacks on rich, privileged African American athletes resonated with his white, working-class base.

A *Politico* reporter who journeyed to Johnstown, Pennsylvania—a onetime coal-mining town that had long since been hollowed out—found that Trump supporters were ecstatic about his vilification of the NFL, and for all the wrong reasons. One Trump voter, the owner of a catering company, griped: "Shame on them. These clowns are out there, making millions of dollars a year, and they're using some stupid excuse that they want equality—so I'll kneel against the flag and the national anthem?" "You're not a fan of equality?" reporter Michael Kruse asked. "For people who deserve it and earn it," he replied. "All my ancestors, Italian,

100 percent Italian, the Irish, Germans, Polish, whatever—they all came over here, settled in places like this, they worked hard and they earned the respect. They earned the success that they got. Some people don't want to do that. They just want it handed to them." So only European immigrants work hard? Professional athletes, who work with superhuman stamina to hone their skills, just want everything "handed to them"? Another Trump supporter—a retired meat packer whose son had died of a heroin overdose—was even more explicit. Do you know what NFL stands for? she asked. "Niggers for life."[6]

No, not all Trump supporters are racist. But virtually all racists, it seems, are Trump supporters. And all Trump supporters implicitly condone his blatant prejudice. At the very least they don't consider racism to be a reason to turn against the president. For a disturbingly large number of Trump voters, it is the primary reason to support him. A 2018 study published by the National Academy of Sciences concluded that support for Trump was not primarily an economic phenomenon—the lowest-income voters actually supported Clinton—but, rather, motivated mainly by the "status threat felt by the dwindling proportion of traditionally high-status Americans (i.e., whites, Christians, and men)."[7] In other words, the study found, it was white anxiety about the looming demographic reality that white people will soon be a minority in America that, more than anything else, drove voters to back a candidate who "emphasized reestablishing status hierarchies of the past."

II. Nativism

Donald Trump wasn't the first president to promise to "make America great again." Ronald Reagan used that very phrase in a speech on Labor Day, 1980, delivered at Liberty State Park in Jersey City with the Statue of Liberty as a backdrop. The difference between the two Republican presidents is that Reagan used much of this speech not to bash immigrants but to hail their contributions to America. "Through this 'Golden Door,' under the gaze of that 'Mother of Exiles,' have come millions of men and women, who first stepped foot on American soil right there, on Ellis Island, so close to the Statue of Liberty . . . ," Reagan said. "They came to make America work. They didn't ask what this country could do for them but what they could do to make this refuge the greatest home of freedom in history." Not only did Reagan celebrate immigrants rhetorically, he also signed legislation in 1986 that legalized three million undocumented immigrants, and he set in motion the negotiations that produced the North American Free Trade Agreement. His dream—never realized—was to allow free travel between the United States, Canada, and Mexico.[8] He wanted to open opportunities, not build walls.

Donald Trump has a very different vision. Far from praising the contributions of immigrants, he regularly cites a poem called "The Snake" about a talking reptile that fatally bites a woman who has taken it in and nurtured it with "milk and honey"; in Trump's telling, the real "snakes" are immigrants. Trump says of the illegal immigrants he is deporting: "These aren't people, these are animals."[9] He claims that he is only speaking of MS-13 gang members, but he is using his denunciations of these criminals to signal his repugnance of all illegal immigrants, indeed of *all* immigrants aside, presumably, from European supermodels. This is exactly the kind of dehumanizing language—labeling minority groups as scum, vermin, subhumans, rats, cockroaches, lice, etc.—employed by dictators and ethnic-cleansers in countries from Nazi Germany to Rwanda. Trump even complains about immigrants in sanctuary cities "breeding" as if they were, yes, animals.[10]

The Department of Homeland Security created, at Trump's

instigation, a Victim of Immigration Crimes Enforcement office to focus on the supposed menace of immigrants, although immigrants, even illegal immigrants, are much less likely to commit crimes than are the native born.[11] But Trump doesn't care about the facts. In early 2018, he told congressional leaders that he prefers immigrants from white countries such as Norway to those from "shithole countries" in Africa and the Caribbean. In point of fact, a study of African immigrants in America found that they "attain higher levels of education than the overall U.S. population as a whole."[12] It is hard to escape the suspicion that what Trump doesn't like about African immigrants is the color of their skin, not the content of their character.

Trump has displayed similar animus against Muslims. He has not only tried to bar newcomers from Muslim nations but has also been quick to label all attacks by Muslims as "terrorism" committed by "animals," while staying quiet about hate crimes against Muslims and labeling mass shootings by non-Muslims as evidence of a "mental health" problem. He even retweeted hateful and false anti-Muslim videos posted by a far-right British leader.

In her landmark book *The Second Sex*, the French philosopher Simone de Beauvoir noted how essential it was for all social groups to differentiate themselves from "the Other": "In small-town eyes all persons not belonging to the village are 'strangers' and suspect; to the native of a country all who inhabit other countries are 'foreigners'; Jews are 'different' for the anti-Semite, Negroes are 'inferior' for American racists, aborigines are 'natives' for colonists, proletarians are the 'lower class' for the privileged."[13] Stigmatizing "the Other" is especially important for authoritarian rulers. For Trump, Mexicans and Muslims have become "the Other" that rally his base behind his leadership despite all of the scandals during his presidency.

The overall number of arrests by the Immigrations and Customs Service increased by 25 percent in Trump's first year in office, and arrests of immigrants without criminal records soared by 164 percent.[14] There are all too many people like Jorge Garcia, a landscaper with a wife and two kids who lived in Detroit for thirty years before being deported to Mexico.[15] Trump even mandated that parents be separated from their children at the border—an unspeakably cruel policy designed to discourage illegal immigration. In the first six weeks alone, some two thousand children were taken away from their parents—sometimes literally ripped out of their arms.[16] Still more deportations may be in the offing because in the fall of 2017 Trump withdrew legal protection from "Dreamers," more than seven hundred thousand immigrants who had been brought illegally to America as young children. Trump claimed to support a deal in Congress to legalize the Dreamers, yet set impossible conditions for Democrats and sabotaged the prospect of compromise at every turn. On Easter Sunday 2018, he tweeted, "NO MORE DACA DEAL!" (DACA stands for Deferred Action for Childhood Arrivals.) Court orders have maintained legal protections for Dreamers, but for how much longer?

The end of DACA hit me particularly hard because almost half of those affected arrived in the United States before their sixth birthday. In other words, they were about the same age I was when I came here. It made me wonder: What would I do now, at nearly fifty years of age, if I were deported to a country that I have not seen in more than forty years and whose language I no longer speak? How would I survive? In my case it would be a particularly pressing problem, given how critical I have been of Russia's current president. (Putin's propaganda outlet, RT, has attacked me by name.)[17] The risk of political persecution would be all too real for me—as it is for Dreamers who might be deported to repressive countries. And what would happen to my family—to my partner, to my children, to my stepchildren? None of them is Russian. A move would be even more jarring for them than for me.

Trump's war on immigrants is making me feel like I am no longer a "real" American. Increasingly I feel like a Jew, an immigrant, a Russian—anything but a normal, mainstream American. That may be precisely what Trump and his most fervent supporters intend. They are redefining what it means to be an American. The old idea that anyone who embraces America's ideals can become an American is out. White House aide Stephen Miller even repudiated the words on the Statue of Liberty that Ronald Reagan celebrated in 1980: "Give me your tired, your poor,/Your huddled masses yearning to breathe free." Instead, American-ness is being redefined in blood-and-soil terms. I find myself increasingly forced to think of my ethnic identity instead of the national identity I adopted as a boy in 1976. That is discomfiting for me and a tragedy for America.[18] Yet most Republicans either excuse or—more frightening—applaud Trump's blatant xenophobia.

III. COLLUSION

We know two things for a fact about the 2016 election. First, Donald Trump won a narrow victory in the Electoral College while losing the popular vote. Second, we know, in the words of the US intelligence community, that "Russian President Vladimir Putin ordered an influence campaign in 2016 aimed at the US presidential election," and that "Putin and the Russian Government aspired to help President-elect Trump's election chances." This "high confidence" intelligence community estimate was subsequently endorsed by a federal grand jury that, at the request of Special Counsel Robert S. Mueller III, indicted twenty-five Russians involved in this influence operation. Trump's former national security adviser, Lieutenant General H. R. McMaster, said that the evidence of Russian tampering was "inconvertible," and his successor, John Bolton, described it as an "act of war." Even the Senate Intelligence Committee's Republican majority admitted that the Russians tried to help Trump.[19]

It strains credulity to claim, as Trump supporters do, that there was no relation between the Kremlin's intervention and Trump's victory. If the Russian operation had no impact on the results, why did Trump mention WikiLeaks—used as a conduit for Democratic Party documents stolen by Russian hackers—141 times during the last month of the campaign? It's true that the Russian spending was only a pittance compared to the $2.4 billion spent on the 2016 presidential campaign, but the Kremlin propaganda blitz reached 126 million Americans via Facebook alone. By all indications, the Russian operation was the most successful foreign attack on America since 9/11. It did not kill anyone, but it did undermine faith in American democracy. What we still do not know is whether there was conscious collusion between the Trump campaign and the Kremlin, but the weight of circumstantial evidence points in that direction.

According to the Moscow Project of the Center for American Progress: "In total, we have learned of at least 80 contacts between Trump's team and Russia linked operatives, including at least 23 meetings. . . . None of these contacts were ever reported to the proper authorities. Instead, *the Trump team tried to cover up every single one of them*."[20] The evidence of collusion grows stronger as more information emerges about these contacts.

Former Trump foreign policy adviser George Papadopoulos learned well in advance of their public release that the Russians had "thousands of emails" with "dirt" on Hillary Clinton; he relayed to the campaign offers of Russian "cooperation." The entire high command of the Trump campaign, including Paul Manafort (himself linked financially to the Russian oligarchy), Donald Trump Jr., and Jared Kushner, met at Trump Tower on

June 9, 2016, with a lawyer from Moscow, closely connected to the Russian government, who promised to "incriminate" Clinton. Trump Jr. communicated with WikiLeaks, and Trump adviser Roger Stone with both WikiLeaks and Guccifer 2.0, a Russian intelligence officer, while Manafort and his deputy, Rick Gates, were in active contact with a former—and possibly current—Russian intelligence officer. After Trump won, his national security adviser, Michael Flynn, held secret conversations with Russian ambassador Sergey Kislyak. An even closer Trump adviser—his son-in-law Jared Kushner—also met after the election with Kislyak and expressed interest in setting up a private back channel to Moscow via the Russian embassy in Washington to bypass the US government.

It is hard to imagine an innocent explanation for all of the Trump-Kremlin contacts—or for all the lying that Trump officials have done about them. It is harder still to imagine that Trump was unaware of what his team was up to. He was, after all, personally involved in putting out a false statement that the June 9 meeting at Trump Tower was about "adoptions." It will not, however, be easy to prove the president's personal complicity.

Trump defenders try to defend him against charges of collusion by citing all of the actions that he has supposedly taken against Russia. "Probably no one has been tougher to Russia than Donald Trump," Donald Trump says, referring to himself in the third-person style favored by monarchs and dictators.[21] In truth his record on Russia has been hard and soft—in a word, incoherent.

Trump can point to the fact that he has authorized the sale of lethal weaponry to Ukraine, expanded sanctions on Russia, launched two pinprick strikes on the Syrian regime allied with Russia, and expelled sixty Russian diplomats in retaliation for the attempted Russian murder of a former Russian agent and his daughter in Britain. But much of this was simply for show: even though the Russians could replace the sixty expelled diplomats, Trump was said to have been furious when he found out that his aides had maneuvered him into so many expulsions.[22] When Putin ordered the elimination of 755 US diplomatic positions in Russia, Trump praised him. When the Russian autocrat won a rigged reelection victory, Trump called to congratulate him, disregarding a briefing paper from his own staff warning him "DO NOT CONGRATULATE." Trump even announced in 2018 that he wanted to invite Russia back to the Group of Seven meetings from which it had been expelled four years earlier after its invasion of Ukraine. The following month, the president was shockingly supine when confronted with Putin's lies at a Helsinki summit, choosing to take the word of the Russian despot over the findings of the US intelligence community.

Just before retiring in April 2018, Trump's national security adviser H. R. McMaster admitted: "We have failed to impose sufficient costs" on Russia. Although Trump hasn't made US policy as pro-Russia as Putin might have hoped, largely because of the Russiagate scandal, his chaotic governance style, hostility to US allies, and aversion to American global leadership have allowed Russia to keep expanding its power from Ukraine to Syria and beyond.[23] Putin could barely conceal his glee in 2018 when Trump launched trade wars with America's NATO allies and called the European Union a "foe."

Imagine what Republican lawmakers would have said if the president accused of colluding with the Kremlin was Hillary Clinton. Charges of "treason" would fill the air. Indeed, such charges are common today, with Republicans peddling specious allegations that Clinton sold American uranium to Russia or somehow conspired with the Kremlin to concoct charges that Trump colluded with the Russians. But rather than thinking worse of Trump as evidence of collusion accumulates, Republicans are starting to think better of Putin because of the coziness between the two men. Gallup found that favorable views of Putin among Republicans jumped twenty points between 2015 and 2017.[24] Admittedly, even in 2017, only 32 percent of Republicans had a positive view of the Russian despot, but that's more than three times higher than among Democrats. And a Pew poll found that only 38 percent of Republicans viewed "Russia's power and influence" as a major threat to the United States compared to 63 percent of Democrats.[25] This is a disturbing indication of how GOP voters are willing to follow Trump wherever he leads—even into the arms of the Kremlin.

IV. THE RULE OF LAW

It is ironic that so many conservatives premise their support for Trump on his willingness to appoint conservative judges because Trump has mounted such a wide-ranging and unprecedented assault on the rule of law. It's not just that he has savaged judges that have ruled against him in cases such as his attempts to limit Muslim immigration, leading his own Supreme Court appointee Neil Gorsuch to denounce his "disheartening" and "demoralizing" attacks on the judiciary.[26] And it's not just that he has abused his pardon power to bypass Justice Department procedures and grant clemency to unrepentant felons such as Dinesh D'Souza and Joe Arpaio because they support him politically—thereby signaling to his own aides who are under criminal investigation that they should not cooperate with the FBI. Even worse, Trump has sought to politicize law enforcement in a way that no president has done in half a century. After the Watergate scandal, rules and regulations were established by the Justice Department to prevent presidential tampering with law enforcement of the kind that Richard Nixon and other presidents had carried out for partisan advantage. Trump shows no awareness that any such restrictions even exist.

The president tried to pressure then-FBI director James Comey into pledging him personal loyalty and going easy in his investigation of Mike Flynn. When Comey refused, he was fired on May 9, 2017, ostensibly for mishandling the Hillary Clinton email investigation. But that cover story swiftly crumbled. On May 11, Trump admitted to Lester Holt of NBC News that he was determined to fire Comey "regardless" of the recommendation from Deputy Attorney General Rod Rosenstein in order to stop the investigation of the "Russia thing." Trump isn't the first president to attempt to obstruct justice. But he is the first to admit what he was doing on national TV, and his admissions led to the appointment of former FBI director Robert S. Mueller as a special counsel.[27]

Trump was only narrowly dissuaded from firing Mueller. Instead he first tried to get Attorney General Jefferson Sessions III to reverse his recusal, which had cleared the way for Mueller's appointment, and then, when Sessions quite properly refused, publicly castigated him for being "very weak," "disgraceful," and an "idiot."[28] This was a spectacle without precedent in US history: a president harshly condemning his own attorney general for refusing to politicize law enforcement. When Sessions would not either quit or accede to Trump's unethical demands, the president vented his "fire and fury" on the FBI, forcing out Comey's deputies Stewart Baker and Andrew McCabe. Trump tweeted: "After years of Comey, with the phony and dishonest Clinton investigation (and more), running the FBI, its reputation is in Tatters—worst in History! But fear not, we will bring it back to greatness."[29] Later he referred to the FBI as a "den of thieves."[30] Trump showed no awareness that the FBI answered to him or that his assault on its reputation could hinder its job of protecting the American public from criminals, spies, and terrorists. When Comey hit back at Trump in a best-selling memoir, Trump called the former FBI director an "untruthful slime ball," "a proven LEAKER & LIAR," and "the WORST FBI Director in history, by far!" and called for him to be prosecuted.[31]

Trump then moved on to attacking the special counsel by name—something that his surrogates at Fox and in Congress had been doing all along. "Why does the Mueller team have 13 hardened Democrats, some big Crooked Hillary supporters, and Zero Republicans?" Trump tweeted. "Another Dem recently added . . . does anyone think this is fair? And yet, there is NO COLLUSION!"[32] In point of fact, Mueller was a Republican just like Trump. Both men also were born into wealth. But there the resemblance ended. Mueller had devoted his life to public service, from volunteering to fight in Vietnam in the 1960s, where he was wounded and earned numerous commendations, to serving as a line prosecutor handling homicide cases in the District of Columbia in the 1990s when he could have been collecting a fat paycheck from a big law firm. Trump, by contrast, had never served any cause greater than his own id.

Mueller is the best of America; Trump the worst. All you need to know about the diseased state of today's Republican Party is that it reviles Mueller and reveres Trump.[33]

SOME REPUBLICANS WARNED Trump not to fire Mueller, but the leaders of the House and Senate refused to move legislation that could have protected the special counsel by adding judicial oversight to any decision to remove him. Republicans not only showed themselves to be unwilling to defend Mueller—some of them also actively joined in Trump's attempts to obstruct his investigation. The foremost culprit was Representative Devin Nunes of California, chairman of the House Intelligence Committee. I had met Nunes before the rise of Trump and had thought him to be thoughtful and reasonable. How misleading first impressions can be! In thrall to Trump, Nunes revealed himself to be an unscrupulous partisan who did not hesitate to misuse his authority to protect the president at all costs.

First Nunes claimed that Obama national security adviser Susan E. Rice had illegally "unmasked" Trump aides in surveillance transcripts. Trump's own national security adviser, H. R. McMaster, concluded that Rice "did nothing wrong." Nunes next directed his staff to prepare a memorandum alleging that the FBI had obtained a surveillance warrant for Trump campaign adviser Carter Page based on former British spy Christopher Steele's work, while hiding Steele's partisan funding. This was false. The Steele dossier was only one piece of evidence among many, and the Justice Department did reveal that Steele was paid by an anti-Trump political entity.

Nunes's failure to make the case did not, of course, lead either him or the White House to retract their scurrilous allegations of a Deep State plot against Trump. Republicans tried embarrassing the FBI with outtakes from the private texts between FBI agent Peter Strzok and his girlfriend, FBI attorney Lisa Page, both of whom had already been removed from the Mueller probe. Trump said their texts were "BOMBSHELLS!" and evidence of "treason"—the kind of accusation of disloyalty that dictators routinely make against their critics. While the Strzok and Page texts critical of Trump and other political figures were embarrassing, the Justice Department's inspector general found that there was no evidence that their personal views influenced any investigation.[34]

When the texts didn't pan out, Nunes opened a new front by effectively outing an informant that the FBI had used to investigate whether Russia was infiltrating the Trump campaign. Trump then hyperbolically claimed that this perfectly proper use of a human source in a counterintelligence investigation, which he dubbed "Spygate," constituted "one of the biggest political scandals in history!"[35] "The day that we can't protect human sources is the day the American people start becoming less safe," said FBI director Christopher Wray. It's safe to say that lickspittle Republicans such as Nunes care more about protecting Trump than they do the American people.[36] Even when their fellow Republican, Representative Trey Gowdy, admitted that the FBI had acted properly, Trump and Nunes kept pushing their conspiracy theory.

Nothing that Nunes unearthed remotely supported the hyperbolic demands of Trump supporters who wanted the leaders of the Justice Department and FBI to be "taken out in cuffs." If anyone was breaking the law, it was Trump with his attempted obstruction of justice. He practically admitted as much in a tweet, writing: "No Collusion or Obstruction (other than I fight back)."[37] That's a pretty big exception!

Yet the dishonest Trump-Nunes campaign of demonization against the FBI was succeeding with Republican voters: an April 2018 survey found that "more than half of Republicans now think that the FBI is actively biased against Trump."[38] Republican candidates for Congress even sought votes by calling for the prosecution of Clinton, Comey, and other enemies of the state. Republicans were casting themselves ever further into dishonor, disgrace, and disrepute by helping the president to undermine the rule of law—the very foundation of the American republic.

V. "FAKE NEWS"

The Washington Post reports that Donald Trump began his presidency by making an average of 4.9 false or misleading statements a day. By his second year in office, like a true Stakhanovite, he had ramped up production to an average of six falsehoods a day. By May 2018, he had uttered the 3,000th falsehood of his presidency and was now serving up nine whoppers a day.[39] Trump made Richard Nixon seem like an honest man by comparison.

Trump did not just lie. He showed reckless disregard for the truth. He boasted that he had told Prime Minister Justin Trudeau that Canada had a trade surplus with the United States even though he didn't know if it did. (It doesn't.) Trump's own US trade representative reports that Canada runs an $8.4 billion trade deficit with the United States.[40] But Trump didn't back down. He tweeted: "We do have a Trade Deficit with Canada, as we do with almost all countries (some of them massive)." And he kept on repeating this fake fact as he imposed steep tariffs on aluminum, steel, and other products manufactured in Canada. Like Trump's claims that General John J. Pershing slaughtered Muslims in the Philippines, or that his inauguration drew record crowds, or that he would have won the popular vote if millions of illegal immigrants had not voted, this is another example of a would-be dictator's desire not just to sneak lies by us but to shove them down our throats. Trump is signaling that he doesn't care what the truth is. From now on the truth will be whatever he says, and he expects every loyal follower to faithfully parrot the official party line, no matter how nonsensical. Trump even had the audacity to claim "I never fired James Comey because of Russia!" a year after having admitted on videotape that, yes, this was precisely why he had fired Comey.[41]

The frightening thing is that Trump's insistence on redefining reality is working, at least with his base. The video news site NowThis posted a hilarious and horrifying clip showing Fox News talking heads hyperventilating over President Barack Obama's promise to meet with the leaders of hostile states such as North Korea (Mike Huckabee: "President Obama likes talking to dictators!"), before going on to effusively praise President Trump for doing just that by meeting with Kim Jong Un. If Trump were to bomb North Korea tomorrow, his cultish followers would praise that decision as avidly as they praised his appeasement of Kim. Trump is sucking a substantial portion of America into his Orwellian universe. The rest of us have to struggle simply to remember that war *isn't* peace, freedom *isn't* slavery, ignorance *isn't* strength.[42] Every lie that is accepted as the truth chips away at the foundations of our democracy. As Rex Tillerson said after his dismissal, in a pointed jab at his ex-boss: "If our leaders seek to conceal the truth or we as people become accepting of alternative realities that are no longer grounded in facts, then we as American citizens are on a pathway to relinquishing our freedom."[43]

HAND IN HAND with Trump's war on the truth has been his campaign against the truth-tellers—the press. All presidents have chafed at critical media coverage and many have lashed out at what they regard as inaccurate reporting, at least in private. But Trump has taken media-bashing to a whole new level.

During the 2016 campaign he called journalists "sick people" and said, "I really don't think they like our country." Reporters covering his rallies said they felt menaced by his incited supporters. As president, Trump tweeted in February 2017: "The FAKE NEWS media (failing @nytimes, @NBCNews, @ABC, @CBS, @CNN) is not my enemy, it is the enemy of the American People!" This was an extraordinary escalation of his assault on the First Amendment. Here was an American president adopting the language used by Adolf Hitler (the Nazis referred to the Lügenpresse, or "lying press") and Josef Stalin, who called the press "vrag naroda" (enemy of the people).[44]

Trump regularly threatened to revoke licenses from broadcast networks that angered him and to loosen the libel laws to make media outlets easier to sue. He is obsessed with Amazon because its CEO, Jeff Bezos, owns the *Washington Post*, where I am a columnist.

Trump repeatedly inveighs against the "Amazon Washington Post" and complains—wrongly—that Amazon does not pay taxes and costs the US Postal Service money. Trump even asked the postmaster general, Megan Brennan, to double the rate Amazon is charged—a demand that Brennan refused because shipping rates are set by contract.[45] In another sign that Trump may be punishing media companies he doesn't like, his attorney, Rudolph Giuliani, said that the president personally intervened to block AT&T's merger with Time Warner, the owner of CNN. (Giuliani later walked back his statement, and a federal judge overruled the administration's objections to the merger.)[46] Trump is following the playbook of strongmen such as Viktor Orban, Vladimir Putin, and Recep Tayyip Erdogan, who silenced the press not by imposing censorship but by imposing financial pressure on independent news organizations to either force them out of business or into the hands of friendly owners.[47]

To be sure, Trump has not actually made good on most of his bloodcurdling threats against the media because the First Amendment provides them such strong protection. If anything, he has been good for the media business, driving newspapers such as the *New York Times* and the *Washington Post* to new circulation highs with their exposés of administration scandals. But he is poisoning the civic culture of the United States, raising distrust of the press, and making it impossible for people on opposing sides of the political divide to agree on a commonly accepted set of facts. In one poll taken in late 2017, more than 60 percent of Trump supporters said that the media are the enemies of the people, while only 19 percent had confidence in the media.[48] Trump's attacks on the media are not just undermining the First Amendment. They are also emboldening authoritarian rulers around the world: the ruling parties in, among other countries, Myanmar, Poland, Egypt, Kuwait, Turkey, Syria, Libya, and the Philippines have adopted the "fake news" mantra to attack press freedom.

Trump does not understand what John McCain, a previous standard-bearer of the GOP, wrote—namely that "journalists play a major role in the promotion and protection of democracy and our unalienable rights, and they must be able to do their jobs freely. Only truth and transparency can guarantee freedom."[49] Trump is intent in discrediting the truth, destroying transparency, and undermining democracy—and he is doing so with nary a protest from most Republicans.

VI. ETHICS

One of the great non-mysteries of the Trump administration is why cabinet members think they can behave like aristocrats at the court of the Sun King. The Department of Housing and Urban Development spent $31,000 for a dining set for Secretary Ben Carson's office while programs for the poor were being slashed. The Environmental Protection Agency paid for Administrator Scott Pruitt to fly first class and be protected by a squadron of bodyguards so he didn't have to mix with the great unwashed in economy class. Two other cabinet secretaries—Veterans Affairs secretary David Shulkin and Health and Human Services secretary Tom Price—were fired over excessive travel expenses. Pruitt eventually got the boot too.

Why would cabinet members act any differently when they are serving in the least ethical administration in our history? The "our" is important because there have been more crooked regimes—but only in banana republics. The corruption and malfeasance of the Trump administration is unprecedented in US history. There are only a few points of comparison: Crédit Mobilier and the Whiskey Ring during the Grant administration, both scandals involving groups of shady businessmen who defrauded the government with the help of federal officials, including reportedly President Grant's private secretary. Teapot Dome during the Harding administration, when the secretary of the Department of the Interior was convicted of taking bribes in return for providing oil companies with leases on federal land, including the Teapot Dome reservation in Wyoming. And, during the Nixon administration, Watergate—a catch-all designation for Nixon's attempts to obstruct an investigation of the burglary of the Democratic National Committee carried out by his campaign and his misuse of the FBI and IRS to spy on his political opponents—along with the bribe taking, extortion, and tax fraud committed by Vice President Spiro Agnew while he was governor of Maryland. There have been other notable scandals, such as Iran-Contra and the Monica Lewinsky affair, but neither rose to the same level—the Iran-Contra affair was not done for the personal profit of the Reagan administration officials who traded arms for hostages to Iran and then funneled some of the proceeds to support Nicaraguan rebels, and, while Bill Clinton was caught lying under oath, it was to conceal a tawdry sexual liaison, i.e., essentially a private matter.

By any historical standard, the Trump administration is in an unethical league of its own—and the president has set the tone.[50] Trump's former national security adviser Mike Flynn and deputy campaign manager Rick Gates have pleaded guilty to felonies; his onetime campaign manager, Paul Manafort, faced thirty-two criminal charges, including conspiracy against the United States; and his personal lawyer was under federal investigation. Manafort even went to prison while out on bail for attempting to tamper with witnesses against him.

Trump skirted nepotism rules by hiring his daughter Ivanka and son-in-law Jared Kushner to work in the White House. Ivanka, who had not divested her ownership stake in her clothing company, has used her high visibility to market her products. In the meantime, according to the *New York Times*, Kushner's family company received hundreds of millions of dollars in loans from companies whose executives met with him in his capacity as a senior White House aide.[51] The *Washington Post* reported that officials in the United Arab Emirates, China, Israel, and Mexico had discussed how they could manipulate Kushner "by taking advantage of his complex business arrangements, financial difficulties and lack of foreign policy experience." It's hard to imagine that anyone who wasn't married to the president's daughter would have received a top-level security clearance under those circumstances—especially after having amended his disclosure forms on numerous occasions to note meetings and income he had "forgotten" to record. But Kushner's father-in-law got away with far worse.

President Trump broke with decades of precedent by refusing to reveal his tax returns, suggesting he has something to hide—whether it's shady money from foreign sources or simply that his net worth is not as high as he claims. Ronald and Nancy Reagan went so far as to donate to charity all of their income from television, radio, and movie residuals so as to avoid any appearance of a conflict of interest. Trump wouldn't even divest himself of his business holdings. He simply turned over the management of the Trump Organization to his two adult sons, Eric and Donald Jr. They continued to promote real-estate developments across the world, many of them involving local businessmen closely connected to governments eager to ingratiate themselves with the Trump administration. When the Trump Organization got into a dispute over a hotel in Panama, its lawyers demanded that the president of Panama intervene to help and warned of "repercussions" for the country if he didn't. The president of Panama had to upbraid Trump's company for acting improperly.[52]

And while Trump was conducting trade negotiations with China, a Chinese state-owned bank provided $500 million in financing for a project in Indonesia that includes "Trump-branded residences, hotels and golf course."[53] China also provided seven new trademarks for products sold by Ivanka Trump.[54] Within days, Trump shocked national security professionals by announcing that he would lift sanctions on the Chinese telecom giant ZTE. At the very least the president was in violation of the Constitution's Emoluments Clause; at worst, this sequence of events gives the impression that China may have been bribing him.

Meanwhile, back in Washington, the Trump International Hotel has become a favored venue for foreign governments, political organizations, and lobbyists to stay while attempting to influence the Trump administration. Citizens for Ethics and Responsibility in Washington calculated that "political groups spent more than $1.2 million at Trump properties during the president's first year in office. Prior to President Trump's 2016 campaign, annual spending by political committees at Trump properties had never exceeded $100,000 in any given year going back to at least 2002." Trump's for-profit "Winter White House," Mar-a-Lago, doubled membership fees to $200,000 as soon as Trump won the presidency; for that money, well-heeled members can have access to the president of the United States.[55]

Trump's sins extend, of course, well beyond the financial sphere. They include sexual affairs followed by payoffs that recall the conduct of Democratic senator John Edwards and allegations of sexual misconduct similar to those that have brought down other public figures from Harvey Weinstein to Charlie Rose. During his first year in office, Trump had on his White House staff a senior aide who was accused of beating his wives. And in the 2017 Alabama US Senate race, he endorsed a candidate who was credibly accused of molesting underage girls. Trump has a propensity to engage in misconduct himself and to excuse it in others—as long as, like him, they are powerful white men.

Republican voters, in turn, have a dismaying propensity to

forgive Trump any sin, including his vulgar, boastful, insulting, and illiterate way of expressing himself—more fitting for an elementary school playground than the Oval Office. Remarkably, according to one poll, 61 percent of Republicans consider Trump a good role model for their children—a view held by only 2 percent of Democrats.[56] What kind of children are these Republicans raising anyway? If Trump is their role model, kids will grow up to be name-calling, lying, narcissistic, ignorant, greedy, prejudiced bullies.

Even those who resist Trump can be contaminated by his conduct. Decades of social science research has revealed that "aggression, bullying and incivility mutate into social super-viruses": "people lie and cheat more after they've seen someone get away with it," "when political leaders are uncivil on social media, it catalyzes aggression in supporters and opponents alike," and "after experiencing incivility at work, 94 percent of us respond with incivility of our own—most commonly with anger and a desire to retaliate."[57] Evidence of the Trump effect is evident in a Pew survey that found 51 percent of Republicans under the age of thirty-four—the ones most influenced by Trump's example—believe that personal insults are sometimes fair game in politics, compared to only 29 percent of young Democrats and fewer than 40 percent of older Republicans.[58] Trump's misbehavior is a stain that will not easily wash away. By legitimating hitherto taboo behavior, he will leave an unsightly mark on American society for decades to come.

Yet conservatives, even (or especially) religious conservatives, couldn't care less: 75 percent of white evangelicals supported Trump in one 2018 poll.[59] The backing of these supposed moralists is Trump's "get out of jail free" card, at least when it comes to matters of morality. It is one big reason why so far, at least, he has avoided the fate of Gary Hart, driven out of the 1988 presidential campaign by evidence of infidelity; Bill Clinton, impeached as a result of his affair with an intern; Bob Livingston, denied the House speakership in 1998 because of his own affairs; or other politicians felled by promiscuity. Liberals, with their live-and-let-live attitude, cannot credibly attack the president for consensual sexual conduct, and conservatives choose not to. Hence, he escapes the consequences of his actions unless he can be shown to have violated the law—no easy matter to establish.

VII. FISCAL IRRESPONSIBILITY

Republicans have long cultivated a reputation—not necessarily deserved—as the party of fiscal austerity. But with Trump's accession, any pretensions to frugality have been tossed into the bonfire, along with the GOP's reputation as the party of law and order and family values. We are a long way removed from 1953, when President Dwight D. Eisenhower said, "There must be balanced budgets before we are again on a safe and sound system in our economy."[60] Or even from 2012, when Representative Paul Ryan said: "We have a debt crisis right in front of us, and what brings down Empires—past and future—is debt."[61]

In 2012, when Ryan spoke those words, federal debt stood at $16 trillion. By 2018 the debt was more than $21 trillion—and climbing, largely because of the spending increases and tax cuts passed by Republicans like Ryan. In 2017 Republicans in Congress approved, on a party-line vote, a tax bill that is projected to add $1.9 trillion to the debt. This was a far cry from the 1986 tax reform act, passed under Ronald Reagan, which was revenue neutral. Then in 2018, a bipartisan coalition in Congress blew through spending caps by approving $300 billion in additional spending over the next two years.

The Committee for a Responsible Federal Budget estimates that, as a result of Republican profligacy, the federal government will be running trillion-dollar deficits "indefinitely." That's roughly double the deficit in Obama's last full year in office—$585 billion. So much for Trump's election-year promise to eliminate the entire federal debt within eight years. The United States is the only major industrialized country whose debt-to-GDP ratio is projected to get worse in the years ahead.[62] Perennial fiscal basket cases such as Greece and Italy are reducing their debt load, while the United States is rapidly expanding it. Republicans are turning economic logic on its head. Periods of economic expansion should be used to balance the budget. Then, when a downturn hits, that's the time for stimulatory spending increases and tax cuts. Running stratospheric deficits while the economy is booming leaves us defenseless to fight a future recession.

It's hard to argue with Senator Rand Paul, who, during a lonely protest on the Senate floor, said, "If you were against President Obama's deficits, and now you're for the Republican deficits, isn't that the very definition of hypocrisy?"[63] But, of course, he's a hypocrite too, having voted for the massive tax cut.

The only way to restore fiscal sanity is to either increase revenue or restrain entitlement spending. Paul Ryan made entitlement reform a centerpiece of his career, but there is no chance of Congress taking badly needed action because Trump, the self-styled "king of debt," couldn't care less. Ryan all but admitted defeat when he announced his retirement in 2018. The president's profligacy is leading the country to fiscal ruin and the Republican Party to intellectual ruin.[64] As former Republican senator Judd Gregg, a onetime chairman of the Senate Budget Committee, writes, the GOP has "no claim any longer to being the party of fiscally responsible government, or to being good stewards of the government and its fiscal health. The Republican Congress now represents a party with very few significant defining principles other than the promotion of the president's impulses at that moment."[65]

VIII. THE END OF THE PAX AMERICANA

Ever since 1945, American foreign policy has been premised on defending and extending political and economic freedom. President after president, both Democrat and Republican, going back to the days of Harry S. Truman, has promoted collective security, international law, free trade, and human rights. Donald Trump has decisively broken from this tradition. He is hostile to both democracy and free trade.

Trump has loudly and repeatedly signaled his intention to abandon more than seventy years of America's commitment to reducing trade barriers and tariffs. With the mindset of a New York real-estate developer used to competing over scarce land, he imagines that every deal has a winner and a loser. He cannot fathom that free trade can be a win for both sides—the country that manufactures a product and the country that buys it. It is doubtful he has ever heard of David Ricardo's theory of "comparative advantage," which holds that countries should specialize and trade in what they are best at producing—cloth for nineteenth-century Britain, wine for Portugal—rather than trying to make everything themselves. Trump imagines that if any country is running a trade surplus with the United States, it is taking advantage of America rather than performing an invaluable service by providing products that Americans want to buy. By the same logic my dentist is ripping me off when he charges $300 for a tooth cleaning unless he buys $300 worth of my books at the same time.

Trump's pullout from the Trans-Pacific Partnership (TPP) was an economic and geopolitical gift to China, which can now pursue its own Regional Comprehensive Economic Partnership, an alternative to the TPP that is designed to facilitate Chinese hegemony over East Asia. Already, China has signed free-trade agreements with twenty-one countries, compared with only twenty for the United States, and it is negotiating more than a dozen additional pacts. Far from lowering trade barriers, as his predecessors did, Trump has demanded changes in existing accords, such as the North American Free Trade Agreement and the Korea-U.S. Free Trade Agreement, while imposing 25 percent tariffs on steel and 10 percent tariffs on aluminum, followed by $37 billion of tariffs on Chinese goods.

Trump welcomes a trade war—he says that "trade wars are good, and easy to win"—but no serious economist would agree. Moody's economists estimate that a trade war with China could cost 190,000 American jobs.[66] Another study finds that steel and aluminum tariffs alone could cost as many as 400,000 American jobs.[67] But Trump seems as oblivious to these grim predictions as he is to the history of trade wars.

The Smoot-Hawley Tariff Act of 1930 triggered a trade war that spread the Great Depression from the United States to the rest of the world. The resulting economic meltdown contributed to the rise of totalitarian regimes in Germany and Japan and led to the outbreak of World War II. After 1945, US policymakers pursued a free-trade policy. They midwifed the creation of the General Agreement on Tariffs and Trade in 1947 and the World Trade Organization in 1995. Free trade became one of the pillars of the Pax Americana, along with support for democracy, international law, and collective security. This altruistic approach paid off: today, the United States has 4.4 percent of the world's population and 24.3 percent of its gross domestic product.[68]

Granted, the impact of free trade has not been uniformly positive; for many Americans it has contributed to the despair they feel.

Even if economic change is primarily driven by technology (one study found that 88 percent of the loss of US manufacturing jobs between 2006 and 2013 was due to automation and related factors),[69] it is easy to blame trade with other countries for hollowing out industrial towns and throwing workers onto the unemployment line. To some extent this is even true—trade does contribute to economic dislocation even if it is not the primary cause. An influx of immigrants also can contribute to the impression among white, working-class Americans that "their" country is being lost. But the right answer is to ameliorate the suffering of those left behind by providing retraining and social welfare benefits—not to shut down free trade and immigration and thereby impose heavy costs on the entire country. There can be no return to some kind of imagined autarkic paradise of the past during which the United States did not depend on the free movement of goods and people. I still believe in the old *Wall Street Journal* slogan so familiar to me from my years at that proudly capitalist publication: "Free People and Free Markets." Too bad so few conservatives are willing to fight for those ideals anymore. Indeed, congressional leaders blocked attempts by some Republican lawmakers, such as Senator Bob Corker, to roll back Trump's steel and aluminum tariffs.

I fear that America's farsighted postwar trade policy—and all of the economic and security benefits it delivered—may not survive Trump's mindless acts of vandalism. Trump has launched a war not just on "unfair" trade practices but also on the very idea of an open, rules-based international system of trade. Trump seems aware of the negative consequences of his tariffs, which is why his commerce department was considering exemptions from steel and aluminum tariffs for companies that claimed they could not find the metals they need domestically. But his case-by-case approach turns trade deals into sweetheart arrangements that undermine the hope of American policymakers going back to the 1940s to create a rules-based trading system under which disputes could be adjudicated impartially and on the merits.

Republicans aren't troubled in the least. A *Washington Post*–ABC News poll in early 2018 showed that 66 percent of Republicans thought that a trade war with China would be good for US jobs, compared to only 36 percent of all adults.[70] Once the party of free trade, the GOP has embraced protectionism because of Trump.

TRUMP'S AVERSION TO free trade is matched by his hostility to America's traditional, democratic allies. He has long believed that the United States was getting ripped off and taken advantage of by its closest friends. In 1990, for example, when the United States was at the height of its power, he said, "Our 'allies' are making billions screwing us."[71] Once in office, Trump allowed his more internationally minded advisers to talk him out of pulling US forces out of South Korea, Japan, or Germany, as he had once threatened to do. He even reluctantly affirmed NATO's Article V mutual-defense provision but then questioned why America's sons should fight for Montenegro. He abandoned not only the TPP but also the Paris climate accord and the Iran nuclear deal. He imposed tariffs on America's NATO allies and abruptly pulled out of a joint communiqué with other world leaders at a Group of Seven summit in Quebec in June 2018. Trump impulsively accepted a summit meeting with North Korean dictator Kim Jong Un and then showered Kim with praise despite not getting any real concessions in return. These are indications of how the administration "grown-ups" could not contain his unilateralist (and erratic) instincts for long.

Trump's words spoke volumes about his contemptuous attitude toward allies. During his first year in office, he had testy exchanges with, among others, the prime minister of Australia and the president of Mexico. Not even America's closest ally was safe from

Trump's animadversions. In June 2017, after a terrorist attack in London, Trump blasted that city's first Muslim mayor, Sadiq Khan, tweeting: "At least 7 dead and 48 wounded in terror attack and Mayor of London says there is 'no reason to be alarmed!'" Trump blatantly misrepresented the mayor's remarks—Khan had said there was no need to be alarmed about a heightened police presence on the streets, not about terrorism. A few months later, in November 2017, Prime Minister Theresa May rebuked Trump for posting anti-Muslim videos produced by a far-right British leader. Trump instantly hit back, lecturing the prime minister, "Don't focus on me, focus on the destructive Radical Islamic Terrorism that is taking place within the United Kingdom. We are doing just fine!"

Trump's relationship with the chancellor of Germany was just as testy as with the prime minister of the United Kingdom. It is perhaps no coincidence that the leaders of both countries are intelligent, strong-willed women; with the notable exception of his own daughter Ivanka, Trump does not appear comfortable dealing with independent women. During the 2016 campaign, Trump bashed Angela Merkel for admitting Muslim refugees into Germany. "I think what she did in Germany is a disgrace," he said, adding that he was no longer "a fan." When the two leaders met at the White House in early 2017, Trump pointedly refused to shake Merkel's hand. Then in May, following a G7 summit in Italy during which Trump clashed with the European leaders over the Paris climate accord, Merkel emerged to say that Europe could no longer count on the United States. "We Europeans truly have to take our fate into our own hands," she declared.

Trump has been even more vitriolic in attacking Canadian prime minister Justin Trudeau, the leader of a country whose troops have fought and bled alongside Americans for more than a century. After Trudeau vowed to retaliate for US tariffs imposed under the pretense that his country posed a "national security

threat" to the United States, Trump blasted him as "very dishonest & weak." Trump's aides piled on, with economic adviser Larry
Kudlow accusing Trudeau of a "betrayal" and trade adviser Peter
Navarro saying there's a "special place in hell" for the Canadian
prime minister.[72] Navarro subsequently apologized, but the contrast between the administration's praise for Kim Jong Un and its
attacks on Justin Trudeau was striking. In Trump's telling, he had
established a "special bond" with Kim but there is a "special place
in hell" for Trudeau.

Just about the only democratic leaders with whom Trump developed cordial relationships were Shinzo Abe of Japan and Emmanuel
Macron of France—the former because he played golf with Trump
(and probably let the American win), the latter because he took
Trump to a military parade in Paris. But not even the budding
Abe-Trump bromance could spare Japan from being included on
the list of nations subject to Trump's ill-advised steel and aluminum sanctions, and Macron could not prevent Trump from pulling
out of the Iran nuclear deal or imposing tariffs on the European
Union. By June 2018, Macron and Trump were exchanging hostile
tweets—and it was entirely Trump's fault.

While clashing with democratic leaders—especially those who
happen to be women or minorities—Trump has gotten along disturbingly well with dictators. He positively purred after the Saudis
in May 2017 projected a five-story-sized photo of him onto the
side of his hotel in Riyadh. In July 2017, Trump had a tête-à-tête
with Vladimir Putin at the G-20 summit in Hamburg that began
with the American president telling the Russian autocrat what an
"honor" it was to see him. In November 2017, Trump was even
more laudatory after a visit with Xi Jinping in Beijing. He said that
his feeling toward Xi is "an incredibly warm one," and described
Xi as a "highly respected and powerful representative of his people." Correction: Xi is not the "representative" of his people. He

is their dictator, and it's impossible to know how respected he is because anyone who is disrespectful to him is likely to be locked up. Xi is currently orchestrating the most intense cult of personality that China has seen since the days of Mao Zedong—and Trump is doing his level best to help. He declared that it's "great" that Xi is making himself president for life and added, supposedly in jest, "maybe we'll have to give that a shot someday."

Trump has a kind word for every strongman he chats with. He congratulated Rodrigo Duterte of the Philippines because "of the unbelievable job" he was doing "on the drug problem"—a problem that Duterte is addressing by unleashing death squads that have killed thousands of Filipinos. He said that Recep Tayyip Erdogan is "getting very high marks" as he was crushing civil society and congratulated him on a rigged referendum that spelled the death knell for Turkish democracy. And, of course, he claimed that North Korea's Kim Jong Un, an odious human-rights violator, loves his people and in turn is loved by them. He even expressed admiration for how "tough" Kim was in accumulating absolute power ("I mean, that's one in 10,000 that could do that")—a feat that Kim pulled off by, among other steps, killing his own uncle and half brother.[73] His relationship with Vladimir Putin is so obsequious that former CIA director John Brennan and former director of National Intelligence James Clapper suggested that Trump might have been compromised by the Kremlin.

All American presidents have been forced to deal with dictators. Recall Franklin Roosevelt's apocryphal aphorism about Anastasio Somoza of Nicaragua: "He's a son of a bitch, but he's our son of a bitch." But no president has been so greasy and extravagant in his blandishments. For Trump, these dictators' attacks on democratic norms are not a problem but rather policies to be praised—and possibly even emulated. "He speaks and his people sit up in attention," Trump said of Kim Jong Un. "I want my people to do the same." In 2018 Freedom House downgraded America in its annual "Freedom in the World" report, which noted that "core institutions were attacked by an administration that rejects established norms of ethical conduct across many fields of activity." Similarly, the watchdog group Reporters Without Borders downgraded America's level of press freedom in 2018, down to forty-fifth in the world, behind Surinam, Burkina Faso, and Rumania.

Trump seemed to have no idea of the damage he was doing to America's standing in the world. But it was profound and long-lasting.

FOR YEARS, AS A SELLER of real estate and star of reality TV, Trump made a living wooing, if not bamboozling, customers and viewers. His selling skills were honed enough that he convinced voters to elect him as president in spite of his near-total lack of qualifications. He is a real-life incarnation of "Professor" Harold Hill, the protagonist of *The Music Man*, who convinces the denizens of a midwestern town that he is a bandleader even though he is bereft of musical skills. Yet once in office Trump has proved to be the worst salesman that America has ever had. Far from winning over other countries, he is actively repelling and repulsing them.

According to Gallup, "approval of U.S. leadership across 134 countries and areas stands at a new low of 30%."[74] That's lower than the 34 percent approval during the last year of George W. Bush's administration in the wake of fiascos such as the Iraq War. Even more ominously, the number of Arab youth who see the United States as an enemy shot up from 32 percent in 2016 to 57 percent in 2018.[75] Meanwhile, a poll found that only 14 percent of Germans consider the United States a reliable partner, compared to 36 percent for Russia and 43 percent for China. That the citizens of one of America's staunchest and most important allies now look more favorably upon our illiberal foes is a testament to Trump's unrivaled wrecking abilities. After Trump pulled out of the Iran nuclear accord over the objections of the Europeans, Donald Tusk, the president of the European Commission, tweeted: "Looking at latest decisions of @realdonaldtrump someone could even think: with friends like that who needs enemies."[76]

Trump is entirely focused on American hard power—military and economic might. An administration official described his worldview as follows: "His dream would be to have a strong military that protects our homeland. We'd wall ourselves off and strike at our discretion and then retreat to defending our homeland."[77] Or, as another administration official put it, the Trump Doctrine is: "We're America, bitch."[78] This type of chest-thumping unilateralism was not a viable policy even in the early twentieth century; it certainly won't work in the twenty-first century in a world that has been brought more closely together by communications and transportation technologies.

What Trump doesn't realize is that much of America's success as a superpower has rested on its "soft power." America is a superpower by invitation: we have troops in more than 170 countries and alliances with at least 60 countries because most other nations do not feel threatened by American power. Anti-Americanism is a fact of life, but the United States simply has not engendered the same kind of fear and loathing that less altruistic, more militaristic would-be hegemons have done—notably, Habsburg Spain, monarchist and Napoleonic France, Wilhelmine and Nazi Germany, and the Soviet Union. Each of those superpowers provoked other nations to ally against its expansionist designs, eventually leading to its downfall. There is no similar international coalition against the United States because it has been viewed as a more benign actor. In the past, America's adversaries—China and Russia—were the isolated ones. These illiberal powers have a few satraps but almost no real friends. They are regarded with suspicion and hostility by their neighbors. But now Trump's unilateralism is leaving an opening for these illiberal states to usurp American power.

Britain was said by the great Victorian historian J. R. Seeley "to have conquered and peopled half the world in a fit of absence of mind." America is losing its global power in the same way. Through ignorance and malice, Trump is destroying the foundations of American influence that previous leaders spent three-quarters of a century erecting. When it comes to "soft power," he is engaging in unilateral disarmament—and that in turn will have dire consequences for American security and prosperity.

American power had been eroding even before Trump came to office, thanks to the growth of competitors such as China and the foreign policy mistakes of George W. Bush, who was too interventionist, and Barack Obama, who was too noninterventionist. Trump has accelerated the decline. He might even have made it irreversible. What ally will trust America ever again? Even if a future president reverts to a more internationalist and free-trade policy, the rest of the world will be acutely conscious of the risk that the American electorate might elect another isolationist and protectionist president in the future. Trump may well be ending the Pax Americana and helping to usher in either a Chinese Century or a new global disorder in which there is no international law and life is "nasty, brutish and short."[79]

6.

THE
TRUMP
TOADIES

*T*HIS IS THE COST THAT AMERICA HAS PAID FOR THE
Trump presidency—so far. His supporters, meaning almost
all Republicans have rationalized the president's racism and nativism, the evidence that his campaign colluded with the Kremlin
to undermine American democracy, his attempted obstruction
of justice and general assault on the rule of law, his efforts to
spread lies and undermine the press, his violations of the most
basic ethical norms, his staggering fiscal irresponsibility, and his
assault on seventy-plus years of American international leadership
in promoting free trade and free societies. Trump is undermining
the foundations of American democracy. And in return they have
gotten . . . what? A few conservative judges, a big but unnecessary tax cut, the repeal of some regulations, some gains against
ISIS, a substance-free summit with North Korea. Trump claims
to be the world's best deal maker, but he is offering his followers
the world's worst deal. Republicans are expected to loyally support him, and in return he traduces most of what they claimed
to believe in.

Yet almost no Republicans are willing to speak out against him.
It is hard to know who is worse: Trump or his enablers. I am inclined
to think it is the latter. Trump does not know any better; he has no
idea of how a president, or even an ordinary, decent human being,
is supposed to behave. But many of his supporters do know better,

and they are debasing themselves to curry favor with him because he controls the levers of power.

Before Trump won the presidency, here is some of what Republicans had to say about him, as compiled by the *New York Times*. They called him a "malignant clown," "national disgrace," "complete idiot," "a sociopath, without a conscience or feelings of guilt, shame or remorse," "graceless and divisive," "predatory and reprehensible," flawed "beyond mere moral shortcomings," "unsound, uninformed, unhinged and unfit," "a character and temperament unfit for the leader of the free world," and "A bigot. A misogynist. A fraud. A bully."[1] Since the election? For the most part the sound of silence—even though all of these characterizations of the president have been validated many times over.

Having become enablers of Trump's transgressions against decency, common sense, and quite possibly the law itself, Republicans find themselves drawn ever deeper into a web of complicity and rationalization. They are defending Trump because they are trying to convince themselves that they have not made a terrible mistake. Like many dupes—for example, the students of Trump University who paid thousands of dollars to be taught the secrets of Trump's success—they do not want to admit that they were conned. Many Republicans overcompensate and wind up praising Trump in unctuous terms more fit for "Dear Leader," the late dictator of North Korea, than for the president of a constitutional republic.

TRUMP HAS DEVELOPED an authoritarian-style cult of personality with the shameful connivance of those around him. At a televised cabinet meeting in June 2017, Trump's appointees took turns lavishing praise on their insecure and needy boss. Vice President Mike Pence told him: "It is the greatest privilege of my life to serve as vice president. The president is keeping his word to the

American people." Agriculture secretary Sonny Perdue said: "I just got back from Mississippi and they love you there." Chief of Staff Reince Priebus: "On behalf of the entire senior staff around you, Mr. President, we thank you for the honor and the blessing that you've given us to serve your agenda and the American people." Labor secretary Alexander Acosta: "I am privileged to be here—deeply honored—and I want to thank you for your commitment to the American workers." Treasury secretary Steven Mnuchin, a Yale-educated, Olympic-class sycophant who had previously opined that the overweight president "has got perfect genes" and is "unbelievably healthy," chipped in: "It was a great honor traveling with you around the country for the last year, and an even greater honor to be here serving on your cabinet."[2]

This nauseating display of toadyism, like something out of an imperial court, was capped by Trump's self-praise. At a time when he had no significant legislative achievements, the president had the gall to boast that he had rivaled the achievements of Franklin Roosevelt's first hundred days—a period of unparalleled legislative activity in which Congress created, among other agencies, the Tennessee Valley Authority, the Agricultural Adjustment Act, the Civilian Conservation Corps, and the Federal Emergency Relief Administration. "I will say that never has there been a president, with few exceptions—in the case of FDR he had a major Depression to handle—who's passed more legislation, who's done more things than what we've done," Trump claimed. "We've been about as active as you can possibly be, and at a just about record-setting pace."

All of that immoderate flattery is almost tame compared to what Trump's outside admirers say about him. After Trump's State of the Union address in 2018—a decent speech by his standards but hardly an oratorical masterpiece—*Washington Times* writer Charles Hurt enthused: "President Trump has officially transformed him-

self from merely a great American president into a historic world
leader keeping lit the torch of freedom for all people around the
world. . . . Mr. Trump joins Reagan, Margaret Thatcher, Pope
John Paul II and Martin Luther King Jr. in the pantheon of great
champions of freedom from the past half-century."[3] Thus did Hurt
do even one better than White House aide Stephen Miller, who
said: "President Trump is the most gifted politician of our time,
and he's the best orator to hold that office in generations."[4] Such
over-the-top praise for Trump's nearly incomprehensible rhetorical
effusions has become standard among his followers.

After Trump's trip to the Middle East in May 2017, Robert
Charles, a veteran of the Reagan and both Bush administrations,
gushed on Fox's website: "The world from which President Trump
returns on his historic trip to Muslim Saudi Arabia, Jewish Israel,
Christian Vatican, and agnostic Brussels, is different from the world
prior to his trip. . . . We have not seen this kind of leadership in a
very long time, not in the Middle East—not anywhere. Hope exists
where it did not before this trip, because of his personal outreach,
resolve and authenticity."[5] It almost seemed like a letdown after the
comparisons to Reagan, Thatcher, the Pope, and Martin Luther King
Jr., but *Washington Examiner* writer Steve Cortes likened Trump to
John Wooden, the UCLA basketball coach who won a record-setting
ten national championships and became known as the "Wizard of
Westwood": "If President Donald Trump has more win streaks like
his present one, he might well become known as the 'Wizard of
Washington.' From the economy to important victories across the
vast Asian continent, America is winning under Trump's leadership."[6]

It is no exaggeration to say that Trump's most pervervid followers literally worship him. Candace Owens, communications
director of a pro-Trump group called Turning Point USA, tweeted:
"I truly believe that @realDonaldTrump isn't just the leader of
the free world, but the savior of it as well."[7] (Trump predictably

extolled her as a "very smart" thinker.)[8] The evangelical leader Franklin Graham actually said: "I just appreciate that we have a man in office that understands the power of prayer and the need for prayer."[9] This, of a president who notoriously revealed that he had never heard of the New Testament book II Corinthians and who reportedly wasn't sure whether Presbyterians like himself are Christians.[10] Representative Jim Jordan, leader of the far-right Freedom Caucus in the House, denied that he had ever heard Trump tell a lie.[11] Indeed, Trump supporters routinely praise him for his "honesty," by which they mean, apparently, not actually telling the truth but making "politically incorrect" remarks—their term of art for racist, xenophobic, or otherwise offensive statements.

Avowals of Trump's infallibility are widespread—just as they have been for other authoritarians. In Fascist Italy, for example, a popular slogan had it: "Il Duce is always right." Trump's economic adviser Peter Navarro updates this refrain when he says: "My function, really, as an economist is to try to provide the underlying analytics that confirm his intuition. And his intuition is always right in these matters."[12] The classicist Victor Davis Hanson, whose historical work I admire, compared Trump to such "tragic heroes" as George S. Patton, Shane, Marshall Will Kaine (Gary Cooper) in *High Noon*, Ethan Edwards (John Wayne) in *The Searchers*, and the protagonists of *The Magnificent Seven*.[13] Some praise for a plutocrat who avoided the draft and has never shown any willingness to sacrifice anything for anyone. Naturally, Trump's followers nominated him for a Nobel Peace Prize even before he met with Kim Jong Un.

All of this extravagant flattery recalls nothing so much as the cult of personality that developed around Marshal Philippe Pétain, the First World War hero who during the Second World War became ruler of France's Vichy regime. As recounted by historian Julian Jackson: "Images of Petain were produced on an industrial scale. One could buy Petain posters, postcards, calendars, plates, cups, chairs, handkerchiefs, stamps, coloring books, matchboxes, tapestries, paperweights, medals, vases, board games, ashtrays, pen-knives, barometers. One could have him in Aubusson tapestry, Baccarat glass, Sèvres porcelain, or plastic."[14] Other despots have had similar merchandising operations: I still have a lighter that I bought years ago in Lebanon's Bekaa Valley, the stronghold of Hezbollah, which projects an image of Hassan Nasrallah, leader of this terrorist organization. In a similar vein, Trump's official website sells "Make America Great Again" hats for a mere twenty-five dollars, water bottles, cups, T-shirts along with a presiden-tial medal, a Trump-Pence flag, "patriotic coolies," a "collectible ornament," lapel pin, and mini-megaphone. The website of the Trump Organization offers Trump-branded knit caps, polo shirts, cocktail glasses, wine glasses, coffee mugs, slippers, robes, chargers, umbrellas, luggage tags, playing cards, "trinket dishes," deodorant, cologne, teddy bears, key chains, clocks, and even pet bandanas, dog throw toys, and dog collars—although sadly not Trump steaks, deodorant, and urine tests, which are no longer on the market.[15]

Just as Trump's followers buy souvenirs of their hero, so too they echo the effusions of Pétain's admirers, who celebrated him as "an envoy from God" and literally sang his praises—one popular ditty labeled him the "savior of France," just as Trump is celebrated as the savior of America. One half-expects some Trump toady to match the rapturous enthusiasm of René Benjamin, author of three hagiographies of Pétain, who grew dizzy with delight after spotting the marshal's overcoat: "After several moving and happy meetings [with Pétain] I had one which I believe was more extraordinary than all the others. I found myself one day alone with his overcoat. Yes, his overcoat, which was lying just like that on the armchair in his study. It was a magnificent moment. I was overcome. Then all of a sudden I become as motionless as the coat when I noticed that the seven stars were gleaming like the seven stars of wisdom of which the ancients tell us."[16]

Whoever pens the first paean to Trump's "really beautiful" and "very classy" overcoat can expect at the very least a positive mention from Fox News if not an actual appointment to the White House staff. Perhaps it will be the anonymous troll who attacked the historian and journalist Jon Meacham, who criticized the president in his typically thoughtful fashion, by tweeting: "Trump isn't an aberration, he is America's savior. He will go down as the greatest president since Washington. Elitist globalist leftists like yourself are a cancer on America's culture & future. You must be eradicated like all disease."[17] To state the obvious: This kind of invective against the president's critics and this kind of worship of the president is not normal or healthy. It is a sign of the corrosion not just of the conservative movement but of our democracy.

IT IS NOT QUITE FAIR to say that all Republicans have become Trump toadies. Only most of them. The consequences for not faithfully toeing the party line can be severe: in April 2018, the conservative website Red State fired, in the words of one source, "everyone who was insufficiently supportive of Trump."[18] In June, South Carolina representative Mark Sanford, who had dared to criticize Trump in the past (while still voting with him), lost his primary election after the president endorsed his opponent.[19] To be an anti-Trump Republican in this climate requires moral courage that few politicians or media personalities display. All too few Republicans are resisting Trump's incipient authoritarianism just as, sadly, too few politicians of any party resisted previous assaults on civil liberties in US history. Assaults such as the Alien and Sedition Act of 1798, which was used by President John Adams's Federalists to prosecute twenty-five prominent Republicans. The Espionage

Act of 1917 and the Sedition Act of 1918, which were used by President Woodrow Wilson to exclude from the mails "disloyal" publications such as *The Nation* and *The Masses*, to deport thousands of radicals such as the anarchist Emma Goldman, and to jail others, including Socialist Party leader Eugene V. Debs, who received nearly a million votes in the 1920 presidential election while sitting in prison. Particularly egregious was Executive Order No. 9066 in 1942, which was used by Franklin Roosevelt to consign 120,000 Japanese Americans to detention camps. Or the McCarthyism in the 1950s, which ruined the lives of numerous civil servants and movie industry figures who were accused of being Communist subversives, often with scant evidence.[20]

Political courage is esteemed so highly precisely because it is so rare. Only one Republican senator publicly upbraided Joe McCarthy early on—Margaret Chase Smith of Maine, the only female member of the Senate. She rose on the Senate floor in 1950 to denounce Republicans for their "selfish political exploitation of fear, bigotry, ignorance and intolerance." She did not name McCarthy, but everyone knew who she had in mind when she spoke about those "who shout loudest about Americanism" while they "by their own words and acts, ignore some of the basic principles of Americanism—the right to criticize; the right to hold unpopular beliefs; the right to protest; the right of independent thought."[21] Her words fell in a vacuum because almost all of her Republican colleagues had calculated that, however boorish McCarthy was, they had to cooperate with him because he had tapped into genuine anti-Communist sentiments in the country shortly after China's fall to Communism, the Soviet Union's acquisition of the atomic bomb, and the outbreak of the Korean War. In such a climate, to defy the Red Scare was judged too great of a risk even for a war hero. On the campaign trail in 1952, Republican nominee Dwight D. Eisenhower planned to criticize McCarthy for casting outrageous aspersions on the loyalty of his mentor, General George C. Marshall, a man who had done as much as anyone to make possible US victory in World War II. Eisenhower's advisers begged him to take out his defense of Marshall—and, at the last minute, he did.

Similarly, today, most Republicans practice situational ethics to convince themselves that there is some advantage to be gained—for their party or their country or themselves—by catering to Trump. One of the few outspoken critics has been Senator Jeff Flake, who in the fall of 2017 eloquently attacked Trump and his Republican enablers. "Mr. President, I rise today to say: enough. We must dedicate ourselves to making sure that the anomalous never becomes the normal," Flake said, while announcing that he would not run for reelection because his views made him toxic for Arizona Republicans. Senator Bob Corker of Tennessee was even more direct, calling Trump "utterly untruthful," warning that his staff has "to figure out ways of controlling him," and noting that "he lowers himself to such a low, low standard and debases our country." But then Corker, too, decided not to seek reelection—before briefly changing his mind and groveling before Trump to secure his support. Even after giving up hopes of staying in office, Corker said he "probably" would still have voted for Trump over Clinton.[22]

Another Republican who did not stay silent was John McCain. He warned in an eloquent speech about the dangers of Trumpism, denouncing the "half-baked, spurious nationalism cooked up by people who would rather find scapegoats than solve problems." And he voted, along with Republican senators Lisa Murkowski and Susan Collins, against a bill strongly supported by Trump to repeal Obamacare. But McCain was a storied Republican leader of yesteryear who had been left behind by his party's embrace of Trumpism.

A few other Republicans, such as Senators Ben Sasse and Lindsay Graham, have occasionally criticized Trump, but most ordinary Republicans seem to adore him, while most of their leaders seethe against him quietly, behind closed doors, not daring to agree in public with his critics. Typical is the Republican congressman who told Erick Erickson: "It's like Forrest Gump won the presidency, but an evil, really fucking stupid Forrest Gump. He can't help himself. He's just a fucking idiot who thinks he's winning when people are bitching about him."[23] Naturally this congressman doesn't want to be quoted by name, because he represents a district that Trump won, and he has regularly defended Trump on Fox News and other outlets. Were this congressman to share his true opinion of Trump publicly, he would have difficulty winning reelection. In the 2018 primaries, Republican candidates routinely accused their opponents of being insufficiently devoted to the Maximum Leader, and those who once criticized Trump tried to explain that they didn't really mean it.

Republican donors have been just as pusillanimous: many of them are troubled by Trump's behavior, but they continue to contribute to Republican candidates as if this were still the party of Paul Ryan rather than of Donald Trump—or as if Paul Ryan were still the high-minded fighter for conservative principles he once appeared to be, rather than another pathetic appeaser of the demagogue in the White House who chose to retire rather than fight for what he supposedly believes in. Donors prefer to ignore what the GOP has actually become—a vehicle for waging a Trump-style culture war, feeding Trump's egomania, and protecting Trump from accountability for his actions. Obstruction of justice has practically become a plank of the new Republican Party. "There is no Republican Party. There's a Trump party," says former House Speaker John Boehner. "The Republican Party is kind of taking a nap somewhere."[24]

One of the few GOP donors who has switched to funding Democrats is the Boston hedge fund billionaire Seth Klarman. Once New England's top GOP donor, he gave more than $222,000 to seventy-eight Democrats running for Congress since 2016. "The Republicans in Congress have failed to hold the president account- able and have abandoned their historic beliefs and values," Klarman told the *Boston Globe*. "For the good of the country, the Democrats must take back one or both houses of Congress."[25] Klarman is right, and it's a disgrace that more Republicans aren't willing to put aside their partisanship for the good of the country.[26]

Republicans in Washington cover their cowardice by claiming they need to appease Trump to pass their policy agenda, but even after the passage of a tax cut, Republicans remained as invertebrate as ever. In a sense, the arch-populist Stephen Bannon is right to exult that "the establishment Republicans are in full collapse."[27] Trumpism is triumphant—at the moment. But Jeff Flake is also right that "this spell will eventually break." At least I hope he's right. And if he is, the judgment of history will not be kind to so many of my old friends and fellow travelers who propitiated a man so unfit for the highest office in the land.[28]

7.

THE

ORIGINS

OF

TRUMPISM

YOU KNOW HOW, AFTER YOU WATCH A MOVIE WITH a surprise ending, you sometimes replay the plot in your head on your way out of the theater to find the clues you missed the first time around? That's what I've been doing lately with the history of conservatism. It would be nice to think that Donald Trump is an anomaly who came out of nowhere to take over an otherwise sane and sober movement. But it just isn't so. Trump is a unique force in American politics, but, in many ways, he is merely the culmination of the right's ruin rather than its cause. Or, put another way, he is a symptom of a deeper, underlying disease.

I have been reading about the origins of the modern conservative movement in books written by liberal scholars such as Geoffrey Kabaservice, E. J. Dionne Jr., Corey Robin, and Rick Perlstein rather than conservative hagiographers, and realizing how much I missed when I was growing up. Upon closer examination, it's obvious that the whole history of modern conservativism is permeated with racism, extremism, conspiracy-mongering, ignorance, isolationism, and know-nothingism. Even those who were not guilty of these sins too often ignored them in the name of unity on the right. I disagree with liberals who argue that these disfigurations define the totality of conservatism; conservatives have also espoused high-minded principles that I still believe in, and the bigotry on the right appeared to be ameliorating in recent decades. But there is no doubt that there has always been a dark underside to conservatism, and one that I chose for most of my life to ignore. It's amazing how little you can see when your eyes are closed!

THE UR-CONSERVATIVES of the 1950s were revolting not against a liberal administration but against the moderate conservatism of Dwight D. Eisenhower—a doctrine that one of his advisers labeled "Modern Republicanism." Ike ended the war in Korea and refused to send US ground troops to Indochina. He preferred to counter Communist advances with covert actions in countries such as the Philippines, Guatemala, and Iran. He balanced the budget in three of his eight years in office, cut federal civilian employment, reduced the debt, and presided over nearly a decade of uninterrupted peace and prosperity. Yet ideological conservatives viewed Eisenhower as a sellout; John Birchers thought he was a Communist agent.

Why the animus against this war hero? Conservatives were furious that Eisenhower made no attempt to liberate the "captive nations" of Eastern Europe, "roll back" Communism, and undo FDR's Yalta "betrayal" because he knew that to do so could have resulted in World War III. They were further enraged that he did not try to repeal the New Deal because he knew that a minimal social safety net was needed for capitalism to maintain popular support. Rather than acting as a conservative revolutionary, Eisenhower marginally expanded government by creating a new Department of Health, Education and Welfare and by building the interstate highway system. Eisenhower further offended the right by working behind the scenes, after his initial appeasement of McCarthyism, to defeat Joseph McCarthy and end his irresponsible Red Scare. Worst of all, from the viewpoint of contemporary conservatives, Eisenhower was a moderate on racial issues. He appointed Chief Justice Earl Warren, a former Republican governor of California who, rejecting Eisenhower's "gradualist" vision of integration, presided over the Supreme Court's unanimous school desegregation decision, *Brown v. Board of Education*. Ike then sent the 101st Airborne Division to Little Rock, Arkansas, to desegregate Central High School in the face of white resistance.

This was the "liberal"—really moderate Republican—status quo against which William F. Buckley Jr., Barry Goldwater, Ronald Reagan, and other conservatives were rebelling in the 1950s. Buckley—yes, my boyhood hero—coauthored a book in defense of Joe McCarthy, *McCarthy and His Enemies* (1954), followed by a defense of the House Un-American Affairs Committee, *The Committee and Its Critics* (1962). Buckley also editorialized in *National Review* against desegregation. One notorious 1957 editorial, "Why the South Must Prevail," claimed that "the white community in the South is entitled to take such measures as necessary to prevail, politically and culturally . . . because, for the time being, it is the advanced race."[1] The editors went on, shockingly enough, to assert: "The great majority of the Negroes of the South who do not vote do not care to vote, and would not know for what to vote if they could." That is as blatant and ugly a statement of racism as one might have the misfortune to read. To his credit, Buckley recanted those views in later years; while running for mayor of New York in 1965, he even endorsed affirmative action.[2] But many other conservatives refused to disown prejudice and bigotry.

Most Republicans in Congress voted in 1964 and 1965 for landmark civil rights legislation, but the conservative hero Barry Goldwater did not. In his 1960 bestseller *Conscience of a Conservative*—ghostwritten by Buckley's brother-in-law, Brent Bozell—Goldwater wrote that "the federal Constitution does not require the states to maintain racially mixed schools. Despite the recent holding of the Supreme Court [*Brown v. Board of Education*], I am firmly convinced—not only that integrated schools are not required—but that the Constitution does not permit any interference whatsoever by the federal government in the field of education."[3] Goldwater was not personally a racist—he had integrated the Arizona National Guard—but he was happy to make common cause with racists in order to wrest the South from the Democrats.

Goldwater was just as extreme when it came to foreign affairs. Abjuring Eisenhower's efforts to maintain the peace, he suggested that Americans needed to overcome their "craven fear of death."[4] If another major uprising occurred in Eastern Europe, like the one in Hungary in 1956, he counseled, "We ought to present the Kremlin with an ultimatum forbidding Soviet intervention, and be prepared, if the ultimatum is rejected, to move a highly mobile task force equipped with appropriate nuclear weapons to the scene of the revolt."[5] In other words, Goldwater was willing to risk nuclear war to free a single "captive nation" from Communist control. I used to think that Goldwater's reputation as an extremist was a liberal libel. Reading his actual words—something I had not done before—reveals that he really was an extremist.

The delegates to the 1964 Republican convention who chose Goldwater as their presidential nominee fully endorsed his far-right views. They voted down planks committing the party to enforce civil rights laws and to repudiate extremist groups such as the Ku Klux Klan and the John Birch Society. The Republicans gathered at the Cow Palace in San Francisco lustily applauded Goldwater's assertion that "extremism in the defense of liberty is no vice" and that "moderation in the pursuit of justice is no virtue," while booing and jeering Governor Nelson Rockefeller of New York when he tried to deliver a more moderate message. Liberal Republicans in attendance were scared by the vehemence of the crowd, comparing it to Nazi rallies. This was the same sort of reaction that Trump would later elicit, and with a message similar in tone. Only in 1964 it didn't work: Goldwater won only six states (all except his home state in the South) and went down to a landslide defeat. But his example continued to inspire conservatives for decades, making clear that extremism is embedded in the DNA of the modern conservative movement.

The Goldwater precedent would prove especially important when it came to civil rights. In 1964, the GOP ceased to be the party of Lincoln and became the party of southern whites. All of the Republican presidential nominees in the future would harvest racist votes, whether consciously or not, because from then on the GOP would be the party of white privilege, and the Democrats, of minority rights. "States' rights"—a euphemism for segregation— became the new Republican rallying cry. As I now look back with the clarity of hindsight, I realize that, whatever Republican candidates claimed to stand for, what a lot of their voters heard was: this is someone who will put minorities in their place. Or who, at the very least, will not grant them any more rights, as the Democrats would do. I am now convinced that coded racial appeals—those dog whistles—had at least as much, if not more, to do with the electoral success of the modern Republican Party than all of the domestic and foreign policy proposals crafted by well-intentioned analysts like me. This is what liberals have been saying for decades in accusing the Republican Party of racism. I never believed them. Now I do, because Trump won by making the racist appeal, hitherto relatively subtle, obvious even to someone like me, who used to be in denial. The polite term for the voters that Republicans appeal to is "Jacksonians" after the populist president, general, and slave-owner Andrew Jackson. The more accurate description is white nationalists.

REPUBLICAN PRESIDENTS, in fairness, have proven a lot more moderate in office than the red-hot rhetoric of the campaign trail would suggest. Richard Nixon pursued a "Southern Strategy" to woo whites in the South and invaded Cambodia, but he also created the Occupational Safety and Health Administration and the Environmental Protection Agency, instituted wage and price controls, launched openings to Moscow and Beijing, and pulled US troops out of Vietnam. Gerald Ford continued Nixon's détente, much to the fury of the right. Ronald Reagan opposed the great civil rights legislation of 1964–1965, vilified "welfare queens" (who were presumably African American), and began his general election campaign in 1980 by proclaiming his adherence to "states' rights" just outside Philadelphia, Mississippi, the very town where in 1964 three civil rights activists had been murdered by the Ku Klux Klan. As president, he delivered on conservative promises by cutting taxes and rebuilding the military, but he also raised taxes, failed to cut spending, legalized undocumented immigrants, and launched negotiations with Soviet leader Mikhail Gorbachev that were viewed as naïve by critics on the right. After leaving office, he even publicly supported a ban on the sale of assault rifles—a position that no prominent Republican dares to espouse today.

His successor, George H. W. Bush, shamefully catered to racist sentiment in 1988 by allowing his campaign, led by the unscrupulous Lee Atwater, to demonize Michael Dukakis by association with Willie Horton—a black convict in Massachusetts who, on furlough, raped a white woman and assaulted her fiancée. (The furlough program had actually been started by Dukakis's Republican predecessor.) But in office, Bush the elder proved to be the consummate moderate. He offended conservative sensibilities by urging the Soviet Union to go slow in its dissolution, refused to march on Baghdad after victory in the Gulf War, signed the Clean Air Act and the Americans with Disabilities Act, and, worst of all from the conservative perspective, agreed to raise taxes in return for spending cuts. A substantial portion of the GOP rebelled against

Bush after he broke his "no new taxes" pledge, even though his willingness to raise taxes and cut spending set the stage for balanced budgets and a robust economic recovery.

His son, George W. Bush, the last "normal" Republican president, called himself a "compassionate conservative" and worked with Democrats to pass the No Child Left Behind Act, an expansion of Medicare, and a bank bailout during the financial meltdown of 2008. Bush even tried to pass immigration reform and went out of his way to visit a mosque after 9/11—acts that probably did as much to alienate the hardcore right as his mishandling of Iraq and Hurricane Katrina did to repel the rest of the country.

The very moderation of Republican presidents has stoked the fury of the right. The pattern was set early on, in 1964, with Phyllis Schlafly's best-selling tract *A Choice Not an Echo*, which would help launch the conservative movement. Her eccentric list of grievances ranged from resurrecting Joe McCarthy's discredited claims that the State Department and CIA were permeated with "Communist agents" to a new complaint: she thought that it was scandalous for President Lyndon Johnson to award the Medal of Freedom to the distinguished literary critic Edmund Wilson because "he has had four wives."

Schlafly was baffled why Republican candidates had lost presidential elections in 1936, 1940, 1944, 1948, and 1960. It could not be that Democrats fielded more attractive candidates or that most Americans did not share her far-right ideology. "It wasn't any accident," she wrote, ominously, of GOP setbacks. "It was planned that way. In each of their losing presidential years, a small group of secret kingmakers, using hidden persuaders and psychological warfare techniques, manipulated the Republican National Convention to nominate candidates who would sidestep or suppress the key issues." These nefarious "kingmakers" were New York financiers who only pretended to be Republicans but in fact favored "a continuation of the Roosevelt-Harry Dexter White-Averell Harriman-Dean Acheson-Dean Rusk policy of aiding and abetting Red Russia and her satellites." Harry Dexter White was a Soviet agent, whereas Harriman, Acheson, and Rusk were Democratic Cold Warriors determined to contain the Soviet threat, but to Schlafly there was no difference between them. And how did these "kingmakers" manipulate the GOP to ensure the defeat of its candidates? By promulgating "false slogans" such as "Politics should stop at the water's edge," "We must unite behind our President who has sole power in the field of foreign affairs," and "Foreign policy should be bipartisan." In other words, for Schlafly the very idea of bipartisanship was evidence of incipient treason.[6]

This was not the ranting of some marginal oddball. Schlafly, the recipient of undergraduate and law degrees from Washington University and a master's degree from Harvard/Radcliffe, was one of the leading lights of the right. In the 1970s she would lead the successful campaign against the Equal Rights Amendment. *A Choice Not an Echo* sold millions of copies. Her work drew on a long tradition of conspiratorial literature that claimed to see the manipulations of the Jesuits, Freemasons, Illuminati, and other bogeymen in the unfolding of American history. Trump's claim that he is going to "Make America Great Again" after it has been betrayed by disloyal elites is only the latest manifestation of this populist derangement.

THE HISTORY OF THE Republican Party over the past several decades is the story of moderates being driven out and conservatives taking over—and then of those conservatives in turn being ousted by those even further to the right. In the 1960s and 1970s there were many liberal or centrist Republicans such as Governors Nelson Rockefeller of New York and George Romney of Michigan (the father of Mitt Romney), New York mayor John Lindsay, and Senators Edward Brooke of Massachusetts, Mark Hatfield of Oregon, William Scranton of Pennsylvania, John Chaffee of Rhode Island, Jacob Javits of New York, and Clifford Case of New Jersey. They supported civil rights and environmental protection while also favoring an internationalist foreign policy, a tough-on-crime policy, and fiscal rectitude, at least in theory. (In practice, Rockefeller and Lindsay proved fiscally profligate, but so did many Republicans who were far more conservative.) Movement conservatives often displayed more venom against these apostates than against liberal Democrats, much as Mensheviks and Bolsheviks hated each other more than they hated their capitalist enemies. One by one, the "Rockefeller Republicans" were driven out, leaving the Democrats in control of most of the northeastern and West Coast states.

The GOP became the party of midwestern isolationists and southern segregationists—a marriage of Robert Taft Jr. and Strom Thurmond—even if the isolationist strain was muted as long as the Communist threat existed. Where once the GOP had been a "big tent" party, it now became an ideological conservative organization, and each generation of the right is more extreme than the one that came before it. A telling moment came in 1996, when the Republican presidential nominee, Bob Dole, visited an aged Barry Goldwater in Arizona. Once upon a time, Dole and Goldwater had defined the Republican right, but by 1996, Dole joked, "Barry and I—we've sort of become the liberals." "We're the new liberals of the Republican Party," Goldwater agreed. "Can you imagine that?"[7]

The rightward lurch of the GOP was symbolized by Newt Gingrich, a conservative firebrand from the South. He waged unrelenting war on Democrats such as House Speaker Jim Wright and masterminded the campaign that allowed Republicans to claim control of the House in 1994 for the first time in forty years. I remember celebrating that glorious occasion at an election-night cocktail party on the Upper West Side with fellow staffers from the *Wall Street Journal* editorial page. For us, the moment felt as glorious as the Bolshevik Revolution in 1917 had been for leftists. Like the radical journalist Lincoln Steffens, we had seen the future and we were convinced that it would work. Only it didn't. Like so many ideologues, Gingrich proved incapable of governing. He forced a government shutdown in 1995 to make President Bill Clinton agree to Republican budget priorities but had to back down after his move proved to be a public relations debacle. Gingrich was then toppled by his own caucus.

Before long, the Republican Party was shaken by a new insurgency, the Tea Party, which arose during the Obama administration. Its zealots made Gingrich seem like a squish by comparison. The new icon of the right, Senator Ted Cruz, forced a government shutdown of his own in 2013 to repeal Obamacare and pave the way for his presidential bid. This was another gambit that failed miserably but did not shake the far right's domination of the Republican Party. As E. J. Dionne noted in *Why the Right Went Wrong*, "between January 1995 and January 2015, the proportion of Republicans who called themselves 'very conservative' nearly doubled, from 19 percent to 33 percent."[8]

The ascendance of these extreme views increasingly made the House Republican caucus ungovernable. The three dozen or so far-right members of the House Freedom Caucus drove House Speaker John Boehner, himself a conservative, into retirement in 2015, after his deputy, House Majority Leader Eric Cantor, lost his reelection bid to a Tea Party insurgent in Virginia the previous year. Boehner's successor as speaker, Paul Ryan, lasted only three years and also found himself accused of being insufficiently conservative in spite of having a perfect score from the National Right to Life Committee and the National Federation of Independent

Business and an 89 percent rating from the American Conservative Union. Ryan's downfall signaled the final repudiation of an optimistic brand of Reaganesque conservatism focused on enhancing economic opportunities at home and promoting democracy and free trade abroad. The Republican Party would now be defined by the tenebrous vision of Donald Trump, with his depiction of Democrats as America-hating, criminal-coddling traitors and his invective against immigrants, Mexicans, and Muslims. Trump had beaten the Republican rabble-rousers at their own game. Completely unrestrained by logic or morality, he could go where even the most extreme conservatives had previously feared to tread.

THE MODERN HISTORY OF the GOP is a warning to be careful of who you pretend to be because sooner or later you will become that person. Republicans have long flirted with populism, conspiracy-mongering, and know-nothingism. This is why they became known as the "stupid party." Stupidity is not an accusation that could be hurled against such early Republicans as Abraham Lincoln, Theodore Roosevelt, Elihu Root, and Charles Evans Hughes. But by the 1950s, it had become an established shibboleth that the "eggheads" were for Adlai Stevenson and the "boobs" for Dwight D. Eisenhower—a view endorsed by Richard Hofstadter's 1963 book *Anti-Intellectualism in American Life*, which contrasted Stevenson, "a politician of uncommon mind and style, whose appeal to intellectuals overshadowed anything in recent history," with Eisenhower—"conventional in mind, relatively inarticulate." The Kennedy presidency, with its glittering court of Camelot, cemented the impression that it was the Democrats who represented the thinking men and women of America.

Rather than run away from the anti-intellectual label, Republicans embraced it for their own political purposes. In his "time for choosing" speech, Ronald Reagan said that the issue in the 1964 election was "whether we believe in our capacity for self-government or whether we abandon the American Revolution and confess that a little intellectual elite in a far-distant Capitol can plan our lives for us better than we can plan them ourselves." Richard M. Nixon appealed to the "silent majority" and the "hard hats," while his vice president, Spiro T. Agnew, issued slashing attacks on an "effete corps of impudent snobs who characterize themselves as intellectuals" and the "nattering nabobs of negativism." (The latter phrase, ironically, was written by speechwriter William Safire, who would go on to establish a reputation as a libertarian columnist and grammarian for the conservatives' bête noire, the *New York Times*.) William F. Buckley Jr. famously said, "I should sooner live in a society governed by the first 2,000 names in the Boston telephone directory than in a society governed by the 2,000 faculty members of Harvard University." More recently, George W. Bush joked at a Yale commencement: "To those of you who received honors, awards and distinctions, I say, well done. And to the C students I say, you, too, can be president of the United States."

Many Democrats took all this at face value and congratulated themselves for being smarter than the benighted Republicans. Here's the thing, though: the Republican embrace of anti-intellectualism was, to a large extent, a put-on—just like their espousal of far-right rhetoric on the campaign trail. In office they proved far more moderate and intelligent. Eisenhower may have played the part of an amiable duffer, but he may have been the best prepared president we have ever had—a five-star general with an unparalleled knowledge of national security affairs. When he resorted to gobbledygook in public, it was in order to preserve his political room to maneuver. Reagan may have come across as a dumb thespian, but he spent decades honing his views on public policy and writing his own speeches. Nixon may have burned with resentment of "Harvard men," but he turned over foreign policy and domestic policy to two Harvard professors, Henry A. Kissinger and Daniel Patrick Moynihan, while his own knowledge of foreign affairs rivaled Ike's.

There is no evidence that Republican leaders have been demonstrably dumber than their Democratic counterparts. During the Reagan years, the GOP briefly became known as the "party of ideas" because it harvested so effectively the intellectual labor of conservative think tanks like the American Enterprise Institute and the Heritage Foundation and publications like the *Wall Street Journal* editorial page, *National Review*, and *Commentary*. Scholarly policymakers such as George P. Shultz, Jeane J. Kirkpatrick, and Bill Bennett held prominent posts in the Reagan administration, a tradition that continued into the George W. Bush administration—amply stocked with the likes of Paul D. Wolfowitz, John J. Dilulio Jr., and Condoleezza Rice. This was the Republican Party that attracted me as a teenager in the 1980s and maintained my loyalty for decades to come.[9]

In recent years, however, the Republicans' relationship to the realm of ideas has become more and more attenuated as talk-radio hosts and television personalities have taken over the role of defining the conservative movement that once belonged to thinkers like William F. Buckley Jr., Irving Kristol, Norman Podhoretz, and George F. Will. The Republicans' populist pose has become all too real. A sign of the times is that Bill Bennett, possessor of a PhD from the University of Texas at Austin and a JD from Harvard Law School, stoops to attack George Will, a Princeton PhD, for his criticism of Vice President Mike Pence by mocking his "penchant for writing columns filled with big words that most Americans never use and can't even define."[10] Presumably a dictionary counts as elitist foppery.

The turning point in the Republican transformation was the

rise of Sarah Palin after John McCain made the mistake of selecting her as his running mate in 2008—a move that he later regretted, wishing he had selected his friend, Democratic senator Joe Lieberman of Connecticut, instead. Palin showed that she was a dim bulb when she was asked during the campaign which sources she relied on for the news. Caught off-guard, she could not answer and had to deflect with unconvincing generalities: "I have a vast variety of sources." This was akin to an admission that she did not read newspapers or magazines beyond, possibly, *Field & Stream* or *Guns & Ammo*. I can't say I was terribly surprised. As a McCain foreign policy adviser, I had briefed her and found her to be nonresponsive and uninterested in foreign policy issues. The most memorable takeaway from our meeting at a midtown Manhattan hotel was that she wore earrings in the shape of the state of Alaska.

Palin's lack of preparation for high office could perhaps be excused as the provincialism of a small-state governor who had not asked for the national spotlight (Alaska's population is smaller than San Francisco's). But rather than return to her duties after the election or try to educate herself on the issues, Palin resigned as governor in 2009 and sought to cash in on her celebrity by becoming a full-time media personality. She then proceeded to litter the land with inanities that have few parallels in our history. There was no malapropism that she did not employ. She even invented a new word—"refudiate"—by conflating "repudiate" and "refute" and tried to suggest that she was a Shakespearean sage who was enlarging our vocabulary. A sample of Palin's other bizarre statements: "Well, if I were in charge, they would know that waterboarding is how we'd baptize terrorists." "But obviously, we've got to stand with our North Korean allies." "We can send a message and say, 'You want to be in America, A, you'd better be here legally or you're out of here. B, when you're here, let's speak American.'" "I think on a national level, your Department of Law there in the

White House would look at some of the things that we've been charged with and automatically throw them out." (There is no Department of Law in the White House or anywhere else.)[11]

Conservatives applauded this inanity, making Palin one of the biggest stars on the right-wing rubber-chicken circuit until she was eclipsed by the rise of the even more vulgar and vacuous Donald Trump. The rise of Palin and now Trump indicates that the GOP really truly has become the stupid party. Its primary vibe has become one of indiscriminate, unthinking, all-consuming anger.

THAT ANGER IS STOKED by the "alternative media" of the right. Its origins can be traced back to the founding of the newspaper *Human Events* in 1944, Regnery Publishing in 1947, and *National Review* in 1955. In later years, two publishing houses—Basic Books and the Free Press—played an important role in producing works of conservative scholarship, including many tomes that I read while growing up, such as Alan Bloom's *The Closing of the American Mind*, Charles Murray's *Losing Ground: American Social Policy, 1950–1980*, George Gilder's *Wealth and Poverty*, and James Q. Wilson's *Bureaucracy*.

The alternative media did not become a mass phenomenon until Ronald Reagan's Federal Communications Commission decided in 1987 to stop enforcing the "fairness doctrine," a 1949 regulation which had mandated that all television and radio broadcast outlets had to present both sides of controversial public issues. This deregulatory decision made possible the debut in 1988 of Rush Limbaugh's national radio show, which did not pretend to offer anything but a conservative perspective on the news. Revealingly, Limbaugh called his fans "dittoheads" because they mindlessly echoed his prejudices—or he theirs; the pandering went both ways. Many other right-wing "talkers" followed.

I worried about the impact of the talk-show populists as far back as 1994, when I wrote a *Wall Street Journal* op-ed headlined "Down with Populism!" shortly after Republicans had taken control of the House for the first time in forty years. I argued that the GOP should not "'Rush' to embrace talk show democracy" because of the dangers of mob rule. I quoted my boyhood favorite, H. L. Mencken: "Least of all do I admire the puerile, paltry shysters who constitute the majority of Congress. But I confess frankly that these shysters, whatever their defects, are at least appreciably superior to the mob." The expression of mob rule I was most worried about was a new conservative TV network called National Empowerment Television that has long since faded away. I had no idea that Fox News Channel would be founded in two years' time and that it would make my worst fears of populism run amok come true.[12] Coincidentally, 1996 was also the year that the Drudge Report, an online bulletin board for right-wing fever dreams, was launched.

Limbaugh, Fox, and Drudge still remain three of the most popular outlets on the right, but they have been joined by radio hosts such as Mark Levin and Michael Savage, celebrity authors and talking heads such as Ann Coulter, Milo Yiannopoulos, and Dinesh D'Souza, and websites such as Breitbart News, TheBlaze, Infowars, and Newsmax. The original impetus for these outlets was to offer a different viewpoint that people could not get from the more liberal TV networks, newspapers, and magazines. But soon the alternative media moved from propounding their own analyses to concocting their own "facts," turning into an incubator of outlandish conspiracy theories such as "Hillary Clinton murdered Vince Foster," "Barack Obama Is a Muslim," or even "Michelle Obama Is a Man."

The career of Dinesh D'Souza, one of the right's biggest media stars in spite of being a convicted felon (who has now been pardoned by President Trump), is indicative of the downward trajectory of conservatism. After a checkered career in conservative journalism at Dartmouth, he made his name with *Illiberal Education*, a well-regarded 1991 book published by the Free Press, which denounced political correctness and championed liberal education. Then he wrote a widely panned 1995 book, also from the Free Press, claiming that racism was no more. It was all downhill from there. In 2014 he pleaded guilty to breaking campaign finance laws. More recently, as the *Daily Beast* notes, he has become a conspiratorial crank who has suggested that the white supremacist rally in Charlottesville was staged by liberals and that Adolf Hitler, who sent fifty thousand homosexuals to prison, "was NOT anti-gay."[13] D'Souza managed to sink even lower in February 2018 by mocking stunned Parkland school-shooting survivors after the Florida legislature defeated a bill to ban assault weapons: "Worst news since their parents told them to get summer jobs."[14] He was joined in this repugnant japery by Laura Ingraham, who made fun of school-shooting survivor David Hogg for not getting into the college of his choice (she later apologized), and by Jamie Allman, a Sinclair broadcasting commentator who was fired for saying that he would like to sexually assault Hogg with a "hot poker."[15]

It is hard to imagine anything more cruel and heartless, but for these opportunists it's all in a day's work. As D'Souza wrote in his 2002 book *Letters to a Young Conservative*, "One way to be effective as a conservative is to figure out what annoys and disturbs liberals the most, and then keep doing it." That, in a nutshell, is the credo of today's high-profile conservatives: say anything to "trigger" the "libtards" and "snowflakes." The dumber and more offensive, the better. Whatever it takes to get on (and stay on) Fox News and land the next book contract! Hence inane outbursts such as this tweet from Fox News's twenty-five-year-old blonde commentator, Tomi Lahren: "Let's play a game! Go to Whole Foods, pick a liberal (not hard to identify), cut them in line along with 10–15 of your family members, then take their food. When they throw a tantrum, remind them of their special affinity for illegal immigration. Have fun!"[16] (I only mention Lahren's appearance because the employment of female hosts in short skirts, and preferably with blonde hair, is such an integral part of Fox's strategy to attract the elderly white men who form its core audience.)

Such rhetorical sallies are as lucrative as they are illogical. D'Souza has grossed tens of millions of dollars with documentaries attacking Hillary Clinton and Barack Obama as anti-American subversives. Sean Hannity makes roughly $30 million a year and flies on his own private jet even while railing against "overpaid" media elites.[17]

Naturally, just as drug addicts need bigger doses over time, these outrage artists must be ever more transgressive to get the attention they crave. Ann Coulter's book titles have gone from accusing Bill Clinton of *High Crimes and Misdemeanors* to accusing all liberals of *Treason*, of being *Godless* and even *Demonic*. Her latest assault on the public's intelligence was called *In Trump We Trust: E Pluribus Awesome!* If this is what mainstream conservatism has become—and it is—count me out.[18]

WHILE DINESH D'SOUZA, Ann Coulter, Laura Ingraham, Alex Jones, and many others have played a role in dumbing down conservatism, no institution has been more harmful in this regard than the Fox News Channel, whose debut must count as one of the most baleful milestones in modern American political history. Fox has turned itself into the American version of RT. Not only does Fox usually go to great lengths to avoid criticizing President Trump but it also regularly peddles insidious conspiracy theories on his behalf. To try to undermine the "incontrovertible" evidence that the Russians hacked into the Democratic National Committee, for example, some Fox commentators pinned the blame on a DNC staffer named Seth Rich, even going so far as to claim that his murder—ascribed by District of Columbia police to a botched robbery—was the work of the Democrats. Rich's parents sued Fox for the "pain and anguish" inflicted on them. (Fox retracted the story and moved on to propagating other crazy claims.)

The Seth Rich hoax is only the tip of the conspiratorial iceberg at Fox, which has also pushed claims that Obama wasn't born in America, that Obamacare would create "death panels," that Hillary Clinton sold America's uranium to Russia, and that a Deep State is plotting against Trump. (Little wonder that, according to one poll, 74 percent of Americans believe in the existence of a Deep State—a concept that Trump borrowed from Egypt and Turkey to suggest that his own government is plotting against him.) Fox, naturally, has taken the lead in smearing Special Counsel Robert Mueller and calling for his investigation—which they call, echoing Trump, "a witch hunt"—to be terminated before its conclusion.[19]

What makes Fox's ravings so scary is that they are not just influencing the public but also the president. Matthew Gertz of Media Matters for America found an insidious feedback loop between Trump and the TV personalities he watches so faithfully.[20] Many of the president's deranged tweets—e.g., his claim that his "nuclear button" is "much bigger & more powerful" than Kim Jong Un's or that Hillary Clinton aide Huma Abedin should be imprisoned—are lifted straight from Fox. When Fox reported that a "caravan" of Central American migrants was about to invade America, Trump echoed its hysteria. On reflection, then, it's not quite right to say that Fox is Trump's RT. Putin is smart enough not to believe his own propaganda. Trump isn't. Fox may be said to have created Trump, but now the president and the network have such a symbiotic relationship that it's not clear who is in charge. Trump even relies on Fox talking heads as trusted advisers. Sean Hannity, the

Washington Post reports, "is so close to Trump that some White House aides have dubbed him the unofficial chief of staff."[21] Hannity even shared a lawyer with Trump—a fact that he did not feel compelled to disclose to his viewers. Such disclosure would be de rigueur for any journalistic organization. But that's not what Fox is—it's a disseminator of disinformation.

I GOT MY OWN SMALL TASTE of Fox's modus operandi in July 2017 when I appeared on Tucker Carlson's show from a studio in Los Angeles. I was there—I thought—to discuss President Trump and US policy toward Russia. Instead, as I later recounted in *Commentary*, I got the equivalent of a barrel of raw sewage dumped on my head. I should have known what I was getting into when the Fox producers refused to give me any makeup; they wanted to make sure that I did not look as good as the heavily powdered and carefully coiffed host in Washington.

Carlson was still smarting from a confrontation the previous night with Ralph Peters, a retired army officer who had accused him of sounding like "Charles Lindbergh in 1938" for his advocacy of an alliance with Russia. Because I had retweeted Peters's comment, Carlson appeared determined to take out his fury on me. His very first question was: "To dismiss anyone who doesn't share your view as a Nazi sympathizer seems cheap and a shortcut and not really befitting a self-described genius like yourself. Why would you say something like that?"

"Well, rest assured, Tucker, I'm not actually saying that you are a Nazi sympathizer," I replied, while wondering when I had described myself as a genius. I went on to state my view that Russia is a major threat to the United States, not a potential ally. I was "very disturbed," I added, to hear Carlson "yukking it up" at the top of his show with guest Mark Steyn—a clever writer I had once invited to write for the *Wall Street Journal* editorial page—about Donald Trump Jr.'s eagerness to accept Russian help in the 2016 election.

During the course of the next ten or so minutes, Carlson and I traded barbs about Russia, Syria, Iran—and my foreign policy perspicacity or lack thereof. I tried to stick to the issues, but he kept interrupting me with smirky sarcasm, obnoxious laughter, and ad hominem insults. My brain raced to formulate retorts as I heard Carlson's rapid-fire abuse in my earpiece, the image on the monitor in front of me disorientatingly delayed by five or six seconds. It was hard to get in a word edgewise. "You have been consistently wrong in the most flagrant and flamboyant way for over a decade," he charged. This turned out to be principally a reference to the invasion of Iraq, which he had also supported before turning against it. "You're humiliating yourself," he said, and "this is why nobody takes you seriously." (If no one takes me seriously, why was I invited on his show?) I was so discredited, Carlson said, that maybe I "should choose another profession. Selling insurance, house painting, something you're good at." Clearly, he had an inflated impression of my house-painting and insurance-selling skills.

Ironically, while dishing out a nonstop stream of invective, Carlson kept accusing *me* of not engaging in substantive debate: "This is precisely the style of debate that prevents people from taking you seriously. . . . It's almost impossible to have a conversation with you because your responses are so childish. . . . You are incapable of giving a factual answer."

Feeling the same adrenaline charge as when I got into fights in elementary school and junior high school, I tried to give as good as I got. For example, when Carlson said that "your judgment has been clouded by ideology," I shot back that *his* "judgment has been clouded by ratings because you feel compelled to be a spokesman for Donald Trump in order to win ratings on the Fox News Channel." I thought the exchange was a draw, despite Carlson's home-court advantage (it's not easy debating with someone you cannot look in the eye), but I left aghast at his rudeness and unprofessionalism. If this is how he treats guests on his TV show, I'm afraid that if I were ever invited to his house—admittedly unlikely—I would be served a hemlock cocktail.

Maybe there's a good case to be made for an "America First" foreign policy, but Carlson wasn't making it. His shtick is sarcasm, condescension, and mock-incredulous double takes. And he doesn't hesitate to lie when it suits his purposes. After our interview, his team posted a clip on Facebook under this headline: "Col. Ralph Peters suggested that anybody who disagrees with him on Russia would also be a Hitler sympathizer. Historian Max Boot agrees." Neither Peters nor I ever said any such thing; in fact, I'd said the opposite on his show.[22]

Carlson's circus act gets ratings and so do the similar performances of Sean Hannity, Laura Ingraham, Lou Dobbs, Jeanine Pirro, and other Fox "personalities." But the cost is high. They are debasing political discourse and degrading our democracy in return for seven- and eight-figure paydays. No one did a better job of revealing what Fox has become than Ralph Peters, a conservative uber-hawk and former army intelligence officer who in early 2018 resigned in disgust as a Fox commentator. In a scorching letter of resignation leaked to BuzzFeed, he wrote, "Fox has degenerated from providing a legitimate and much-needed outlet for conservative voices to a mere propaganda machine for a destructive and ethically ruinous administration." He went on: "Four decades ago, I took an oath as a newly commissioned officer. I swore to 'support and defend the Constitution,' and that oath did not expire when I took off my uniform. Today, I feel that Fox News is assaulting our constitutional order and the rule of law, while fostering corrosive and unjustified paranoia among viewers. Over my decade with Fox, I long was proud of the association. Now I am ashamed."[23]

I TOO AM ASHAMED—not because I've ever been a Fox employee but because I used to view it as a benign force that was merely selling the conservative agenda, developed by policy wonks like myself, to a larger audience. Now I know better. This is part of my general awakening to disturbing trends not just in the conservative movement but also in the larger American society that conservatism grows out of and reflects.

In college, as I first recounted in *Foreign Policy*, I used to be one of those smart-alecky young conservatives who would scoff at the notion of "white male privilege" and claim that anyone propagating such concepts was guilty of "political correctness." As a Jewish refugee from the Soviet Union, I felt it was ridiculous to expect me to atone for the sins of slavery and segregation, to say nothing of the household drudgery and workplace discrimination suffered by women. I wasn't racist or sexist. (Or so I thought.) I hadn't discriminated against anyone. (Or so I thought.) My ancestors were not slave owners or lynchers; they were more likely to have been victims of the pogroms.

I saw America as a land of opportunity, not a bastion of racism or sexism. I didn't even think that I was a "white" person—the catchall category that has been extended to include everyone from a *Mayflower* descendant to a recently arrived illegal immigrant from Ireland. I was a newcomer to America who was eager to assimilate into this wondrous new society, and I saw its many merits while blinding myself to its dark side.

Well, live and learn. A quarter-century is enough time to examine deeply held shibboleths and to see if they comport with reality. In my case, I have concluded that my beliefs were based more on faith than on a critical examination of the evidence. In the last few years, in particular, it has become impossible for me to deny the reality of discrimination, harassment, even violence that people of color and women continue to experience in modern-day America from a power structure that remains for the most part in the hands of straight white males. People like me, in other words. Whether I realize it or not, I have benefited from my skin color and my gender—and those of a different gender or sexuality or skin color have suffered because of it.

This sounds obvious, but it wasn't clear to me until recently. I have had my consciousness raised. Seriously.

This doesn't mean that I agree with America's harshest critics—successors to the New Left of the 1960s who saw this country as an irredeemably fascist state that they called "Amerikkka." Judging by historical standards or those of the rest of the world, America remains admirably free and enlightened. Minorities are not being subject to ethnic cleansing like the Rohingya in Burma. Women are not forced to wear all-enveloping garments like in Saudi Arabia. No one is jailed for criticizing our supreme leader as in Russia.

We are becoming more aware of oppression and injustice, which has long permeated our society, precisely because of growing agitation to do something about it. Those are painful but necessary steps toward creating a more equal and just society. But we are not there yet, and it is wrong to pretend otherwise. It is even more pernicious to cling to the conceit, so popular among Donald Trump's supporters, that straight white men are the "true" victims, because their unquestioned position of privilege is now being challenged by "uppity" women, gays, and people of color.

Similarly, I reject the premise, so popular in conservative circles, that the white identity politics promoted by Trump is simply an understandable response to the identity politics of African Americans, Latinos, Asians, and other minorities. That is only a compelling argument if your historical consciousness begins in the sixties—the decade that conservatives like to blame for everything they dislike about modern America. In fact, white identity politics has been pervasive ever since the European settlement of North America in the sixteenth century. Southern states had apartheid policies that lasted legally until the 1960s, backed up by racist police and terrorist groups such as the Ku Klux Klan that stood ready to imprison, lynch, or otherwise eliminate anyone who ran afoul of the white power structure. The civil rights revolution was a long-overdue attempt to right the scales and deliver justice for Americans of color, but it was only partially successful—and it left a long legacy of smoldering white resentment that was exacerbated by measures designed to promote integration such as school busing and affirmative action. Seen in the context of the long sweep of history, the identity politics of African American, Latino, or Asian American activists in recent years is a reaction to, rather than the cause of, white-nationalist sentiment. Again, this isn't news to many people. But it is a new realization for me.

I used to take a reflexively pro-police view of arguments over alleged police misconduct, thinking that cops were getting a bum rap for doing a tough, dangerous job. I still have admiration for the huge majority of police officers, but there is no denying that some are guilty of mistreating the people they are supposed to serve. Not all the victims of police misconduct are minorities—witness a blonde Australian woman shot to death by a Minneapolis police officer after she called 911, or an unarmed white man shot to death by a Mesa, Arizona, officer while crawling down a hotel hallway— but a disproportionate share are. The videos do not lie. One after another, we have seen the horrifying video evidence of cops arresting, beating, even shooting black people who were doing absolutely nothing wrong or who were stopped for trivial misconduct. For African Americans, and in particular African American men, infractions like jaywalking or speeding or selling cigarettes without tax stamps can incite corporal, or even capital, punishment without benefit of judge or jury. African Americans have long talked about being stopped for "driving while black." I am ashamed to admit I did not realize what a serious and common problem this was until the videotaped evidence emerged. The iPhone may well have done more to expose racism in modern-day America than the NAACP.

Of course, the problem is not limited to the police; they merely reflect the racism of our society, which is not as severe as it used to be but remains real enough. I realized how entrenched this problem remains when an African American friend—a well-educated, well-paid, well-dressed woman—confessed that she did not want to walk into a department store carrying in her purse a pair of jeans that she planned to give to a friend later in the day. Why not? Because she was afraid that she would be accused of shoplifting! This is not something that would occur to me, simply because the same suspicion would not attach to a middle-aged, middle-class white man. Likewise, I would never be asked to leave a Starbucks, much less arrested for loitering, even if I didn't buy anything. But that was the fate of two African American men in Philadelphia in 2018. Trump's victory has revealed that racism and xenophobia are more widespread than I had previously realized. Previous Republicans may have dog-whistled to the racist right; with Trump it's more of a wolf whistle.

As for sexism, its scope has been made plain by the horrifying revelations of widespread harassment, assault, and even rape perpetrated by powerful men from Hollywood to Washington. As with the revelations of police brutality, so too with sexual harassment: I am embarrassed and chagrined that I did not understand how bad the problem is. I had certainly gotten some hints from my female friends of the kind of harassment they have endured, but I never had any idea it was this bad or this common—or this tolerated. I now realize, thanks to the #MeToo movement, something I should have learned long ago: that feminist activists had a fair point when they denounced the corrosive impact of a "patriarchal society," even if choosing to become a mother and homemaker is hardly evidence of oppression, as some radicals might suggest. While the abuse of, and discrimination against, women is less severe than it used to be, it remains a major problem in spite of the impressive strides the United States has taken toward greater gender equality.

This doesn't mean that I am about to join the academic brigade in protesting "microaggressions" and "cultural appropriations" and agitating against free speech. I remain a classical liberal, and I am disturbed by attempts to infringe on freedom of speech in the name of fighting racism, sexism, or other ills. But I no longer think, as I once did, that "political correctness" is a bigger threat than the underlying racism and sexism that continues to disfigure our society decades after the civil rights and women's rights movements. If the Trump era teaches us anything, it is how far we still have to go to realize the "unalienable Rights" of all Americans to enjoy "Life, Liberty and the pursuit of Happiness," regardless of gender, sexuality, religion, or skin color.[24]

WHEN I FIRST WROTE about my "awakening" to "white privilege" in December 2017, I got a lot of positive responses from moderate liberals and honest conservatives—but also quite a bit of blowback. The far right naturally mocked me for "virtue signaling" and diagnosed me as suffering from "Trump derangement syndrome"—ironic charges given that if anyone has been deranged by Trump, it is all of the conservatives who jettisoned their supposed beliefs to support him. Tucker Carlson sneered: "Max Boot will say anything if they just let him invade Iran."[25] (I never advocated invading Iran, but of course if Trump did invade, Tucker would support him.) But the far left was also unimpressed, basically taking the attitude of "What took you so long?" A self-described "anarcho-psychonaut" (whatever that is) wrote in a blog post that I was "spectacularly evil" underneath the headline: "Iraq-Raping Neocons Are Suddenly Posing as Woke Progressives to Gain Support."[26] Former CNN anchor Soledad O'Brien tweeted a more civilized version of the leftist lament: "Sorry, but why is this 'gutsy'? Admitting you've walked around your whole life oblivious to even the basic experiences of women and people of color is just . . . pathetic."[27]

O'Brien may be surprised to hear me say it, but she has a good point (even if I wasn't the one who claimed that my writing was "gutsy"). It is pathetic, I suppose, that I didn't focus on the underbelly of American society—and of the conservative movement in particular—until relatively recently. But then, as George Orwell wrote: "To see what is in front of one's nose needs a constant struggle." I don't expect any commendations for seeing what should have been obvious all along. All I can say in my own defense is that many never see it at all, even when what is in front of their noses is a president who evinces sympathy for neo-Nazis, dictators, alleged child molesters, and accused wife-beaters.

Most conservatives appear willing, even eager, to shed earlier attempts to moderate their movement and to make it more acceptable to polite society. They are embracing the kind of extremism personified in the past, in their different ways, by the likes of Joe McCarthy, Barry Goldwater, Strom Thurmond, and Phyllis Schlafly. Trump benefits from, and accelerates, this move to the fringe, and he channels it in a white-nationalist, rather than a libertarian, direction. But he did not start the trend—and it won't end when he is gone. Indeed, if the modern history of conservatism is any guide, Trump's successors might actually be worse than he is. If Trump has a saving grace, it is that he is so ignorant and impetuous. He is incapable of effectively implementing his worst impulses in the face of entrenched resistance from government professionals, the judiciary, and the press corps. A future Trump might be smarter and more disciplined, and thus more dangerous. That's a frightening thought, given how much damage even the scattershot Trump has done.

Epilogue

THE VITAL CENTER

I AM NO LONGER A REPUBLICAN. AM I STILL A CONSER-
vative? Honestly, I'm not sure, because I don't know what conservatism stands for anymore beyond reflexive support of Donald
Trump and all his malign works. I certainly don't like to call myself
a conservative anymore because the movement has been so thoroughly taken over by Trump and his amen chorus. Even before the
rise of Trump, however, the tide of extremism was rising on the
right, although I chose to ignore the warning signs.

You tell me where I belong on the political spectrum:

★ I am socially liberal. I am pro-LGBTQ rights and pro-choice.
   I am not religious but am respectful of those who are—as
   long as their beliefs do not impinge on anyone's individual rights.

★ I am fiscally conservative. I think we need to reduce the
   deficit and get entitlement spending under control without, however, shredding the social safety net. The bipartisan
   Simpson-Bowles Commission came up with a plan in 2010
   to accomplish this objective.

★ I am in favor of free markets *and* the welfare state. Far from
   being incompatible, the latter ensures the success of the for-

mer. Markets aren't perfect, and government has a responsibility to ameliorate their failings. The welfare state is an inherently conservative institution, as its creator, Otto von Bismarck, realized: the German chancellor pioneered in the 1870s governmental programs to take care of the sick, aged, and disabled in order to forestall the advance of socialism.[1]

★ I am pro–free trade. I think we should be concluding new trade treaties rather than pulling out of old ones, because free trade has not only contributed to America's prosperity but also enriched the entire world. But I have been reminded by Trump's victory that globalization has left many of our fellow citizens behind. They deserve government aid not only because it is the right thing to do but also, on Bismarckian grounds, because if they do not receive it they are more likely to fall prey to populist nostrums that will damage the entire country—and the world.

★ I am pro-environment. I think that climate change is a major threat that we need to address, and I don't want to indiscriminately open federal lands to strip mining and oil digging.

★ I am pro–gun control. I don't see any legitimate reason why civilians should be able to buy military-grade assault weapons or to buy any gun at all without passing an extensive background check and a test in firearms safety—the kind of requirements routinely imposed in other democracies that have much lower rates of gun violence.

★ I am pro-immigration. As an immigrant myself, I think that immigrants are the source of America's greatness and that we would benefit from more of them. Rather than trying to kick out eleven million undocumented immigrants, we should offer them a path to citizenship so that they can become full-fledged members of our society. And rather than reduce legal immigration, we should increase it to address a shortage of native-born workers. But I am newly cognizant that the policies I favor could exacerbate a populist backlash—as has happened not only in the United States but also in a number of European countries. It is imperative to screen newcomers carefully and to make the case to white Americans that changing demography is no threat to their wellbeing.

★ I am in favor of free speech and oppose the identity politics of both minority groups and the white majority. I believe in the melting pot, integration, and color blindness, while recognizing that America must struggle to erase the stain of racism. I oppose both overly restrictive campus speech codes *and* the NFL's ban on kneeling to protest while the national anthem is played.

★ I am strong on defense: I think we need to maintain a capable military to cope with multiple enemies—from near-peer threats such as China and Russia, to rogue states like Iran and North Korea, to non-state actors like Al Qaeda and ISIS. I believe it is imperative to maintain America's military deployments in the three centers of global power and wealth—Europe, the Middle East, and East Asia—to keep the peace and deter aggressors. But, as a chastened hawk, I also recognize that we should be cautious about the use of force and shy away from preventive wars.

★ I am an internationalist: I believe it is in America's self-interest to promote and defend freedom and a rules-based international order, as we have been doing in one form or another since at least 1942. Above all, I believe that America needs to stand with our allies, especially democratic allies. Isolationism was not a viable option even in the 1930s; it is certainly not possible in today's interconnected world.[2]

You would think these political views would make me unexceptional. Taken individually, each of these opinions scores overwhelming support from the American public. But there is no party that reflects this compendium of convictions. Because I hold these views, I am a political pariah—a man without a party. Neither Democrats nor Republicans are appealing to someone of my center-right outlook. I am politically homeless.

After years of thinking of myself as a "movement conservative," I now realize that I am actually a "Rockefeller Republican," although "Eisenhower Republican" is a better description, because Ike was a more competent and impressive figure. Whatever the name, this is a breed of centrist Republican that is as extinct as the dodo, at least at the national level. (There are still some Rockefeller Republicans, such as Maryland governor Larry Hogan and Massachusetts governor Charlie Baker, in blue states.) Which is why I'm not registered as a Republican anymore. Ironically, given how far to the right the GOP has moved, even earlier icons of conservatism such as Barry Goldwater and Ronald Reagan, if they were still alive, would now be derided as RINOs—Republicans in name only.

One sign of my isolation is that I am regularly pilloried by both the far left and far right, often in terms that are virtually indistinguishable. I'm used to being described by the far left as a bloodthirsty neocon warmonger for the original sin of having supported the invasion of Iraq, along with 72 percent of the American public. This is the same mindset exhibited by Randa Jarrar, the California

State University, Fresno, professor who celebrated the death of First Lady Barbara Bush, writing "I'm happy the witch is dead," because she "raised a war criminal."[3] This kind of intolerance and incivility from the left only encourages more of the same from the Trumpist right. If Jarrar did not exist, Fox News Channel would have to invent her, so perfectly does she fit its narrative of the loony left.

While still being excoriated by the far left as a war criminal, I am simultaneously vilified by the far right as a dangerous left-winger. David Horowitz's *FrontPage* magazine accused me of going "full leftist" for acknowledging that racism and sexism remain pervasive problems. (Horowitz went from being a leftist radical in the 1960s to a rightist radical in more recent years; his ideology changes, but he remains consistent in his embrace of immoderation.) *Breitbart* called me, with ironic quotation marks, the "Washington Post's ostensibly new 'conservative' columnist," because, among other apostasies, I support gun control and immigration. *American Greatness* wrote that I am a "soulless, craven opportunist" whose "brain is broken," because I compared President Trump's indifference to the 2016 Russian election assault to a president ignoring 9/11. For the same offense, Jack Posobiec—an Internet troll notorious for pushing the theory that Hillary Clinton was running a child-sex ring out of a Washington pizza parlor—said I was "sick" and a "Russian propagandist." In the Orwellian language of the far right, someone who wants to combat Russian aggression is a "Russian propagandist," whereas someone who echoes Russian propaganda is putting "America first."[4]

I respect #NeverTrumpers such as Bill Kristol and Tom Nichols who have remained Republicans because they hope to wrest that party back from the extremists. But I have concluded that the battle is lost, at least for the time being. Sadly, David Horowitz and Laura Ingraham, Dinesh D'Souza and Jack Posobiec, Donald Trump and Devin Nunes are far more representative than I am of the right today—and quite probably in the past too, even if it's taken me a long time to realize it.

Every day that goes by, I am ever more thankful that, after spending my entire adult life as a Republican, I left the GOP the day after Trump's election. I now ardently wish harm upon my former party because it has become an enabler of Trump's assault on the rule of law and the norms of civilized society. In the republic's hour of peril, most Republicans are either cheering the president's attack on liberal democracy or pretending it doesn't exist. I agree with my friends the centrist writers Benjamin Wittes and Jonathan Rauch when they call for voters to support Democrats "mindlessly and mechanically" because "the Republican Party, as an institution, has become a danger to the rule of law and the integrity of our democracy."[5] I would not, however, call this option "mindless": supporting the opposition party is a mindful and considered response to a grotesque situation in which the majority party in Congress refuses to resist presidential abuses.

My fondest hope is that the Republican Party is soundly defeated in elections to come. And, yes, I know there are some "decent" Republicans who are inwardly cringing at what their party has become. But the key word is "inwardly": few Republican officeholders or media personalities are willing to oppose Trumpism publicly because to do so would likely be ruinous to them personally. So these invertebrates become accomplices to misdoing on a scale that would have revolted the Founding Fathers. For the time being, I echo the thirteenth-century French abbot who, when asked by Crusaders how to tell devout Catholics from apostates, reportedly advised them to kill them all and let God sort them out. Voters should simply vote against *all* Republicans as long as Trumpism remains such a dire threat to our republic. And they should keep on doing so however long it takes to purge the taint of Trumpism. Republican candidates must realize how wrong it is—morally wrong if not politically wrong—to appeal for votes by demonizing minorities or undermining the rule of law.

IF I AM NOT A REPUBLICAN, why am I not a Democrat? I became an independent instead because, although Democrats are sounding a lot more sensible than Republicans these days, I cannot fully embrace their party either.

To Democrats' credit, they have been rightly outraged by Trump's conduct, and they have tried to hold him to account despite their minority status in Congress. Trump's embrace of Vladimir Putin has even led many Democrats to adopt the kind of tough-on-Russia foreign policy that many once criticized. Democrats certainly understand the imperative of American global leadership on issues such as climate change and gay rights. But many still don't seem to get the importance of a strong defense or free trade. Few Democrats protested when Trump left the Trans-Pacific Partnership, thereby handing China a big foreign policy win. Even Hillary Clinton, who must know better, felt compelled to oppose TPP to appease the Democratic base.

Still, if the Clintons' moderate views represented the Democrats' center of gravity, I would feel comfortable becoming a Democrat. But increasingly it's obvious that it's more Bernie's party than Hillary's. There are Democrats I admire and support—particularly young centrists, many of them with military backgrounds, such as Representatives Seth Moulton of Massachusetts, Conor Lamb of Pennsylvania, and Stephanie Dang Murphy of Florida, and Mayor Pete Buttigieg of South Bend, Indiana. Virginia senators Tim Kaine and Mark Warner also fit the bill. But they are, sad to say, marginal figures, even if Kaine was a vice presidential nominee. But then so was Joe Lieberman—and he was driven out of the Democratic Party for being too conservative.

It's hard to name a single prominent centrist leader in the Democratic Party. Where is the Scoop Jackson of today? He or she simply doesn't exist. The heart of the party lies with figures of the left such as Senators Elizabeth Warren and Bernie Sanders, the heirs to such firebrands of the sixties and seventies as Eugene McCarthy and George McGovern. All of these "progressives" had great youth appeal because they offered sweeping and idealistic, if impractical, proposals. In the case of Sanders, he proposes free medical care and free education, along with federal jobs, without calculating the price tag of this vast experiment with socialism.

In 2017 Sanders introduced a Medicare for All bill that sounds great—who wouldn't want free health care for all?—but that would necessitate a sweeping, government-driven restructuring of 17 percent of the economy. Among the consequences: 155 million Americans who currently have employer-funded health insurance would have to move to Medicare.[6] Presumably all of the insurance companies that currently provide health coverage would go bankrupt unless they could find a new business model. That is the kind of ambitious social engineering that governments can never pull off without causing massive problems and disruptions.

Sanders has not bothered to calculate the price tag of his single-payer plan, but it would obviously be a budget-buster in spite of his claims to squeeze out unnecessary overhead. His bill is, in fact, considerably more generous than Canada's health system, which he cites as a model. The best estimate is that the Sanders bill would cost $1.4 trillion a year.[7] Keep in mind that the 2018 federal budget already calls for spending $4 trillion and that soon the *annual* budget deficit will exceed $1 trillion. Through such profligacy, we have accumulated more than $21 trillion in federal debt—and climbing. The Sanders bill, by increasing federal spending 35 percent, would either add to the mountain of debt or cause tax rates to spike. Either way, our economic prospects would be put in peril.

The Medicare for All plan would also endanger our national security by further crowding out the defense budget, scientific research, the arts, education, foreign aid, environmental protection, infrastructure, law enforcement, and all the other spending programs that are classified as "discretionary."[8]

And yet at least a third of all Democratic senators have endorsed his legislation, including potential presidential candidates such as Elizabeth Warren, Cory Booker, Kirstin Gillibrand, and Kamala Harris. Other Democrats support other versions of the same idea—of opening up Medicare to any American who wants it. The *Washington Post*'s liberal blogger Paul Waldman writes that "we're getting awfully close to a consensus among Democratic politicians, on that one basic idea."[9] This is an idea far more radical and costly than President Obama's Affordable Care Act, which simply subsidized private insurance for people who can't afford it and was based on a plan first implemented by Mitt Romney in Massachusetts.

Free health care is only part of the basket of benefits that the progressive wing of the Democratic Party is now promising to provide at no charge. Sanders has also introduced, with Senator Warren's support, a College for All Act that would provide free tuition at public universities for students from families that make less than $125,000 a year and that would make community colleges tuition-free for everyone. The estimated cost of this subsidy: $47 billion a year.[10] In addition, Sanders advocates offering a $15-an-hour job with the federal government to every worker "who wants or needs one," as well as providing full health care benefits. Senators Gillibrand and Booker have joined in supporting this make-work plan even though Sanders has no idea of how much it will cost or how to pay for it.[11]

Even Kevin Drum, a blogger for *Mother Jones*, describes Sanders's make-work scheme as "damn close to insane": "It's about 3–10 percent of the labor force effectively nationalized forever by the federal government, which makes it roughly comparable to the emergency labor force employed for a few years by the WPA during the depths of the Depression. This is why even our lefty comrades in social democratic Europe don't guarantee jobs for everyone. It would cost a fortune; it would massively disrupt the private labor market; it would almost certainly tank productivity; and it's unlikely in the extreme that the millions of workers in this program could ever be made fully competent at their jobs."[12]

Yet progressive ideologues want to go even further. The influential writer Jedediah Purdy advocates taking advantage of an anti-Trump backlash to push for a socialist wish list, including raising tax rates to 70 percent, creating universal family leave and child care, mandating compulsory unionization, and giving noncitizens the right to vote.[13] None of Purdy's ideas will be enacted anytime soon, but his writing may be indicative of where the Democratic Party is heading. Senator Sanders's proposals for government-run health care, federal jobs, and free education are radical enough, and they are attracting mainstream support. When I raise questions about the practicality of Sanders's schemes, I am often met with withering scorn from progressives claiming that I'm in favor of people dying in the streets for lack of health care. This is the mirror image of the kind of invective, questioning the motives of political opponents, that Trump and other right-wing populists specialize in.

Note, also, that Sanders and many other progressives actually agree with Trump on many of the issues—they, too, are sympathetic to protectionism and isolationism or at least nonintervention-ism. A Warren/Sanders administration could be nearly as hostile to American global leadership—save on issues such as global warming and LBGT rights—as the Trump administration has been. Don't get me wrong: we need to lead on climate change and LBGT rights. But we also need to lead on other issues as well.

All of this suggests that the Democratic Party is drifting leftward as the Republican Party is drifting rightward. The polarization of US politics leaves anyone who is not a socialist or a far-right populist feeling increasingly disenfranchised.

WHAT AMERICA NEEDS IS a center-right party—either a reborn GOP or an entirely new party—free of any taint of Trumpism. Such a party would not necessarily reflect all of my policy preferences, as outlined at the start of this chapter: socially liberal, fiscally conservative, pro-environment, internationalist, pro-defense, pro–gun control, pro-immigration. While I would love it if a political party would espouse as many of these views as possible, I am willing to compromise on some issues because that's the messy, unsatisfying nature of democratic politics. For example, I could make common cause with more socially conservative or more fiscally profligate voters—and in fact I have done so in the past because the Republican Party has long included both factions. But I could not possibly compromise one inch on support for the rule of law or on opposition to racism, sexism, xenophobia, and other forms of prejudice. Above all, the party I envision would need to be optimistic and inclusive rather than hateful and divisive. It would need to speak for what Arthur Schlesinger Jr. in 1949 called "the vital center."

Unfortunately, the last time a successful third party was created in America was 1854, when the Republican Party was started by disenchanted members of the Whig Party. Our entire political system is designed to entrench the Republican-Democratic duopoly and marginalize third parties. It may be possible to create a new third party in California, where, at least in statewide races, the Republican Party has all but ceased to exist. But in the rest of the country it is simply too difficult to start a third-party movement from the grassroots level, as libertarians can attest. There may be, however, an outside chance of doing so from the top down. Admittedly it would take a moonshot to succeed—but we really did reach the moon once.

The example of Emmanuel Macron could point the way. France is another country that is riven between the far left and far right—a situation that is increasingly common across the democratic world. In the first round of presidential balloting in 2017, the neo-fascist Marine Le Pen and the neo-Marxist Jean-Luc Mélenchon together won more than 40 percent of the vote. But the leading vote-getter, who was eventually elected in a second round of balloting over Le Pen, was Macron—a former Socialist who had left his old party to launch an independent bid on a centrist platform. Once elected, Macron selected a slate of candidates to support his agenda in the National Assembly. Republic on the March, as his party is called, won a landslide victory, enabling Macron to push his reformist agenda through the legislature, notwithstanding obstructionism from labor unions that object to his attempts to loosen work rules so as to get the economy moving.

We could use an American Macron—someone who can make centrism sexy. Such a candidate would need name recognition, funding, charisma, and above all, policy knowledge. If such a candidate were to win the presidency on a third-party ticket, he or she could shatter the two-party system from the top down by leading Democratic and Republican officeholders to abandon their old parties while drawing fresh faces into politics. Alternatively, such an outsider could capture the Republican nomination much as Trump himself did despite his lack of party credentials—or, in a much more optimistic vein, as Eisenhower did in 1952. If the Republican Party's shameless embrace of Trump shows anything, it is how malleable its agenda is. Having embraced white nationalism, protectionism, deficit spending, immorality, obstruction of justice, and isolationism under Trump's leadership, Republicans could just

as easily reverse themselves again should a charismatic centrist win
the presidency under their banner. The GOP tribe, seemingly, will
do whatever its chief instructs. That's a big problem under Trump
but could be a big advantage under a more reasonable successor.

Given how entrenched the two-party system is in America,
rehabilitating the GOP, following a series of cleansing defeats,
seems the more likely path toward establishing a principled center-
right party. The way to start the process would be with a credible
challenge to Trump's renomination in 2020. An insurgent campaign would be almost certain to lose but, as historian Matthew
Dallek argues, it could severely harm the incumbent and change
the direction of the party. That's what previous challengers did:
Eugene McCarthy's 1968 run against Lyndon Johnson made the
Democratic Party dovish on foreign policy and forced Johnson out
of the race, Ronald Reagan's 1976 run helped defeat Gerald Ford
and led the Republican Party to embrace his brand of conservatism,
Ted Kennedy's 1980 run helped defeat Jimmy Carter and made
the Democratic Party more liberal and coastal, and Pat Buchanan's
1992 run helped defeat George H. W. Bush and advanced the "culture war" agenda that Trump later picked up.[14]

By comparison, the third-party option is less likely—but not
impossible. Look at how much support H. Ross Perot won as a
third-party candidate running on a deficit-reduction platform in
1992. He garnered 18.9 percent of the vote even though he left the
campaign in the middle, knew little about politics, and was more
than a touch screwy. Of course, we don't need another Perot—in
Trump, we have an even more noxious version of the conspiracy-
mongering, know-nothing tycoon. What we could use is someone
like Dwight D. Eisenhower. The more I study him, the more I like
Ike. As a young man, I was critical of Eisenhower for being a plod-
ding general and president who disdained bold gestures whether
on the battlefield or in the political process: his forces did not cut

off the escape of German troops from Normandy in 1944 and, as president in the 1950s, he did not take the lead in fighting segregation or McCarthyism. But as I have matured, I have come to appreciate Eisenhower's virtues. He wasn't a military genius like Douglas MacArthur or a political genius like Franklin Roosevelt, but he was smart and steady. Above all, he had a first-class temperament that allowed him to grapple with the most difficult problems while maintaining an air of equanimity—an emotional state far removed from Trump's manic rage. Trump is disorganized and chaotic; Eisenhower was a consummate manager who ran the White House more effectively than anyone before or since. Trump is a divider; Eisenhower was a uniter.

We don't necessarily need a president to be a retired general officer, although there are potential candidates such as former Admirals William McRaven and James Stavridis and former Generals Stanley McChrystal and Jim Mattis (now, of course, the secretary of defense) who might fill that role. We do need someone who can appeal to the forgotten middle, where I find myself stranded along with other voters. Oprah Winfrey, as bright as she is, Mark Cuban, Dwayne Johnson, or some other celebrity won't cut it: they don't know enough about government to be a competent president, and after Trump we can't afford another amateur in the Oval Office. The ideal candidate would be a younger, more charismatic Michael Bloomberg. John Kasich, the Ohio governor, congressman, and presidential candidate, who has become much too moderate for the Republican Party, could fit the bill. So might Senators Ben Sasse or Jeff Flake. Any of them could either challenge Trump for the nomination or run as a third-party candidate and name a centrist Democrat such as Seth Moulton as a running mate. Of course, the danger of a third-party candidacy is that it could split the anti-Trump vote and reelect the president—but it could also drain away conservative votes that Trump needs to win.

Perhaps this is simply a fantasy. Maybe it's impossible for a centrist candidate to emerge out of our increasingly polarized politics. If that's the case, I fear the Democrats will continue to drift left and the Republicans right—a trend that will do more to imperil our country's future than any external threat because it will make it impossible to solve our problems on a bipartisan basis. As Pogo put it, we have met the enemy and he is us.

Of one thing I am sure: the Republican Party as currently constituted does not deserve to survive. The more quickly it expires, the faster it can be replaced with a more responsible center-right party. That day is not as far off as you might imagine, notwithstanding Republicans' electoral success in 2016. Given the extent to which the Trumpified GOP is alienating young people and minorities, it seems to have a death wish. Indeed, the national party may be following the example of the California GOP, which can no longer win statewide races, and even has trouble qualifying candidates for the ballot, because it became so identified with anti-immigrant bias under Governor Pete Wilson in the 1990s. By 2015, Latinos in California had come to outnumber non-Hispanic whites. If California is a trendsetter, as it has been in the past, Republicans in the rest of the country have good cause to fear for the future.

Republicans can continue to win elections nationally for a few more years by relying on a base of older, less educated white voters, but that strategy will prove less and less successful as the number of people of color continues to grow. By 2044, whites are expected to be a minority in America—very bad news for a party that has alienated everyone who isn't white. The GOP is turning off the young just as quickly: a 2017 poll found that only 19 percent of respondents between the ages of 18 and 34 approved of Trump's presidency while 67 percent disapproved.[15]

I grew up in the 1980s when Reagan-style conservatism was

cool. Young people today are growing up in a world where Trump-style conservatism is deservedly unfashionable. I am not surprised that my own kids—ranging in age from sixteen to twenty—are not becoming conservatives. I hardly blame them. Indeed, I would wonder what was wrong with them if they embraced conservatism at a time when the movement has become virtually synonymous with Trumpism.

HAVING LEFT THE Republican Party and even the conservative movement behind, I will not eagerly or quickly embrace *any* party or movement in the future. I have spent most of my life as part of a political movement that has revealed itself to be morally and intellectually bankrupt. That is a chastening lesson about the price of loyalty.

I am happy, then, to make common cause with like-minded individuals in the struggle to maintain democracy in the face of a populist onslaught. At a time of extreme crisis such as this one, the normal policy differences between the center-left and center-right fade into insignificance. All people of goodwill must come together to defend liberal democracy from the populist threat. And, indeed, one of the most salutary developments of the Trump era is how it has brought the president's critics, from both the left and the right, together. I find myself retweeting *Mother Jones* contributors—and they me (often with the preface, "I can't believe I'm retweeting Max Boot"). I had to laugh when I saw this tweet from someone who goes by the handle Digitalist: "It is deeply disturbing that the current US political climate is so abnormal that Max Boot and I have ended up on the same side of this many issues."[16] It's funny—and true.

I have also become involved in starting a centrist group called the Renew Democracy Initiative, along with former world chess champion Garry Kasparov, historian Anne Applebaum, financier Richard Hurowitz, novelist and columnist Richard North Patterson, former German defense minister Karl-Theodor zu Guttenberg, and many others. This is one of a panoply of civil-society groups on both the center-left and center-right that have arisen to protest Trump and other populists who are an affront to democracy and decency. Many of these organizations were represented at the National Summit for Democracy held in a Washington office building in February 2018. It was an invigorating event where civil-society activists came together to figure out how to protect our institutions from the threat of Trumpism. I spent my time, for example, in a working group brainstorming ideas for protecting the United States from the kind of influence operation that Russia mounted in 2016. For someone like me, who feels aghast at the direction of the Trumpified Republican Party, it was reassuring to meet so many on the left and right who share my horror of what the president is doing to the country we love.[17]

But, after leaving my old tribe, I am in no hurry to join a new one. For now, I am content to remain a party of one. Having become first an American and then a conservative, I was eager in the past to adopt a group identity. It wasn't easy to do: it required first learning English and then the language of "movement conservatism." I spent decades immersed in conservative thought and society, advancing from a lowly high school volunteer for a Senate campaign in California to a *Wall Street Journal* editor, an adviser to Republican presidential candidates, and a regular contributor to leading conservative publications. Now I prefer to think for myself rather than subscribe to the groupthink that previously defined my existence.

I did not even realize until the crisis of 2016, when I left the Republican Party, the extent to which my thinking in the past had been circumscribed by my allegiance to the conservative movement. Like oxygen, the pressure to conform is something that you only notice when it's gone. For the first time since I was twenty-four years old—a quarter of a century ago—I do not draw any pay from any conservative organization. There is something frightening but also energizing about becoming a free agent at last. Having escaped the corrosion of conservatism, I am a political Ronin, and will swear allegiance to no master in the future. I will fight for my principles wherever they may lead me.

ACKNOWLEDGMENTS

THIS BOOK IS THE BRAINCHILD OF MY EXTRAORDINARY editor, Robert Weil, to whom it is dedicated. This is the third book in a row I have worked on with Bob, and by this point I cannot imagine working with another editor. He is quite simply the best—not only at editing but also at coming up with book ideas. This volume was his inspiration; I hope I have done justice to his vision. I am also grateful to the entire team at Norton/Liveright, including Marie Pantojan, Nick Curley, Bill Rusin, Peter Miller, Cordelia Calvert, Steven Pace, Brendan Curry, Anna Oler, and Steve Attardo—all of whom are as dedicated to books as Bob is.

I am blessed to have in my corner not only the world's greatest editor but also the greatest literary agent—Tina Bennett of WME. She has shepherded this book from conception to publication and offered valuable advice and support along the way. Her assistant Svetlana Katz has also been extraordinarily helpful.

My friends Gary Rosen, Bill Kristol, and Richard North Patterson read the manuscript and helped me to improve the book in all sorts of ways. I cannot thank them enough for taking time from their own labors to assist me.

Some of the arguments advanced in this book first appeared in my articles, in somewhat different form, and I am grateful to my editors for running them: Fred Hiatt, Jackson Diehl, and Ruth Marcus at the *Washington Post*, where I now have the privilege of being a columnist; David Rothkopf and Jonathan Tepperman at *Foreign Policy*, where I was previously a columnist; Susan Brenneman at the *Los Angeles Times*, where I have written off and on since I was in college; Jill Lawrence at *USA Today*; and John Podhoretz at *Commentary*, where I was a regular blogger for a decade. At all those publications, extraordinary line editors improved my prose; I am particularly grateful to Christian Caryl at the *Post*. Not long after signing to write this book, I agreed to become a global affairs analyst at CNN, and I am grateful to my colleagues there—especially to CNN president Jeff Zucker, Vice President Rebecca Kutler, and the producers and hosts of *Anderson Cooper 360*, *New Day*, and *CNN Tonight*—for allowing me to comment on the news. Previously I was a regular commentator at MSNBC and greatly appreciate the opportunity that so many of its hosts and producers provided to me.

The Council on Foreign Relations remains my professional home, as it has been since 2002, and I cannot imagine a more congenial place to work or better bosses than Council president Richard Haass and Director of Studies James Lindsay. They have always supported me and never told me what to say or write. The Council's mission of fostering America's engagement with the world is needed now more than ever, and I am proud to be a small part of this distinguished organization. My research associate, Sherry Cho, provided invaluable support throughout.

Finally I am grateful to my partner, Sue Mi Terry, not only for her trenchant comments on the manuscript, which helped to improve it, but also for everything else that she has done to help keep me on an even keel amid the choppy currents of our contemporary politics.

NOTES

ABBREVIATIONS

FP: *Foreign Policy*
LAT: *Los Angeles Times*
MB: Max Boot
NYT: *New York Times*
WP: *Washington Post*
USAT: *USA Today*

PROLOGUE: NOVEMBER 8, 2016

1. "Here's Donald Trump's Presidential Announcement Speech," *Time*, June 16, 2015, http://time.com/3923128/donald-trump-announcement-speech/.
2. Ben Schreckinger, "Trump attacks McCain: 'I like people who weren't captured,'" *Politico*, July 18, 2015, https://www.politico.com/story/2015/07/trump-attacks-mccain-i-like-people-who-werent-captured-120317.
3. "Donald Trump Criticized for Mocking Disabled Reporter," *Snopes*, Jan. 11, 2017, https://www.snopes.com/2016/07/28/donald-trump-criticized-for-mocking-disabled-reporter/.
4. Barry Goldwater, *Conscience of a Conservative* (LaVergne, TN: Bottom of the Hill Publishing, 2010).

1. The Education of a Conservative

1. Gal Beckerman, *When They Come for Us We'll Be Gone: The Epic Struggle to Save Soviet Jewry* (Boston: Houghton Mifflin Harcourt, 2010).
2. William F. Buckley Jr., "On Donald Trump and Demagoguery," *National Review*, Jan. 22, 2016, https://www.nationalreview.com/2016/01/william-f-buckley-donald-trump-demagoguery-cigar-aficionado/.
3. "On the Meaning of Life," *Letters of Note*, Jan. 31, 2012, http://www.lettersofnote.com/2012/01/on-meaning-of-life.html.
4. German Lopez, "America's Unique Gun Violence Problem, Explained in 17 Maps and Charts," *Vox*, Oct. 2, 2017, https://www.vox.com/policy-and-politics/2017/10/2/16399418/us-gun-violence-statistics-maps-charts.
5. David Corn, "Remember How Dinesh D'Souza Outed Gay Classmates—and Thought It Was Awesome?," *Mother Jones*, Jan. 24, 2014, https://www.motherjones.com/politics/2014/01/dinesh-dsouza-indictment-dartmouth-outed-gay-classmates/.

2. The Career of a Conservative

1. MB, "Americans Need to Overcome Partisan Enmity—But Our President Is Stoking It," *WP*, May 29, 2018, https://www.washingtonpost.com/news/global-opinions/wp/2018/05/29/americans-need-to-overcome-partisan-enmity-but-our-president-is-stoking-it/?utm_term=.686bc7bf396e.
2. MB, "The Case for American Empire," *Weekly Standard*, Oct. 15, 2001, https://www.weeklystandard.com/max-boot/the-case-for-american-empire.
3. MB, "To Help Restore U.S. Standing, Rumsfeld Must Take the Fall," *LAT*, May 13, 2004, http://articles.latimes.com/2004/may/13/opinion/oe-boot13.

3. The Surrender

1. MB, "Donald Trump's Remarkably Consistent Inconsistency," *Commentary*, Aug. 18, 2015, http://maxboot.net/donald-trumps-remarkably-consistent-inconsistency/.
2. Philip Elliott, "Donald Trump Brags His Way through New Hampshire," *Time*, Feb. 5, 2016, http://time.com/4208870/donald-trump-brags/.

3. MB, "Does Donald Trump Know the Right General Can't Save a Failed Foreign Policy?," *Commentary*, Sept. 9, 2015, http://maxboot .net/does-donald-trump-know-the-right-general-cant-save-a-failed-foreign-policy/.

4. Chris Cillizza, "A Fact Checker Looked into 158 Things Donald Trump Said. 78 Percent Were False," *WP*, July 1, 2016, https:// www.washingtonpost.com/news/the-fix/wp/2016/07/01/donald-trump-has-been-wrong-way-more-often-than-all-the-other-2016-candidates-combined/?utm_term=.6df3fedaf473.

5. MB, "Max Boot: Trump Is a Character Test for the GOP," *USAT*, Feb. 29, 2016, https://www.usatoday.com/story/opinion/2016/02/29/ trump-tests-republicans-max-boot/81123934/.

6. MB, "'Sheriff Joe' and Donald Trump Are Emblems of Racism and Lawlessness," *LAT*, Aug. 28, 2017, http://www.latimes.com/opinion/ op-ed/la-oe-boot-arpaio-pardon-20170827-story.html.

7. MB, "Trump Bows to Russia Again: Max Boot," *USAT*, Feb. 6, 2017, https://www.usatoday.com/story/opinion/2017/02/06/trump-interview-putin-killer-innocent-thug-moral-relativism-max-boot-column/97525480/.

8. Jeremy Diamond, "Donald Trump on Protester: 'I'd Like to Punch Him in the Face,'" *CNN*, Feb. 23, 2016, https://www.cnn.com/2016/02/23/ politics/donald-trump-nevada-rally-punch/index.html.

9. Gordon F. Sander, "When Nazis Filled Madison Square Garden," *Politico*, Aug. 23, 2017, https://www.politico.com/magazine/story/2017/08/23/ nazi-german-american-bund-rally-madison-square-garden-215522.

10. MB (@MaxBoot), Twitter, Nov. 22, 2015, https://twitter.com/ maxboot/status/668447756512456705?lang=en.

11. John McNeill, "How Fascist Is Donald Trump? There's Actually a Formula for That," *WP*, Oct. 21, 2016, https://www.washingtonpost .com/posteverything/wp/2016/10/21/how-fascist-is-donald-trump-theres-actually-a-formula-for-that/?utm_term=.4b86d9a226e9.

12. MB, "Donald Trump's Honesty Problem," *Commentary*, Feb. 22, 2016, http://maxboot.net/donald-trumps-honesty-problem/.

13. MB, "There Is No Escape from Trump," *Commentary*, Mar. 3, 2016, http://maxboot.net/there-is-no-escape-from-trump/.

14. MB and Benn Steil, "Selling America Short," *Weekly Standard*, Feb. 26, 2016, https://www.weeklystandard.com/max-boot-benn-steil/ selling-america-short.

15. Publius Decius Mus [Michael Anton], "The Flight 93 Election," *Claremont Review of Books*, Sept. 5, 2016, http://www.claremont.org/crb/ basicpage/the-flight-93-election/.

16. "Open Letter on Donald Trump from GOP National Security

Leaders," *War on the Rocks*, Mar. 2, 2016, https://warontherocks
.com/2016/03/open-letter-on-donald-trump-from-gop-national-
security-leaders/.

17. "Against Trump," *National Review*, Jan. 22, 2016, https://www.national
review.com/2016/01/donald-trump-conservative-movement-menace/.

18. MB, "Trump vs. Mueller is a Battle for America's Soul," *WP*, Feb. 26,
2018, https://www.washingtonpost.com/opinions/trump-vs-mueller-
is-a-battle-for-americas-soul/2018/02/26/0979904c-1b19-11e8-9de1-
147dd2df3829_story.html?utm_term=.5ab69d72bd8a.

19. Alexander Burns, "Anti-Trump Republicans Call for a Third-Party
Option," *NYT*, Mar. 3, 2016, https://www.nytimes.com/2016/03/03/
us/politics/anti-donald-trump-republicans-call-for-a-third-party-
option.html.

20. Hadas Gold and Oliver Darcy, "Salem Executives Pressured Radio
Hosts to Cover Trump More Positively, Emails Show," *CNN*, May
9, 2018, http://money.cnn.com/2018/05/09/media/salem-radio-
executives-trump/index.html.

21. David Frum, "Conservatism Can't Survive Donald Trump Intact,"
The Atlantic, Dec. 19, 2017, https://www.theatlantic.com/politics/
archive/2017/12/conservatism-is-what-conservatives-think-say-and-
do/548738/.

22. MB, "Max Boot: Trump Is a Character Test for the GOP," *USAT*,
Feb. 29, 2016, https://www.usatoday.com/story/opinion/2016/02/29/
trump-tests-republicans-max-boot/81123934/.

23. David A. Graham, "Which Republicans Oppose Donald Trump? A
Cheat Sheet," *The Atlantic*, Nov. 6, 2016, https://www.theatlantic
.com/politics/archive/2016/11/where-republicans-stand-on-donald-
trump-a-cheat-sheet/481449/.

24. Richard Brookhiser, "WFB Today," *National Review*, Feb. 17, 2018,
https://www.nationalreview.com/magazine/2018/02/17/william-f-
buckley-trump-conservatism-needs-rebuilding/.

25. MB, "The Republican Party Is Dead," *LAT*, May 8, 2016, http://
www.latimes.com/opinion/op-ed/la-oe-boot-republicans-in-exile-
20160508-story.html.

26. Matthew Yglesias, "New Report Details Trump-Inspired Surge in
Anti-Semitism," *Vox*, Oct. 19, 2016, https://www.vox.com/policy-
and-politics/2016/10/19/13326336/trump-antisemitism.

27. "Anti-Semitic Incidents in US More than Doubled within 2
Years—Report," *Times of Israel*, Feb. 27, 2018, https://www
.timesofisrael.com/anti-semitic-incidents-in-us-more-than-
doubled-within-2-years-report/?utm_source=The+Times+of

+Israel+Daily+Edition&utm_campaign=fe43d6c8aa-EMAIL_
CAMPAIGN_2018_02_27&utm_medium=email&utm_term=0_
adb46cec92-fe43d6c8aa-55237393.

28. Yochi Dreazen, "It's Time to Acknowledge Reality: Donald Trump
Talks Like an Anti-Semite," *Vox*, Oct. 14, 2016, https://www.vox
.com/world/2016/10/14/13288138/donald-trump-anti-semite-israel-
david-duke-racism-misogny-clinton.

29. MB, "Trump's Opposition Research Firm: Russia's Intelligence
Agencies," *LAT*, July 25, 2016, http://www.latimes.com/opinion/
op-ed/la-oe-boot-trump-russian-connection-20160725-snap-story
.html.

30. Eugene Scott, Ashley Killough, and Daniel Burke, "Evangelicals 'Disgusted' by Trump's Remarks, But Still Backing Him," *CNN*, Oct.
21, 2016, https://www.cnn.com/2016/10/07/politics/donald-trump-
evangelical-leaders/index.html.

31. MB, "This Lifetime GOP Voter Is with Her," *FP*, Nov. 6, 2016,
http://foreignpolicy.com/2016/11/06/this-lifetime-gop-voter-is-with-
her-why-republicans-should-vote-for-hillary-clinton/.

32. Philip Bump, "Donald Trump Will Be President Thanks to
80,000 People in Three States," *WP*, Dec. 1, 2016, https://www
.washingtonpost.com/news/the-fix/wp/2016/12/01/donald-trump-
will-be-president-thanks-to-80000-people-in-three-states/?utm_
term=.e836b07cbc2e.

33. Heather Boushey, "The Appealing Logic that Underlies Trump's Economic Ideas," *The Atlantic*, March 15, 2017, https://www.theatlantic
.com/business/archive/2017/03/trumps-economic-logic/519381/.

34. Ian Bremmer, *Us vs. Them: The Failure of Globalism* (New York: Portfo-
lio/Penguin, 2018), 17.

35. The bipartisan Financial Crisis Inquiry Commission concluded that "it
was the collapse of the housing bubble—fueled by low interest rates,
easy and available credit, scant regulation, and toxic mortgages—that
was the spark that ignited a string of events, which led to a full-blown
crisis in the fall of 2008." *Conclusions of the Financial Crisis Inquiry Commission*, http://fcic-static.law.stanford.edu/cdn_media/fcic-reports/
fcic_final_report_conclusions.pdf.

36. Donald J. Trump (@realDonaldTrump), Twitter, Jan. 20, 2017, https://
twitter.com/realdonaldtrump/status/822502450007515137.

37. Jonah Goldberg, Max Boot, Michael Brendan Dougherty, William
Voegeli, and Emily Ekins, "Conservatives Ponder the Future of the
GOP under Trump," *LAT*, Nov. 13, 2016, http://www.latimes.com/
opinion/op-ed/la-oe-gop-future-roundtable-20161113-story.html.

4. The Chaos President

1. MB, "Why a Trump Presidency Might Not Be as Awful as We Fear," *FP*, Nov. 9, 2016, http://foreignpolicy.com/2016/11/09/why-a-trump-presidency-might-not-be-as-awful-as-we-fear/.

2. MB, "NeverTrumpers Should Not Shun Trump: Max Boot," *USAT*, Nov. 13, 2016, https://www.usatoday.com/story/opinion/2016/11/13/never-trumpers-should-not-shun-trump-national-security-checks-balances-max-boot/93767170/.

3. MB, "The Grave Dangers and Deep Sadness of 'America First,'" *FP*, Jan. 23, 2017, http://foreignpolicy.com/2017/01/23/the-grave-dangers-and-deep-sadness-of-america-first-donald-trump/.

4. MB, "Slapdash Trump Order Ignores Real Danger: Max Boot," *USAT*, Jan. 29, 2017, https://www.usatoday.com/story/opinion/2017/01/29/slapdash-trump-order-ignores-real-danger-max-boot-column/97211882/.

5. Kathryn Dunn Tenpas, "Why Is Trump's Staff Turnover Higher than the 5 Most Recent Presidents?," *Brookings*, Jan. 19, 2018, https://www.brookings.edu/research/why-is-trumps-staff-turnover-higher-than-the-5-most-recent-presidents/.

6. Philip Bump, A Quarter of Trump's 'Highest IQ' Cabinet Has Been Replaced," *WP*, Mar. 28, 2018, https://www.washingtonpost.com/news/politics/wp/2018/03/28/a-quarter-of-trumps-highest-iq-cabinet-has-been-replaced/?utm_term=.9e981e387e1f.

7. Aaron Blake, "'It's Chaos. . . . It's Not Good for Anything': After Rejecting Trump's Offer, Ted Olson Admonishes Him," *WP*, Mar. 26, 2018, https://www.washingtonpost.com/news/the-fix/wp/2018/03/26/its-chaos-its-not-good-for-anything-after-snubbing-trump-ted-olson-admonishes-him/?utm_term=.284eb538f93c.

8. Trump Golf Count, http://trumpgolfcount.com/.

9. Patrick Radden Keefe, "McMaster and Commander," *New Yorker*, Apr. 30, 2018, https://www.newyorker.com/magazine/2018/04/30/mcmaster-and-commander.

10. Susan B. Glasser, "The Price of Getting Inside Trump's Head," *New Yorker*, May 11, 2018, https://www.newyorker.com/news/news-desk/the-price-of-getting-inside-trumps-head.

11. Arelis R. Hernandez, "New Puerto Rico Data Shows Deaths Increased by 1,400 after Hurricane Maria," *WP*, June 1, 2018, https://www.washingtonpost.com/national/new-puerto-rico-data-shows-deaths-increased-by-1400-after-hurricane-maria/2018/06/01/43bb4278-65e2-11e8-99d2-0d678ec08c2f_story.html?utm_term=.

12. John Harwood (@JohnJHarwood), Twitter, Apr. 2, 2018, https://twitter.com/johnjharwood/status/980900978789675008?s=11.

13. Brian Klaas (@brianklaas), Twitter, Apr. 25, 2018, https://twitter.com/brianklaas/status/989127820420026369.

14. Robert Shapiro, "Trump Lags behind His Predecessors on Economic Growth," *Brookings*, May 17, 2018, https://www.brookings.edu/blog/fixgov/2018/05/17/trump-lags-behind-his-predecessors-on-economic-growth/?utm_campaign=Brookings%20Brief&utm_source=hs_email&utm_medium=email&utm_content=63022866.

15. Julian E. Barnes, "Pompeo Says Iran Nuclear Deal Could Only Be Preserved with a 'Substantial Fix,'" *WSJ*, Apr. 28, 2018, https://www.wsj.com/articles/pompeo-begins-first-official-foreign-trip-amid-uncertainty-over-iran-deal-1524821386.

16. Alan Levin and Jesse Hamilton, "Trump Takes Credit for Killing Hundreds of Regulations That Were Already Dead," *Bloomberg*, Dec. 11, 2017, https://www.bloomberg.com/news/features/2017-12-11/trump-takes-credit-for-killing-hundreds-of-regulations-that-were-already-dead.

17. Jeffry Bartash, "Trump's Regulatory Rollback for the U.S. Economy Is a Dud—So Far," *MarketWatch*, Feb. 12, 2018, https://www.marketwatch.com/story/trumps-regulatory-rollback-for-the-us-economy-is-a-dud-so-far-2018-02-12.

18. Eliana Johnson, Emily Stephenson, and Daniel Lippman, "'Too Inconvenient': Trump Goes Rogue on Phone Security," *Politico*, May 21, 2018, https://www.politico.com/story/2018/05/21/trump-phone-security-risk-hackers-601903.

5. The Cost of Capitulation

1. Marshall Frady, "How George Wallace Harnessed Hate," *Daily Beast*, Apr. 3, 2016, https://www.thedailybeast.com/how-george-wallace-harnessed-hate.

2. James Madison, "The Utility of the Union as a Safeguard against Domestic Faction and Insurrection (continued)," *The Federalist*, No. 10, Nov. 22, 1787, http://www.constitution.org/fed/federa10.htm.

3. Louis Jacobson, "Steele Says GOP Fought Hard for Civil Rights Bills in 1960s," *PolitiFact*, May 25, 2010, http://www.politifact.com/truth-o-meter/statements/2010/may/25/michael-steele/steele-says-gop-fought-hard-civil-rights-bills-196/.

4. MB, "The Difference between George Washington and Robert E. Lee," *FP*, Aug. 18, 2017, http://foreignpolicy.com/2017/08/18/the-

difference-between-george-washington-and-robert-e-lee-trump-
sedition-slavery-confederate-monuments/.

5. Veronica Stracqualursi, "Trump: NFL Players Who Don't Stand
during National Anthem Maybe 'Shouldn't Be in the Country,'"
CNN, May 24, 2018, https://www.cnn.com/2018/05/24/politics/
trump-nfl-national-anthem/index.html.

6. Scott Goldsmith, "Johnstown Never Believed Trump Would Help.
They Still Love Him Anyway," *Politico*, Dec. 11, 2008, https://www
.politico.com/magazine/story/2017/11/08/donald-trump-johnstown-
pennsylvania-supporters-215800.

7. Diana C. Mutz, "Status Threat, Not Economic Hardship, Explains the
2016 Presidential Vote," *Proceedings of the National Academy of Sciences
of the United States of America*, Apr. 23, 2018, http://www.pnas.org/
content/early/2018/04/18/1718155115.

8. "Ronald Reagan on Immigration," *On the Issues*, http://www
.ontheissues.org/celeb/Ronald_Reagan_Immigration.htm.

9. Julie Hirschfeld Davis, "Trump Calls Some Unauthorized Immigrants 'Animals' in Rant," *NYT*, May 16, 2018, https://www.nytimes
.com/2018/05/16/us/politics/trump-undocumented-immigrants-
animals.html?smtyp=cur&smid=tw-nytimes.

10. Z. Byron Wolf, "Trump Blasts 'Breeding' in Sanctuary Cities. That's a
Racist Term," *CNN*, Apr. 24, 2018, https://www.cnn.com/2018/04/18/
politics/donald-trump-immigrants-california/index.html.

11. Chris Nichols, "MOSTLY TRUE: Undocumented Immigrants Less
Likely to Commit Crimes than U.S. Citizens," *PolitiFact*, Aug. 3,
2017, http://www.politifact.com/california/statements/2017/aug/03/
antonio-villaraigosa/mostly-true-undocumented-immigrants-less-
likely-co/.

12. "Immigrants from Africa Boast Higher Education Levels than Overall
U.S. Population," *New American Economy*, Jan. 11, 2018, http://www
.newamericaneconomy.org/press-release/immigrants-from-africa-
boast-higher-education-levels-than-overall-u-s-population/.

13. Simone de Beauvoir, *The Works of Simone de Beauvoir: The Second Sex
and the Ethics of Ambiguity* (CreateSpace, 2011).

14. Tal Kopan, "Arrests of Immigrants, Especially Non-Criminals, Way
Up in Trump's First Year," *CNN*, Feb. 23, 2018, https://www.cnn
.com/2018/02/23/politics/trump-immigration-arrests-deportations/
index.html.

15. Geneva Sands, "'A Nightmare': Family Bids Goodbye as Undocumented Father of 2 Is Deported to Mexico," *ABC News*, Jan. 16,
2018, http://abcnews.go.com/US/nightmare-family-bids-goodbye-
undocumented-father-deported-mexico/story?id=52367022.

16. Seung Min Kim, "Trump Is Blaming Democrats for Separating Migrant Families at the Border. Here's Why This Isn't a Surprise," *WP*, May 27, 2018, https://www.washingtonpost.com/politics/trump-is-blaming-democrats-for-separating-migrant-families-at-the-border-heres-why-this-isnt-a-surprise/2018/05/27/c07810d8-61d3-11e8-a69c-b944de66d9e7_story.html?utm_term=.b23debbc9f5a.

17. "Neocons & Russiagaters Unite! New Think Tank Will Protect Democracy from Russia, Sell Books," *RT*, Apr. 27, 2018, https://www.rt.com/usa/425303-renew-democracy-initiative-neocons-rdi/.

18. MB, "I Came to this Country 41 Years Ago. Now I Feel Like I Don't Belong Here," *WP*, Sept. 5, 2017, https://www.washingtonpost.com/news/democracy-post/wp/2017/09/05/i-came-to-this-country-41-years-ago-now-trump-is-making-me-feel-like-i-dont-belong-here/?utm_term=.dd6600ee508f.

19. Amber Phillips, "The Senate's New Russia Report Just Undercut Trump in Two Big Ways," *WP*, May 16, 2018, https://www.washingtonpost.com/news/the-fix/wp/2018/05/16/the-russia-report-trump-likes-best-just-took-a-big-credibility-hit/?utm_term=.d98dec7b542a.

20. "Trump's Russia Cover-Up By the Numbers—76+ Contacts with Russia-Linked Operatives," *The Moscow Project*, May 17, 2018, https://themoscowproject.org/explainers/trumps-russia-cover-up-by-the-numbers-70-contacts-with-russia-linked-operatives/.

21. Brett Samuels, "Trump: Nobody Has Been Tougher on Russia than Me," *The Hill*, Apr. 3, 2018, http://thehill.com/homenews/administration/381437-trump-nobody-has-been-tougher-on-russia-than-me.

22. Greg Jaffe, John Hudson, and Philip Rucker, "Trump, a Reluctant Hawk, Has Battled His Top Aides on Russia and Lost," *WP*, Apr. 15, 2018, https://www.washingtonpost.com/amphtml/world/national-security/trump-a-reluctant-hawk-has-battled-his-top-aides-on-russia-and-lost/2018/04/15/a91e850a-3f1b-11e8-974f-aacd97698cef_story.html?__twitter_impression=true.

23. MB, "Trump Is Ignoring the Worst Attack on America Since 9/11," *WP*, Feb. 13, 2017, https://www.washingtonpost.com/opinions/trump-is-ignoring-the-worst-attack-on-america-since-911/2018/02/18/5ad888f2-14f3-11e8-8b08-027a6ccb38eb_story.html.

24. Dylan Matthews, "Trump Has Changed How Americans Think about Politics," *Vox*, Jan. 30, 2018, https://www.vox.com/policy-and-

politics/2018/1/30/16943786/trump–changed–public–opinion–russia–immigration–trade.

25. Kristen Bialik, "Putin Remains Overwhelmingly Unpopular in the United States," *Pew Research Center*, Mar. 26, 2018, http://www.pewresearch.org/fact–tank/2018/03/26/putin–remains–overwhelmingly–unpopular–in–the–united–states/.

26. Abby Phillip, Robert Barnes, and Ed O'Keefe, "Supreme Court Nominee Gorsuch Says Trump's Attacks on Judiciary Are 'Demoralizing,'" *WP*, Feb. 8, 2017, https://www.washingtonpost.com/politics/supreme–court–nominee–gorsuch–says–trumps–attacks–on–judiciary–are–demoralizing/2017/02/08/64e03fe2–ee3f–11e6–9662–6eedf1627882_story.html?utm_term=.ad67c8244fc2.

27. For a timeline of Trump's obstruction attempts up to early 2018, see Artin Afkhami, "Timeline of Trump and Obstruction of Justice: Key Dates and Events," *Just Security*, Jan. 25, 2018, https://www.justsecurity.org/45987/timeline–trump–obstruction–justice–key–dates–events/.

28. Michael S. Schmidt and Julie Hirschfeld Davis, "Trump Asked Sessions to Retain Control of Russia Inquiry after His Recusal," *NYT*, May 29, 2018, https://www.nytimes.com/2018/05/29/us/politics/trump–sessions–obstruction.html.

29. Donald J. Trump (@realDonaldTrump), Twitter, Dec. 3, 2017, https://twitter.com/realdonaldtrump/status/937305615218696193?lang=en.

30. Linda Qiu, "Key Moments in Trump's Interview on 'Fox and Friends,' with Fact Checks," *NYT*, June 15, 2018, https://www.nytimes.com/2018/06/15/us/politics/trump–fox–and–friends–interview.html.

31. Donald J. Trump (@realDonaldTrump), Twitter, Apr. 13, 2018, https://mobile.twitter.com/realDonaldTrump/status/984767560494313472.

32. Peter Baker, "Trump Assails Mueller, Drawing Rebukes from Republicans," *NYT*, Mar. 18, 2018, https://www.nytimes.com/2018/03/18/us/politics/trump–mueller.html.

33. MB, "Trump vs. Mueller Is a Battle for America's Soul," *WP*, Feb. 26, 2018, https://www.washingtonpost.com/opinions/trump–vs–mueller–is–a–battle–for–americas–soul/2018/02/26/0979904c–1b19–11e8–9de1–147dd2df3829_story.html.

34. Natasha Bertrand, "How Trumpworld Is Spinning the FBI Report," *The Atlantic*, June 15, 2018, https://www.theatlantic.com/politics/archive/2018/06/how–trumpworld–is–spinning–the–fbi–report/562922/.

35. Donald J. Trump (@realDonaldTrump), Twitter, May 23, 2018, https://twitter.com/realDonaldTrump/status/999246677549768704.

36. MB, "Here Are the Political Norms that Trump Violated in Just

the Past Week," *WP*, May 21, 2018, https://www.washingtonpost
.com/news/global-opinions/wp/2018/05/21/here-are-the-political-
norms-that-trump-violated-in-just-the-past-week/?utm_term=
.c083021c230d.

37. Donald J. Trump (@realDonaldTrump), Twitter, Apr. 11, 2018, https://twitter.com/realDonaldTrump/
status/984020136255541248?ref_src=twsrc%5Etfw&ref_
url=https%3A%2F%2Fwww.mediaite.com%2Fonline%2Ftrump-on-
fbis-cohen-raid-no-collusion-or-obstruction-other-than-i-fight-
back%2F&tfw_creator=KenMeyer91&tfw_site=mediaite.

38. Philip Bump, "An Increasing Number of Americans See the
FBI as Biased against Trump," *WP*, Apr. 17, 2018, https://www
.washingtonpost.com/news/politics/wp/2018/04/17/an-increasing-
number-of-americans-see-the-fbi-as-biased-against-trump/?utm_
term=.b82c4635332c.

39. Glenn Kessler, Salvador Rizzo, and Meg Kelly, "President Trump Has
Made 3,001 False or Misleading Claims So Far," *WP*, May 1, 2018,
https://www.washingtonpost.com/amphtml/news/fact-checker/
wp/2018/05/01/president-trump-has-made-3001-false-or-misleading-
claims-so-far/?utm_term=.086753215f1b&__twitter_impression=true.

40. Office of the United States Trade Representative, "Canada: U.S.-Can-
ada Trade Facts," https://ustr.gov/countries-regions/americas/canada.

41. Donald J. Trump (@realDonaldTrump), Twitter, May 31, 2018,
https://twitter.com/realDonaldTrump/status/1002160516733853696.

42. MB, "Trump Is Perfecting the Art of the Big Lie," *WP*, Mar. 17,
2018, https://www.washingtonpost.com/news/global-opinions/
wp/2018/03/17/trump-is-perfecting-the-art-of-the-big-lie/?utm_
term=.ffdd48a2b483.

43. Anne Gearan and Carol Morello, "Rex Tillerson Says 'Alternative Realities' Are a Threat to Democracy," *WP*, May
16, 2018, https://www.washingtonpost.com/politics/
former-trump-aide-rex-tillerson-says-alternative-realities-
are-a-threat-to-democracy/2018/05/16/4d0353f0-594b-11e8-8836-
a4a123c359ab_story.html?utm_term=.7ec476c7256a.

44. Lucia Graves, "How Trump Weaponized 'Fake News' for His Own
Political Ends," *Pacific Standard*, Feb. 26, 2018, https://psmag.com/
social-justice/how-trump-weaponized-fake-news-for-his-own-
political-ends.

45. Damian Paletta and Josh Dawsey, "Trump Personally Pushed Postmaster General to Double Rates on Amazon, Other Firms," *WP*,
May 18, 2018, https://www.washingtonpost.com/business/economy/
trump-personally-pushed-postmaster-general-to-double-rates-

on-amazon-other-firms/2018/05/18/2b6438d2-5931-11e8-858f-
12becb4d6067_story.html?utm_term=.782a0e7dd5a7.

46. Brian Stelter, "Giuliani Says Trump 'Denied' the AT&T-Time Warner Deal, then Backtracks," *CNN*, May 11, 2018, http://money.cnn
.com/2018/05/11/media/rudy-giuliani-trump-att-time-warner/index
.html.

47. MB, "Here Are the Political Norms that Trump Violated in Just the
Past Week," *WP*, May 21, 2018, https://www.washingtonpost.com/
news/global-opinions/wp/2018/05/21/here-are-the-political-norms-
that-trump-violated-in-just-the-past-week/?utm_term=.932ecf0a5d07.

48. Avery Anapol, "Poll: Majority of Trump Supporters Say Media Is
'Enemy of American People,'" *The Hill*, Dec. 4, 2017, http://thehill
.com/blogs/blog-briefing-room/363098-poll-majority-of-trump-
backers-say-media-is-enemy-of-american-people.

49. John McCain, "Mr. President, Stop Attacking the Press," *WP*, Jan.
16, 2018, https://www.washingtonpost.com/opinions/mr-president-
stop-attacking-the-press/2018/01/16/9438c0ac-faf0-11e7-a46b-
a3614530bd87_story.html?utm_term=.da6354624854.

50. MB, "The Trump Administration Is in an Unethical League
of Its Own," *WP*, Mar. 1, 2018, https://www.washingtonpost
.com/opinions/the-trump-administrations-no-good-very-bad-
wednesday/2018/03/01/7dc60fd2-1d69-11e8-ae5a-16e60e4605f3_
story.html?utm_term=.a7d55d2d0376.

51. Jesse Drucker, Kate Kelly, and Ben Protess, "Kushner's Family Business Received Loans after White House Meetings," *NYT*, Feb. 28,
2018, https://www.nytimes.com/2018/02/28/business/jared-kushner-
apollo-citigroup-loans.html.

52. Ana Cerrud and David A. Fahrenthold, "Warning of 'Repercussions,' Trump Company Lawyers Seek Panama President's Help,"
WP, Apr. 9, 2018, https://www.washingtonpost.com/world/warning-
of-repercussions-trump-company-lawyers-seek-panama-presidents-
help/2018/04/09/9e3fbb8e-3c2f-11e8-8d53-eba0ed2371cc_story.html.

53. "Trump Indonesia Project Is Latest Stop on China's Belt and Road,"
South China Morning Post, May 11, 2018, http://www.scmp.com/news/
asia/southeast-asia/article/2145808/trump-indonesia-project-latest-
stop-chinas-belt-and-road.

54. Julia Horowitz, "Ivanka Trump Granted Seven New Trademarks in
China," *CNN*, May 28, 2018, http://money.cnn.com/2018/05/28/
news/ivanka-trump-china-trademarks/index.html.

55. "CREW Releases Report: Profiting from the Presidency: A Year's
Worth of President Trump's Conflicts of Interest," *Citizens for
Responsibility and Ethics in Washington*, Jan. 19, 2018, https://www

.citizensforethics.org/press-release/crew-releases-report-profiting-presidency-years-worth-president-trumps-conflicts-interest/.

56. Jenna Johnson, "As Stormy Daniels Tells Her Story, Six Conservative Americans Debate Whether Trump Is a Role Model," *WP*, Mar. 3, 2018, https://www.washingtonpost.com/politics/as-stormy-daniels-tells-her-story-six-conservative-americans-debate-whether-trump-is-a-role-model/2018/03/28/bb4f258a-2f86-11e8-b0b0-f706877db618_story.html?utm_term=.b5a8c6b91dde.

57. Ashley Merryman, "President Trump's Worst Behaviors Can Infect Us All Just Like the Flu, According to Science," *WP*, Mar. 3, 2018, https://www.washingtonpost.com/news/inspired-life/wp/2018/03/29/president-trumps-worst-behavior-can-spread-among-us-just-like-the-flu-according-to-science/?utm_term=.e0da8a510bf8.

58. Hannah Hartig, "Few Americans See Nation's Political Debate as 'Respectful,'" *Pew Research Center*, May 1, 2018, http://www.pewresearch.org/fact-tank/2018/05/01/few-americans-see-nations-political-debate-as-respectful/.

59. Ian Bremmer (@ianbremmer), Twitter, Apr. 18, 2018, https://twitter.com/ianbremmer/status/986683408611971072.

60. "Dwight D. Eisenhower: 12—The President's News Conference, February 17, 1953," *The American Presidency Project*, http://www.presidency.ucsb.edu/ws/index.php?pid=9623.

61. Paul Ryan (@SpeakerRyan), Twitter, Feb. 9, 2012, https://twitter.com/speakerryan/status/167647060957462528.

62. Catherine Rampell, "The United States Is Mortgaging Its Future," *WP*, Apr. 19, 2018, https://www.washingtonpost.com/opinions/the-united-states-is-mortgaging-its-future/2018/04/19/daa35554-4409-11e8-ad8f-27a8c409298b_story.html?utm_term=.9e5905badcbb.

63. Eugene Scott, "Rand Paul Calls Out Hypocrisy of GOP in the Trump Era," *WP*, Feb. 9, 2018, https://www.washingtonpost.com/news/the-fix/wp/2018/02/09/rand-paul-calls-out-hypocrisy-of-gop-in-the-trump-era/?utm_term=.4f98c7af3c92.

64. MB, "Republicans Are Making a Mockery of Their Reputations," *WP*, Feb. 11, 2018, https://www.washingtonpost.com/opinions/republicans-are-making-a-mockery-of-their-reputations/2018/02/10/866aefe0-0eaa-11e8-8890-372e2047c935_story.html?utm_term=.db9678716864.

65. Judd Gregg, "Judd Gregg: The GOP Abandons Fiscal Responsibility," *The Hill*, Apr. 9, 2018, http://thehill.com/opinion/finance/382219-judd-gregg-the-gop-abandons-fiscal-responsibility?amp&__twitter_impression=true.

66. Steve LeVine, "Economist: Trump Trade War Will Cost 190,000

Jobs," *Axios*, Apr. 4, 2018, https://www.axios.com/economist-trump-trade-war-will-already-cost-190k-jobs-1522857360-0d8f5f65-8334-45f7-a2e6-d8251d5c5884.html.

67. Alexandra Hutzler, "Trump's Unpopular Tariffs Could Cost U.S. 400,000 Jobs, Economists Estimate," *Newsweek*, June 6, 2018, http://www.newsweek.com/donald-trump-tariffs-trade-job-loss-961988.

68. MB, "Imposing Tariffs Is Stupid Policy," *WP*, Mar. 5, 2018, https://www.washingtonpost.com/opinions/imposing-tariffs-is-stupid-policy/2018/03/05/b5512ea0-2093-11e8-86f6-54bfff693d2b_story.html.

69. Ian Bremmer, *Us vs. Them: The Failure of Globalism* (New York: Portfolio/Penguin, 2018), 16.

70. "Washington Post–ABC News Poll April 8–11, 2018," *WP*, Apr. 15, 2018, https://www.washingtonpost.com/page/2010-2019/Washington Post/2018/04/15/National-Politics/Polling/question_20289 .xml?uuid=DEOE8kCWEeiy3LCkA-RyCg.

71. Thomas Wright, "Trump's 19th Century Foreign Policy," *Politico*, Jan. 20, 2016, https://www.politico.com/magazine/story/2016/01/donald-trump-foreign-policy-213546.

72. MB, "Trump Turns the G-7 into the G-6 vs. G-1," *WP*, June 10, 2018, https://www.washingtonpost.com/opinions/trump-turns-the-g-7-into-the-g-6-vs-g-1/2018/06/10/1d3b7276-6ccc-11e8-afd5-778aca903bbe_story.html?utm_term=.43c3e878d2ba.

73. John Wagner, "'He's a Tough Guy': Trump Downplays the Human-Rights Record of Kim Jong Un," *WP*, June 14, 2018, https://www.washingtonpost.com/politics/hes-a-tough-guy-trump-downplays-the-human-rights-record-of-kim-jong-un/2018/06/14/90ed487e-6fbb-11e8-bf86-a2351b5ece99_story.html?utm_term=.8240 ea13c377.

74. Julie Ray, "World's Approval of U.S. Leadership Drops to New Low," *Gallup*, Jan. 18, 2018, http://news.gallup.com/poll/225761/world-approval-leadership-drops-new-low.aspx.

75. Haley Britzky, "Arab Youth See the U.S. as an Enemy," *Axios*, May 8, 2018, https://www.axios.com/arab-youth-see-us-as-an-enemy-a4415c65-e096-4904-b32e-921ef54651a6.html.

76. Donald Tusk (@eucopresident), Twitter, May 16, 2018, https://twitter.com/eucopresident/status/996731038062862336?ref_src=twsrc%5Etfw&ref_url=https%3A%2F%2Fwww.washingtonpost .com%2Fnews%2Fworldviews%2Fwp%2F2018%2F05%2F16% 2Fe-u-leader-lights-into-trump-with-friends-like-that-who-needs-enemies%2F&tfw_creator=michaelbirnbaum&tfw_site=WashingtonPost&tid=a_mcntx.

77. Greg Jaffe, "Trump Tries to Appear Strong in Syria Even as He Plans to Withdraw," *WP*, Apr. 14, 2018, https://www.washingtonpost.com/world/national-security/trump-tries-to-appear-strong-in-syria-even-as-he-plans-to-withdraw/2018/04/14/4bb75fe6-400f-11e8-8d53-eba0ed2371cc_story.html?utm_term=.2126ce5bc304.

78. Jeffrey Goldberg, "A Senior White House Official Defines the Trump Doctrine: 'We're America, Bitch,'" *The Atlantic*, June 11, 2018, https://www.theatlantic.com/politics/archive/2018/06/a-senior-white-house-official-defines-the-trump-doctrine-were-america-bitch/562511/.

79. MB, "Trump Is the Worst Salesman America Has Ever Had," *FP*, Jan. 22, 2018, http://foreignpolicy.com/2018/01/22/trump-has-already-destroyed-americas-soft-power/.

6. The Trump Toadies

1. "The President Is Not above the Law," *NYT*, Apr. 15, 2018, https://www.nytimes.com/interactive/2018/04/15/opinion/editorials/president-above-rule-law.html?action=click&pgtype=Homepage&clickSource=image&module=opinion-c-col-top-region&region=opinion-c-col-top-region&WT.nav=opinion-c-col-top-region.

2. Julie Hirschfeld Davis, "Trump's Cabinet, with a Prod, Extols the 'Blessing' of Serving Him," *NYT*, June 12, 2017, https://www.nytimes.com/2017/06/12/us/politics/trump-boasts-of-record-setting-pace-of-activity.html.

3. Charles Hurt, "Trump the Orator Outlines the Greatness of America to Democrats' Disgust," *Washington Times*, Feb. 1, 2018, https://www.washingtontimes.com/news/2018/feb/1/donald-trump-highlights-americas-freedom/.

4. Chris Cillizza, "Donald Trump Talks Like No Politician Has Ever Talked Before," *CNN*, Aug. 9, 2017, https://www.cnn.com/2017/08/09/politics/stephen-miller-trump-orator/index.html.

5. Fox News, June 1, 2017, http://www.foxnews.com/opinion/2017/06/01/donald-trump-miracle-worker.html.

6. Steve Cortes, "Trump's Winning Streak Rivals One of the Greatest Streaks in Sports," *Washington Examiner*, May 15, 2018, https://www.washingtonexaminer.com/opinion/op-eds/trumps-winning-streak-rivals-one-of-the-greatest-streaks-in-sports.

7. Candace Owens (@RealCandaceO), Twitter, Apr. 16, 2018, https://twitter.com/realcandaceo/status/986066422399774720?s=11.

8. Mallory Shelbourne, "Trump Praises Conservative Activist Candace Owens as a 'Very Smart Thinker,'" *The Hill*, May 9, 2018, http://thehill.com/homenews/administration/386857-trump-praises-candace-owens-as-a-very-smart-thinker.

9. Fox News (@FoxNews), Twitter, Apr. 15, 2018, https://twitter.com/foxnews/status/985500401976971267?s=11.

10. MB, "Donald Trump Is Proving Too Stupid to Be President," *FP*, June 16, 2017, http://foreignpolicy.com/2017/06/16/donald-trump-is-proving-too-stupid-to-be-president/.

11. Rebecca Savransky, "Anderson Cooper Confronts GOP Lawmaker: You Haven't Heard the President Lie?," *The Hill*, Apr. 17, 2018, http://thehill.com/homenews/media/383471-anderson-cooper-confronts-gop-lawmaker-you-havent-heard-the-president-lie.

12. Peter Coy, "After Defeating Cohn, Trump's Trade Warrior Is on the Rise Again," *Bloomberg*, Mar. 8, 2018, https://www.bloomberg.com/news/articles/2018-03-08/after-defeating-cohn-trump-s-trade-warrior-is-on-the-rise-again.

13. Victor Davis Hanson, "Donald Trump, Tragic Hero," *National Review*, Apr. 30, 2018, https://www.nationalreview.com/magazine/2018/04/30/donald-trump-tragic-hero/.

14. Julian Jackson, *France: The Dark Years, 1940–1944* (New York: Oxford University Press, 2001), 278.

15. Zane Anthony, Kathryn Sanders, and David A. Fahrenthold, "Whatever Happened to Trump Neckties? They're Over. So Is Most of Trump's Merchandising Empire," *WP*, Apr. 13, 2018, https://www.washingtonpost.com/politics/whatever-happened-to-trump-ties-theyre-over-so-is-most-of-trumps-merchandising-empire/2018/04/13/2c32378a-369c-11e8-acd5-35eac230e514_story.html?utm_term=.3592a997c0b9.

16. Jackson, *France*, 279.

17. Jon Meacham (@jmeacham), Twitter, May 1, 2018, https://twitter.com/Trump4American1/status/991318857343258624.

18. Brian Stelter, "'Mass Firing' at Conservative Site RedState," *CNN*, Apr. 27, 2018, http://money.cnn.com/2018/04/27/media/redstate-blog-salem-media/index.html?sr=twmoney042718redstate-blog-salem-media1227PMStory.

19. Karen Tumulty, "'Republicans Don't Want the Tweet That I Got': Mark Sanford Says Trump Sealed His Loss," *WP*, June 13, 2018, https://www.washingtonpost.com/opinions/republicans-dont-want-the-tweet-that-i-got-mark-sanford-says-trump-sealed-his-loss/2018/06/13/d36a9fe2-6f0e-11e8-afd5-778aca903bbe_story.html?utm_term=.af88900f3abf.

20. Geoffrey R. Stone, *Perilous Times: Free Speech in Wartime* (New York: W. W. Norton, 2004).

21. David M. Oshinsky, *A Conspiracy So Immense: The World of Joe McCarthy* (New York: Free Press, 1983), 163–65.

22. Ben Terris, "Bob Corker Is Free to Speak His Mind about Trump. If He Could Only Make It Up," *WP*, Apr. 16, 2018, https://www .washingtonpost.com/lifestyle/style/bob-corker-is-free-to-speak-his-mind-about-donald-trump-if-he-could-only-make-it-up/2018/04/16/ cc4f2d58-3da0-11e8-974f-aacd97698cef_story.html?utm_term= .8cfe2eb63bcf.

23. Erick Erickson, "A Congressman's Profanity Laced Tirade in a Safeway Grocery Store," *The Maven*, Apr. 11, 2018, https://www.themaven.net/ theresurgent/erick-erickson/a-congressman-s-profanity-laced-tirade-in-a-safeway-grocery-store-SeHI2l5bIECGQn4gmnzGaw/?mc_ cid=10d8170a1d&mc_eid=3cc50e048e&full=1.

24. Cristiano Lima, "Boehner: 'There Is No Republican Party. There Is a Trump Party,'" *Politico*, May 31, 2018, https://www.politico.com/ story/2018/05/31/john-boehner-republican-trump-party-615357.

25. Annie Linskey, "In the Era of Donald Trump, New England's Biggest GOP Donor Is Funding Democrats," *Boston Globe*, Apr. 14, 2018, https://www.bostonglobe.com/news/politics/2018/04/14/era-donald-trump-new-england-biggest-gop-donor-funding-democrats/ QzyFs3i3Yq3o6Ae7QIkhVP/story.html.

26. MB, "It's a Disgrace More Republicans Aren't Willing to Choose Country over Partisanship," *WP*, Apr. 23, 2018, https://www .washingtonpost.com/news/global-opinions/wp/2018/04/23/its-a-disgrace-more-republicans-arent-willing-to-choose-country-over-partisanship/?utm_term=.9e7c7dcd18ff.

27. Demetri Sevastopulo (@Dimi), Twitter, Oct. 25, 2018, https://twitter .com/dimi/status/923144727700099074.

28. MB, "On Trump, GOP Hasn't Learned Churchill's Lesson: War Is Preferable to Appeasement," *USAT*, Oct. 26, 2017, https://www .usatoday.com/story/opinion/2017/10/26/trump-gop-hasnt-learned-churchills-lesson-war-preferable-to-appeasement-max-boot-column/799914001/.

7. The Origins of Trumpism

1. "Why the South Must Prevail," *National Review*, Aug. 24, 1957, https:// adamgomez.files.wordpress.com/2012/03/whythesouthmustprevail-1957.pdf.

2. Alvin Felzenberg, "How William F. Buckley, Jr., Changed His Mind on Civil Rights," *Politico*, May 13, 2017, https://www.politico.com/ magazine/story/2017/05/13/william-f-buckley-civil-rights-215129.

3. Barry Goldwater, *Conscience of a Conservative* (LaVergne, TN: Bottom of the Hill Publishing, 2010), 20.

4. Goldwater, *Conscience*, 51.

5. Goldwater, *Conscience*, 72.

6. Phyllis Schlafly, *A Choice Not an Echo* (Alton, IL.: Pere Marquette Press, 1964), https://www.metabunk.org/files/Schlafly%20-%20A%20 Choice%20Not%20an%20Echo%20-%20The%20Inside%20Story%20 of%20How%20American%20Presidents%20are%20Chosen%20(1964) .pdf.

7. E. J. Dionne, *Why the Right Went Wrong: Conservatism—From Goldwater to Trump and Beyond* (New York: Simon & Schuster, 2016), loc. 2257, Kindle.

8. Dionne, *Why the Right Went Wrong*, loc. 91, Kindle.

9. MB, "How the 'Stupid Party' Created Donald Trump," *NYT*, July 31, 2016, https://www.nytimes.com/2016/08/01/opinion/how-the-stupid-party-created-donald-trump.html.

10. William J. Bennett, "William Bennett: George Will Scorns Pence for the High Crime of Decency," *Fox News*, May 12, 2018, http://www .foxnews.com/opinion/2018/05/12/william-bennett-george-will-scorns-pence-for-high-crime-decency.html.

11. "10 of Sarah Palin's Most Amazingly Stupid Quotes," *Wow247*, Jan. 20, 2016, http://www.wow247.co.uk/2016/01/20/sarah-palin-quotes/.

12. MB, "Down with Populism!," *WSJ*, Dec. 8, 1994.

13. Andrew Kirell, "Dinesh D'Souza Mocked Shooting Survivors. Why Is He Still on the 'National Review' Masthead?," *Daily Beast*, Feb. 21, 2018, https://www.thedailybeast.com/dinesh-dsouza-national-review-parkland-shooting-survivors-racist-bigot.

14. MB, "If This Is What Conservatism Has Become, Count Me Out," *WP*, Feb. 25, 2018, https://www.washingtonpost.com/ opinions/if-this-is-what-conservatism-has-become-count-me-out/2018/02/25/853685c6-19bd-11e8-92c9-376b4fe57ff7_story .html.

15. Tim Stelloh, "Sinclair Talk Show Canceled after Host Appears to Threaten Parkland Survivor David Hogg," *NBC News*, Apr. 9, 2018, https://www.nbcnews.com/news/us-news/sinclair-talk-show-canceled-after-host-appears-threaten-parkland-survivor-n864211.

16. Tomi Lahren (@TomiLahren), Twitter, May 14, 2018, https://twitter .com/tomilahren/status/996106261283270656?s=11.

17. Derek Hawkins, "Hannity—with His $29 Million Salary and Private Jet—Slams 'Overpaid' Media Elites," *WP*, Sept. 28, 2016, https://www.washingtonpost.com/news/morning-mix/wp/2016/09/28/hannity-slams-overpaid-media-elites-then-journalists-respond-noting-his-29m-salary-and-private-jet/?utm_term=.91607e317873.

18. MB, "If This Is What Conservatism Has Become, Count Me Out," *WP*, Feb. 25, 2018, https://www.washingtonpost.com/opinions/if-this-is-what-conservatism-has-become-count-me-out/2018/02/25/853685c6-19bd-11e8-92c9-376b4fe57ff7_story.html.

19. MB, "A Conservative Commentator Revolts against Fox News," *WP*, Mar. 21, 2018, https://www.washingtonpost.com/news/global-opinions/wp/2018/03/21/a-conservative-commentator-revolts-against-fox-news/.

20. Matthew Gertz, "I've Studied the Trump-Fox Feedback Loop for Months. It's Crazier than You Think," *Politico*, Jan. 5, 2018, https://www.politico.com/magazine/story/2018/01/05/trump-media-feedback-loop-216248.

21. Robert Costa, Sarah Ellison, and Josh Dawsey, "Hannity's Rising Role in Trump's World: 'He Basically Has a Desk in the Place,'" *WP*, Apr. 4, 2017, https://www.washingtonpost.com/politics/hannitys-rising-role-in-trumps-world-he-basically-has-a-desk-in-the-place/2018/04/17/e2483018-4260-11e8-8569-26fda6b404c7_story.html?utm_term=.ffe2d91a3d5e.

22. MB, "Useful Idiocy," *Commentary*, July 17, 2017, https://www.commentarymagazine.com/politics-ideas/tucker-carlson-russia-putin-neoconservatism/.

23. Tom Namako, "Commentator Just Quit the 'Propaganda Machine,'" *BuzzFeed*, Mar. 20, 2016, https://www.buzzfeed.com/tomnamako/ralph-peters?utm_term=.jspZ2WnAj#.wdPe7wpMO.

24. MB, "2017 Was the Year I Learned About My White Privilege," *FP*, Dec. 27, 2017, http://foreignpolicy.com/2017/12/27/2017-was-the-year-i-learned-about-my-white-privilege/.

25. Tucker Carlson (@TuckerCarlson), Twitter, Dec. 27, 2017, https://twitter.com/TuckerCarlson/status/946158361241968640.

26. Caitlin Johnstone, "Iraq-Raping Neocons Are Suddenly Posing as Woke Progressives to Gain Support," *Medium*, https://medium.com/@caityjohnstone/iraq-raping-neocons-are-suddenly-posing-as-woke-progressives-to-gain-support-289fa527f3f8.

27. Soledad O'Brien (@soledadobrien), Twitter, Dec. 28, 2017, https://twitter.com/soledadobrien/status/946268253277577216?lang=en.

Epilogue: The Vital Center

1. Bruce Bartlett, "A Conservative Case for the Welfare State," *Dissent*, Apr. 24, 2015, https://www.dissentmagazine.org/online_articles/bruce-bartlett-conservative-case-for-welfare-state.

2. MB, "I Would Vote for (a Sane) Donald Trump," *FP*, Sept. 20, 2017, http://foreignpolicy.com/2017/09/20/i-would-vote-for-a-sane-donald-trump/.

3. Bob Fredericks, "This College Professor Is Happy 'Racist' Barbara Bush Is Dead," *New York Post*, Apr. 18, 2018, https://nypost.com/2018/04/18/this-college-professor-is-happy-racist-barbara-bush-is-dead/?utm_campaign=iosapp&utm_source=mail_app.

4. MB, "If This Is What Conservatism Has Become, Count Me Out," *WP*, Feb. 25, 2018, https://www.washingtonpost.com/opinions/if-this-is-what-conservatism-has-become-count-me-out/2018/02/25/853685c6-19bd-11e8-92c9-376b4fe57ff7_story.html.

5. Jonathan Rauch and Benjamin Wittes, "Boycott the Republican Party," *The Atlantic*, Mar. 15, 2018, https://www.theatlantic.com/magazine/archive/2018/03/boycott-the-gop/550907/.

6. Jonathan Chait, "Bernie Sanders's Bill Gets America Zero Percent Closer to Single Payer," *New York*, Sept. 13, 2017, http://nymag.com/daily/intelligencer/2017/09/sanderss-bill-gets-u-s-zero-percent-closer-to-single-payer.html.

7. Tami Luhby, "Sanders' Last 'Medicare for All' Plan Cost Nearly $1.4 Trillion," *CNN*, Sept. 12, 2017, http://money.cnn.com/2017/09/12/news/economy/sanders-medicare-for-all/index.html.

8. MB, "I Would Vote for (a Sane) Donald Trump," *FP*, Sept. 20, 2017, http://foreignpolicy.com/2017/09/20/i-would-vote-for-a-sane-donald-trump/.

9. Paul Waldman, "The Next Big Thing for Democrats: Medicare for All," *WP*, Apr. 19, 2018, https://www.washingtonpost.com/blogs/plum-line/wp/2018/04/19/the-next-big-thing-for-democrats-medicare-for-all/?utm_term=.cad8ad33eae1.

10. Mitchell Wellman, "Here's How Much Bernie Sanders' Free College for All Plan Would Cost," *USAT*, Apr. 17, 2017, http://college.usatoday.com/2017/04/17/heres-how-much-bernie-sanders-free-college-for-all-plan-would-cost/.

11. Mairead Mcardle, "Bernie Sanders Has No Cost Estimate on His Guaranteed-Jobs Plan," *National Review*, Apr. 24, 2018, https://www.nationalreview.com/news/bernie-sanders-has-no-cost-estimate-on-his-guaranteed-jobs-plan/.

12. Kevin Drum, "Need a Job? Just Call Bernie," *Mother Jones*, Apr. 23, 2018, https://www.motherjones.com/kevin-drum/2018/04/need-a-job-just-call-bernie/.

13. Jedediah Purdy, "Normcore," *Dissent*, Summer 2018, https://www.dissentmagazine.org/article/normcore-trump-resistance-books-crisis-of-democracy.

14. Matthew Dallek, "Why the GOP Needs Someone—Anyone—to Challenge Trump in 2020," *WP*, May 18, 2018, https://www.washingtonpost.com/amphtml/outlook/why-the-gop-needs-someone--anyone--to-challenge-trump-in-2020/2018/05/18/1127f014-59ed-11e8-b656-a5f8c2a9295d_story.html?tid=ss_tw&utm_term=.068d00a0bc86&__twitter_impression=true.

15. Matt Lewis, "Donald Trump Is Turning Young Voters Off the GOP—and Maybe Forever," *Daily Beast*, June 13, 2017, https://www.thedailybeast.com/donald-trump-is-turning-young-voters-off-the-gopand-maybe-forever.

16. Digitalist (@SomeDigitalist), Twitter, May 19, 2018, https://twitter.com/somedigitalist/status/997816270056648705?s=11.

17. MB, "The Political Center Is Fighting Back," *WP*, Apr. 25, 2018, https://www.washingtonpost.com/opinions/global-opinions/the-political-center-is-fighting-back/2018/04/25/6170f646-489b-11e8-827e-190efaf1f1ee_story.html.

INDEX

ABOUT THE AUTHOR

Max Boot is a historian, best-selling author, and foreign policy analyst who has been called one of the "world's leading authorities on armed conflict" by the International Institute for Strategic Studies. He is the Jeane J. Kirkpatrick Senior Fellow in National Security Studies at the Council on Foreign Relations, a columnist for the *Washington Post*, and a global affairs analyst for CNN. His most recent books are the *New York Times* bestsellers *The Road Not Taken: Edward Lansdale and the American Tragedy in Vietnam* and *Invisible Armies: An Epic History of Guerrilla Warfare from Ancient Times to the Present Day.*